Also by Stephen M. Pollan and Mark Levine

Surviving the Squeeze

The Total Negotiator

The Big Fix-Up: Renovating Your Home Without Losing Your Shirt

The Business of Living

Your Recession Handbook: How to Thrive and Profit During Hard Times

The Field Guide to Starting a Business

The Field Guide to Home Buying in America

Stephen Pollan's Foolproof Guide to Selling Your Home

Lifescripts

*What to say to get what you want
in life's toughest situations*

STEPHEN M. POLLAN

MARK LEVINE

Wiley Publishing, Inc.
10475 Crosspoint Boulevard
Indianapolis, Indiana 46256

Wiley and the Wiley logo are trademarks or registered trademarks of Wiley Publishing, Inc. Lifescripts is a trademark of Stephen M. Pollan.

Library of Congress Control Number: 2002105853

Printed in the United States of America

20   19   18   17   16   15   14

Book design by Nick Anderson

Dedication

This book is dedicated to our friend and agent,
Stuart Krichevsky, who's never at a loss for words.

ACKNOWLEDGMENTS

The authors would like to thank Natalie Chapman for her vision, Jane Morrow for her support, and Deirdre Martin Levine and Corky Pollan for their understanding and patience.

PART II: LIFESCRIPTS FOR BUSINESS

The Secret of Using *Lifescripts*

I've been giving advice to people for most of my adult life.

Usually it's in my capacity as an attorney and financial advisor; but other times it's as a son, husband, father, or friend. Most often I'm being asked for help with vital legal and financial matters; but sometimes I'm asked how to persuade a husband to lose weight or how to borrow money from a parent.

I suppose I've become a source of advice on these diverse areas because of my long and varied experience in the law and business, my reputation as an effective negotiator, my notoriety as an author and television commentator, and the uniquely personal brand of service and attention I offer clients, readers, and viewers.

I like to take people by the hand and lead them through a process; helping them plan and preparing them for potential obstacles. Whether it's helping a young couple buy their first home, an experienced corporate executive negotiate an employment contract, or my father complain to his insurance company, I try to break every project down into manageable steps. But despite my best efforts at explaining and coaching there's always one last question: "But what do I say?" People always want to know what words they should use and how they should deal with possible responses.

To ease their anxiety, I tell the person to telephone me before the event so we can create a "lifescript" for the whole conversation: an outline of the entire conversation including counters, responses, and rejoinders. Usually the lifescript is used verbatim, but some times it simply serves as the extra measure of confidence the person needs to face a difficult, unpleasant, or awkward situation. Many of my clients are amazed at how effective these lifescripts can be, and how much better they fare using them.

I could claim that the reason my lifescripts work so well is that I'm the best negotiator on the planet. But that would be boastful and untrue. I am an experienced professional negotiator. But the secret behind lifescripts isn't my skill—it's that they're comprehensive plans for situations we usually don't plan for.

When a couple decides to have a formal wedding, they don't just wing it. They sit down, either with a party planner or on their own, and plan out the whole affair. They make sure that there will be enough food, that the napkins will match the centerpieces, and that Aunt Muriel and Aunt Hettie, who have been feuding for 35 years, aren't sitting at the same table. By the day of the wedding, little is left to chance. The reason my lifescripts work so well is that I bring the same kind of planning and attention to a conversation that a bride and groom bring to their wedding day.

If we plan out our interpersonal exchanges—whether they involve work, business, or our family lives—not only will they be easier to deal with but, more often than not, they'll turn out the way we want. With a lifescript, either directly in front of you or just in your head, you'll never be surprised. You'll have a plan that leads inexorably to your goal, regardless of what obstacle is thrown in your way. You'll have an answer to every question, a comeback to every crack, and a defense for every attack.

HOW TO USE LIFESCRIPTS

In the following pages I've tried to offer lifescripts for 101 of the most perplexing and problematic dialogues you might face in the course of your work, business, and personal lives.

Each lifescript begins with a general discussion of the overall *strategy* you should use in the dialogue, usually highlighting what your goal should be. Then I briefly describe the *attitude* you should adopt—for example, righteous indignation or contrition. I touch on what kinds of *preparation* you need before using the script—perhaps some research or the drafting of a memo. Next I offer tips on *timing*—whether it's better to have this conversation during the workweek or on the weekend, for instance. Then, I touch on what your *behavior* should be like. This could involve body language or whether to sit or stand during the conversation.

On the next page I present the lifescript itself in flowchart form. I offer icebreakers, pitches, possible responses, counters, and retorts. Obviously, each lifescript is different because each conversation takes a different form.

After the flow chart I offer some ideas for *adaptations*—other situations where, with some minor modifications, you could use the same lifescript. Finally, I've provided a few *key points* for each lifescript. You can use these as crib notes to bring with you to the dialogue.

These lifescripts can be used verbatim. I've picked the words very carefully and each has been chosen for a reason. However, I think its best if you take the words I offer and play around with them until they sound like your own. That's because everyone has different diction and sentence structure. There's nothing wrong with sounding prepared— as long as you sound like yourself.

With 101 scripts and possible adaptations more than doubling that number, I think this book offers help in nearly every common situation. However, I'm sure there are important situations I've left out either because I simply didn't think of them, or because they're unique to you and the circumstances of your life.

Rather than require you to call me on the telephone to help you prepare a personal script, I thought I'd give you a brief course in the five rules behind these lifescripts. That way you'll be able to draft your own. (Though of course, you are welcome to call me if you get in a real pickle.)

Rule #1: Take control of the situation

If you gain nothing else from this book, let it be an understanding of this rule. The single most important element in getting these conversations to turn out the way you want is to take control of them. That doesn't mean you monopolize the conversation or bully the other person. It simply means that, through your choice of words and reactions, you frame and steer it in the direction you want it to go.

In many cases that means you make the first move, and by so doing, force the other person to respond. In other situations, it means responding in such a way that the other person is forced into retorts that you've already prepared to address. Unlike most icebreakers, mine aren't written just to make the person delivering them more comfortable. They're written to force the other party into a position where he or she has a limited number of options. That way we can prepare responses to each of those limited options.

Rule #2: Say what you want

I'm continually amazed at the inability of most people to come out and say exactly what they want. Whether it's because we don't want to be viewed as demanding or we're afraid of being turned down, most of us beat around the bush, imply, and drop hints, rather than coming right out and saying what's on our mind.

In almost every lifescript I've included what I call a pitch. That's a direct, specific request. You can't rely on other people to infer what you're after or to pick up on your hints. And besides, if you don't come right out and ask directly, you're giving the other party a chance to sidestep the whole issue. Make them respond directly. It's easier to deal with an outright rejection than you might imagine.

Rule #3: Show your power before you use it

Subtle demonstrations of power are often just as effective as the outright use of that power. For instance, if you're a restaurant patron you have two powers: your ability to make a scene and your willingness to pay your bill. By calling over a waiter or maître d' and whispering that you're unhappy with your meal and would like another, you demonstrate that you're aware of your power to make a scene, but are holding it in check until they've had a chance to respond. If you actually raise your voice and make a scene immediately you have far less power since you've used up all your ammunition.

Other ways of displaying your power include saying things like, "I'm a long-time customer and would like to continue our relationship," or "The last thing I want to do is hire someone else to finish this project." In both cases you're showing an awareness of your power but a willingness not to use it. That's far more likely to work than an outright threat. Though if push comes to shove, you may have to make such a threat.

Rule #4: Absorb or deflect anger

That doesn't mean you should get angry, however. Displays of anger are just as self-defeating as gratuitous exercises of power. The actual message you send when you get angry is "I've no real power so all I can do is make noise." Therefore, hold your temper whenever possible.

Similarly, when you're met with anger, the best response is to disarm the other party by either absorbing or deflecting it. You absorb anger by acknowledging it and refusing to respond in kind. ("I can understand your being angry. I would be too.") You deflect anger by suggesting that it's an odd reaction and must therefore be based on something other than your request. ("I don't understand why you're getting angry at me. Have I done something else to bother you?")

Rule #5: Have the last word

In almost every situation it's to your advantage to have the last word in a dialogue. That means either expressing thanks for getting what you wanted, asking for reconsideration of a rejection, pushing for another meeting, or saying that you'll call back if you couldn't get a definite answer. Having the last word does two things: It makes sure you retain the control over the dialogue that you seized when you broke the ice; and it allows you to close the conversation on advantageous terms.

The only exceptions to having the last word are in situations where it's important for you to give the other party a chance to "save face." In effect, by giving them the last word you're letting them think they're still in control, even though they're not.

TWO PHILOSOPHICAL THOUGHTS

Before you jump into the lifescripts themselves, I need to touch on two important philosophical issues: the ethics of scripting conversations in advance, and the question of whether or not you use "white lies" to your advantage.

Some of the people I've helped develop lifescripts have voiced concerns about the ethics of scripting some dialogues, particularly those involving spouses and family members. While they have no problem with preparing for a meeting with their boss or a client, they feel uneasy about doing the same for a talk with their husband or mother.

Personally, I don't see anything wrong with preparing for such talks. In fact, I think it's an excellent idea.

One of the major reasons people tell me they like my lifescripts is that they work. By using them, my clients have been able to get what they want out of life. But that's not the only advantage to lifescripts. When you plan a conversation out to this extent you avoid a lot of the ancillary problems of human interaction. By scripting you avoid getting sidetracked into a discussion of why you don't come to visit as often as you should, or why you leave the toilet seat up all the time. Granted, those are two valid topics for discussion. But they should be topics in and of themselves, not background noise in a talk about estate planning or relocating to another city. By scripting you ensure that the conversation will stay on track and in the process avoid falling into the argumentative patterns of the past. I think that, far from being unfair or unethical, lifescripts help pave the way for smoother family relations and better communications.

Finally, let's look at the issue of white lies. In a few of the lifescripts you'll notice lines such as, "I've already notified the boss about this," which effectively disarm threats from the other party. I'm assuming that you're actually going to do what the lifescript says—in this case, speak to your boss before the meeting. Of course, that doesn't mean you have to in order to use the line. That's something you'll have to decide for yourself. But if I can offer one more word of advice in parting, it's this: The most effective lifescripts are truthful.

I

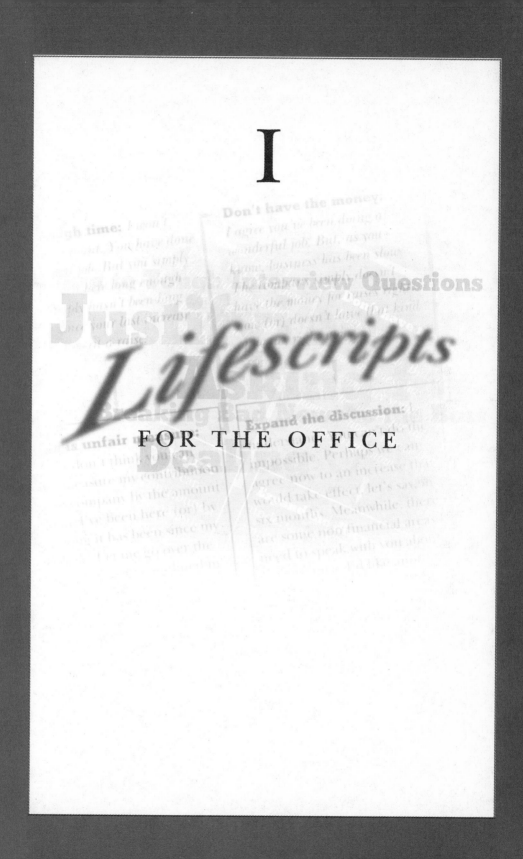

Lifescripts

FOR THE OFFICE

CHAPTER ONE

Lifescripts for Job Hunting

Cold Calling for an Informational Interview

1.

STRATEGY

Cold calling—contacting someone with no forewarning—is always difficult. It's even more of a problem when the call is about your career. The objective of this script is to make contact *inside* the organization. That way you'll only have to make one cold call.

TACTICS

- **Attitude:** Don't look on what you're doing as demeaning. Consider that you're actually offering the other party a wonderful opportunity—the other party just doesn't know yet how wonderful a chance it really is! If you're feeling desperate, you'll get nowhere. Feel confident and you'll get surprisingly far.

- **Preparation:** You definitely need a name to drop for the other party's security and comfort. Obviously, the more impressive and familiar the name the better . . . but any name is better than none. Even a headhunter or secretary will do in a pinch. Before making the telephone call, it's important to discover everything you possibly can about the organization (especially its recent history). Your knowledge of the company may help compensate for your lack of a contact. It certainly won't hurt.

- **Timing:** Many individuals in supervisory positions come to the office early in an effort to get work done before regular business hours, then spend the first hour or so launching their staff. From 11:30 A.M. until 2:00 P.M. they're either thinking about, traveling to or from, or eating, lunch. From 3:00 P.M. on they're thinking about bringing the day to a close. That gives you two small but decent windows of opportunity to make your call: from 10:00 A.M. until 11:30 A.M. and from 2:00 P.M. until 3:00 P.M.

- **Behavior:** The more comfortable, friendly, and relaxed you sound the more likely you'll be able to connect.

1. Cold Calling for an Informational Interview

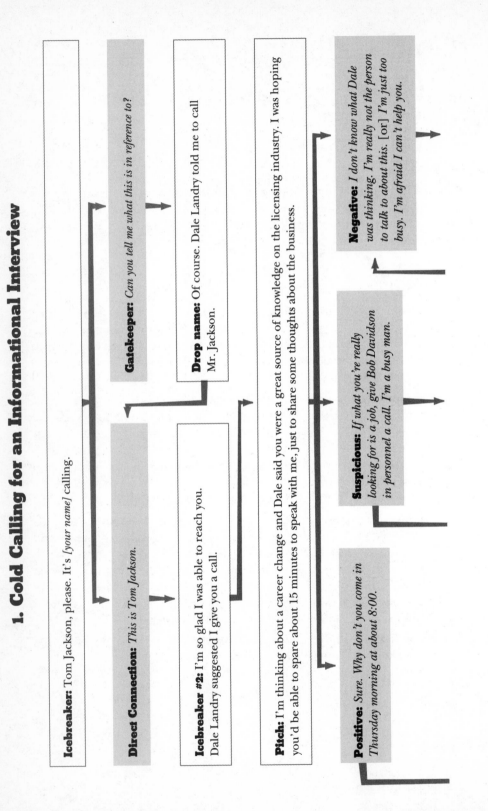

Icebreaker: Tom Jackson, please. It's *[your name]* calling.

Direct Connection: *This is Tom Jackson.*

Gatekeeper: *Can you tell me what this is in reference to?*

Drop name: Of course. Dale Landry told me to call Mr. Jackson.

Icebreaker #2: I'm so glad I was able to reach you. Dale Landry suggested I give you a call.

Pitch: I'm thinking about a career change and Dale said you were a great source of knowledge on the licensing industry. I was hoping you'd be able to spare about 15 minutes to speak with me, just to share some thoughts about the business.

Positive: *Sure. Why don't you come in Thursday morning at about 8:00.*

Suspicious: *If what you're really looking for is a job, give Bob Davidson in personnel a call. I'm a busy man.*

Negative: *I don't know what Dale was thinking; I'm really not the person to talk to about this.* [or] *I'm just too busy. I'm afraid I can't help you.*

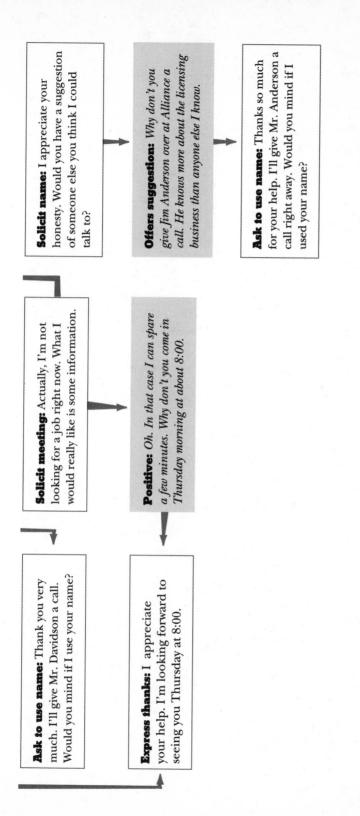

Ask to use name: Thank you very much. I'll give Mr. Davidson a call. Would you mind if I use your name?

Solicit meeting: Actually, I'm not looking for a job right now. What I would really like is some information.

Positive: *Oh. In that case I can spare a few minutes. Why don't you come in Thursday morning at about 8:00.*

Express thanks: I appreciate your help. I'm looking forward to seeing you Thursday at 8:00.

Solicit name: I appreciate your honesty. Would you have a suggestion of someone else you think I could talk to?

Offers suggestion: *Why don't you give Jim Anderson over at Alliance a call. He knows more about the licensing business than anyone else I know.*

Ask to use name: Thanks so much for your help. I'll give Mr. Anderson a call right away. Would you mind if I used your name?

ADAPTATIONS

This script can be modified to:

- Obtain information about an industry
- Solicit new business for your company
- Raise money for an organization

KEY POINTS

- Use words like "need" and "told" with gatekeepers; they imply you're on a definite mission rather than a fishing expedition.
- Flatter them shamelessly and ask for a very short amount of time . . . at their convenience.
- Stressing you're looking for knowledge, not a job, improves your chances for a face-to-face meeting enormously. However, if they offer a personnel contact, grab it.
- If they decline, solicit another name and ask to use them as a reference. Having turned you down once, they're unlikely to do so again.

Asking a Manager for Job-Hunting Advice

2.

STRATEGY

Right from the start, it's essential for you to understand that there's no way to ask for job-hunting advice from a manager without potentially putting your present job in danger. Most managers only do this kind of favor for employees who are their relatives, or who they treat as relations. Even though from day one it was probably made clear to you that there was no long-term future for you at the company (if there was, you wouldn't be having this dialogue), your boss could have forgotten all about that . . . especially if you've become valuable to him, the company, or both. If he does remember the original terms of your employment with the company, this will be more an annoyance than a shock. Your leaving runs counter to his needs. In both cases you're in for an uphill battle that should only be taken on if your direct supervisor is your only good link to future jobs. Your goal in this dialogue is to keep him from canning you, and then, get him to invest time and effort on your behalf.

TACTICS

- **Attitude:** Treat this as a discussion between mentor and protégé, not supervisor and staffer. But realize that you may have to either retreat into employee mode or use guilt to force him into mentor mode.

- **Preparation:** Conduct your own performance review. Try to ensure that you've maximized all your internal possibilities and have been successful at everything that's been handed to you. Any shortcomings, even those so minor to have been ignored in a performance review, will be brought to your attention the moment you talk about having outgrown your job.

- **Timing:** Do not, repeat, do not have this dialogue shortly after your supervisor has done you any kind of favor. It's a sure thing he will still be thinking about what a wonderful guy he is long after you've moved on to other things. Favors should be so far in the past that he won't throw them in your face and accuse you of ingratitude.

- **Behavior:** Have this meeting outside of the work environment in order to stress your personal rather than professional relationship. Be ready to stand up for yourself if you're met by anger. You've already dropped the bombshell so there's nothing to be gained by backing down. Restate what you know to be the original terms of your employment and directly ask if they've been changed.

2. Asking a Manager for Job-Hunting Advice

Icebreaker and pitch: I'm glad you accepted my invitation to lunch. It's not much, but I wanted to thank you for all you've taught me and done for me. You've been an important part of my professional growth. That's why I wanted to ask for your advice and help in planning the next step in my career.

Grudging acceptance: As your boss I'm not happy you're looking to move on . . . but as your friend I'll do what I can to help.

Has plans: Actually, I'm glad you brought this up. I've got some plans for you and I don't think you'll need to move up.

Make things clear: I'm sorry, I must not have been clear. I'm not telling you I'm leaving. I would never leave you or the company on such short notice. This lunch is about my gratitude and my request was for your help in setting a direction for my future. I was wondering whether you thought it was a good idea for me to speak with Jack Smith from the national association?

Gets angry: So, this lunch was a set up! Is this how you show your gratitude, by leaving me in the lurch?

Restate terms of employment: The last thing I thought was that you'd get angry. Don't you remember telling me when you hired me that this was a great first job? We both understood this position was a stepping stone. Still, I've given 110 percent. Have your feelings changed? Do you see me taking over a department [or] becoming a partner?

Not ready: You've done a great job. And you have grown. But I don't think you're quite ready to move on just yet.

Express thanks: You're probably right. Thanks so much for your wisdom and encouragement. I'd like to talk to you about this again. And when we both agree the time has come for me to move on, I'm glad to know I'll have your help and support.

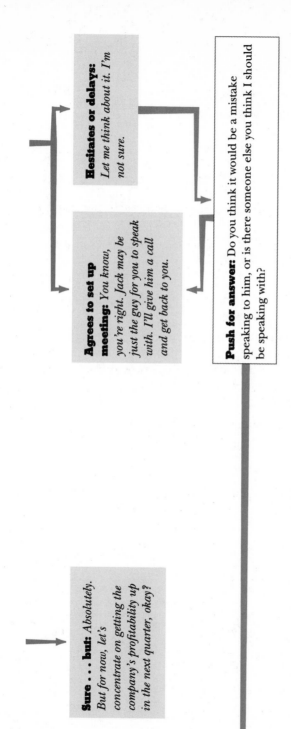

Push for answer: Do you think it would be a mistake speaking to him, or is there someone else you think I should be speaking with?

Agrees to set up meeting: *You know, you're right. Jack may be just the guy for you to speak with. I'll give him a call and get back to you.*

Hesitates or delays: *Let me think about it. I'm not sure.*

Sure . . . but: *Absolutely. But for now, let's concentrate on getting the company's profitability up in the next quarter, okay?*

ADAPTATIONS

This script can be modified to:

- Have a planning session with a mentor
- Indirectly solicit a job at a networking meeting
- Indirectly solicit a raise

KEY POINTS

- Present this as a personal request for guidance from a grateful and humble protégé.
- If he says you're not ready, take it as a positive. He has agreed you'll need to move on some day . . . just not today. Thank him and try to establish this as an ongoing dialogue.
- If he gets angry, restate the original terms of your employment and directly ask if there has been a change.
- If he says he has plans for you and thinks you're giving notice, stress that you're only in the early stages of your career planning, don't intend to leave tomorrow, and would like his advice on others you can speak with. Offer a specific suggestion.
- If he won't commit to helping arrange a meeting for you, push for a reason. Accept your not being ready as a sound reason.

Asking a Current Supervisor for a Job Recommendation

3

STRATEGY

Asking your current supervisor for a job recommendation can be extremely dangerous. The moment you tell him you're a candidate for another job, he mentally starts replacing you. And at the same time, he may be able to sabotage your future position. The objective of this script is to minimize his anger at you and ensure he'll put in a good word—or at least won't put in a bad word—with your future employer.

TACTICS

- **Attitude:** Don't look on this as asking for a favor or help. That makes it seem a big deal and gives him more of an opportunity to withhold his recommendation. You're simply asking for a professional courtesy—that's very difficult to withhold. Also, if he seems remote, you want nothing but the truth. Be aware that, by law, employers must be very careful about what they say about you.

- **Preparation:** Before having this conversation, you need to be able to put your finger on an inarguable reason for taking the job—something the new job offers that your current job can never provide. You also need to be prepared to say how long you'll be able to stick around.

- **Timing:** Due to the danger involved in this script, you need to wait until you're sure the only remaining hurdle to your getting the new job is a positive reference from your current employer. Of course, that means surprising your current supervisor . . . but you've really no choice.

- **Behavior:** The more you frame this as an unsolicited offer which you simply cannot refuse—and which no one who truly has your best interests at heart would advise you to refuse—the more likely you are to avoid a problem.

3. Asking a Current Supervisor for a Job Recommendation

Icebreaker: I need to talk to you about some news I've just gotten. I've been given an incredible job offer——an opportunity I can't pass up. Working with you has meant a tremendous amount to me and I've given your name as my most important reference. I'd really appreciate it if you would speak with them.

Gets annoyed: *This is awfully short notice. I would've expected more.*

Goes ballistic: *You ungrateful SOB. This company trained you, put you through grad school, and spent a fortune on you. And this is how you say thanks?*

You're making mistake: *I think you're making a mistake. You've got a wonderful future here. Are you sure you want to give it all up?*

Accepting: *Look, as long as I get enough time to find your replacement I'm happy for you.*

No choice: I realize that and I'll do whatever I can to help. This was completely unexpected, but it's a once-in-a-lifetime opportunity. A positive recommendation from you would mean a great deal to me.

Also taught me: It's true that the company has done a lot for me. It has also taught me to be ambitious. And you taught me to take advantage of my opportunities.

Not really: I've had a wonderful career here, but this offers me [something current job can't], and we both know I could never get that here. That's why I need your help.

Reassure: I've told them you were both my mentor and my friend and that I'd need to give you as much time as you need. They're eager to talk to you.

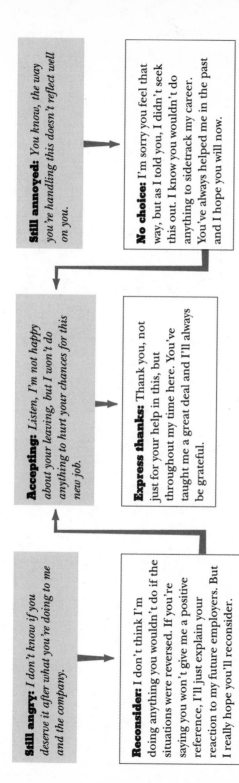

Still annoyed: *You know, the way you're handling this doesn't reflect well on you.*

No choice: I'm sorry you feel that way, but as I told you, I didn't seek this out. I know you wouldn't do anything to sidetrack my career. You've always helped me in the past and I hope you will now.

Accepting: *Listen, I'm not happy about your leaving, but I won't do anything to hurt your chances for this new job.*

Express thanks: Thank you, not just for your help in this, but throughout my time here. You've taught me a great deal and I'll always be grateful.

Still angry: *I don't know if you deserve it after what you're doing to me and the company.*

Reconsider: I don't think I'm doing anything you wouldn't do if the situations were reversed. If you're saying you won't give me a positive reference, I'll just explain your reaction to my future employers. But I really hope you'll reconsider.

ADAPTATIONS

This script can be modified to:

- Use a manager as a personal reference for a club, co-op, or part-time job
- Use a manager's contacts for networking
- Ask a supervisor to help you gain a promotion within the company

KEY POINTS

- Present it as wonderful news you want to share.
- If he gets annoyed, stress the suddenness and uniqueness of your opportunity, as well as your willingness to do all you can to help concerning your replacement.
- If he says you're making a mistake, show him how the new job offers something this position cannot.
- If he explodes, counter his attacks and then show how the new job offers something your present position cannot.
- If he remains angry, reiterate the suddenness and uniqueness of your opportunity, frame his attitude as damaging to your future, and stress your willingness to do without his help.

Responding to a Salary Offer

STRATEGY

Most job seekers are so happy to have been chosen for a job that they immediately jump at the first salary offer. In their understandable eagerness, they're failing to recognize that the number is just the first card being dealt, not necessarily the best. The goal of this script is to ensure that you get as much as you possibly can when you're first being offered a job. That is important because your starting salary will be the major factor in determining your short- and long-term compensation (since increases are generally based on percentages of your starting salary).

TACTICS

- **Attitude:** While your first sentiment may be relief that you've finally landed a job, don't fall into the trap of complacency. You will never be more powerful in this company than you are right now. They picked you because you're the best person to satisfy a need they have. In this period between selection and actually starting the job, your potential is limitless. Your attitude should be one of confidence.

- **Preparation:** The most important preparation you can do is finding out what the market range is for the position in question. Assume there's a range of 25 percent from the lowest salary paid to the highest ($75,000 to $100,000 or $30,000 to $40,000). You can also assume the other party wants to get away with paying you a salary in the bottom third of that range. Your goal, on the other hand, should be a salary in the top third of the range. That will let you jump into the next range when you shift positions in the future. In addition, come up with a list of nonfinancial compensations you are interested in, such as added vacation days, a company car, or a clothing allowance.

- **Timing:** You have only a little bit of time to work with here, but in order to maximize your return you need to push it as far as possible. That means, regardless of the offer that's on the table at the end of the conversation, ask to think about it overnight. This gives the other party one last chance to increase his offer in exchange for your immediate acceptance.

- **Behavior:** Your behavior should undergo a subtle transition when you move from job seeker to "anointed one"—you've shifted from seller to buyer. Obviously you should still remain polite and interested, but you no

4. Responding to a Salary Offer

Makes job offer: *We'd like to offer you the job. What kind of salary are you looking for?*

Deflect approach: I'm delighted that you've offered me the job. I want you to know I'm 100 percent committed to the company. As for salary, I'm looking for the market. What do you think that is now?

Won't name figure: *Well, what do you think that is?*

Name figure: Stream of income is important to me, but I also want to be fair. My research has led me to believe a salary of *[figure in top third of range]* would be appropriate for this position and someone of my experience.

Too much: *I'm not quarreling with your value, but I'm afraid we can only afford to pay [a figure in the bottom third of the range].*

Too big a jump: *That would be quite a jump for you. In your last job you were making 15 percent less than that. I'm willing to offer you an increase of 10 percent.*

Names figure: *We're prepared to offer you . . .*

Much too low: I really don't know how to respond. I expected an offer more in line with the marketplace which I think is *[upper end of range]*. Perhaps our perceptions of the job profile are different.

A bit low: I believe that's in the low end of the range for this position. I was thinking that with my experience and this job profile a salary of *[15 percent higher]* would be appropriate.

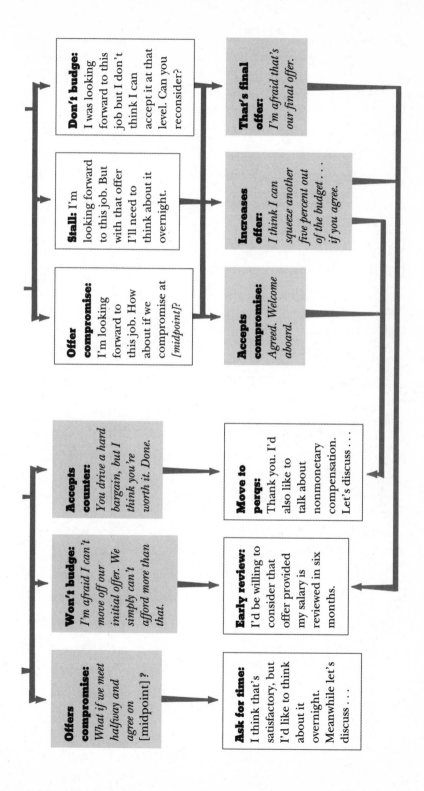

Offers compromise: *What if we meet halfway and agree on [midpoint]?*

Won't budge: *I'm afraid I can't move off our initial offer. We simply can't afford more than that.*

Accepts counter: *You drive a hard bargain, but I think you're worth it. Done.*

Ask for time: I think that's satisfactory, but I'd like to think about it overnight. Meanwhile let's discuss . . .

Early review: I'd be willing to consider that offer provided my salary is reviewed in six months.

Move to perqs: Thank you. I'd also like to talk about nonmonetary compensation. Let's discuss . . .

Offer compromise: I'm looking forward to this job. How about if we compromise at [midpoint]?

Stall: I'm looking forward to this job. But with that offer I'll need to think about it overnight.

Don't budge: I was looking forward to this job but I don't think I can accept it at that level. Can you reconsider?

Accepts compromise: *Agreed. Welcome aboard.*

Increases offer: *I think I can squeeze another five percent out of the budget . . . if you agree.*

That's final offer: *I'm afraid that's our final offer.*

longer need to appear as eager and active. You can now sit back in your seat. You can break eye contact for longer periods of time. Most important of all, you no longer need to fill gaps in the conversation. While you don't want to play hard to get, a little resistance will encourage further offers. It's good to take notes during the dialogue.

ADAPTATIONS

This script can be modified to:

- Respond to a promotion, transfer, emergency assignment, or a significant increase in responsibility

KEY POINTS

- Try, if at all possible, to force the other party into making the first offer. If that happens, the only direction it can go is up. If you are forced to name the first number, it can only go down. That's why, if you're cornered, you should come back with a figure close to the very top of the market range.
- If the first offer is below what you know to be the market range, say so, and suggest your perceptions of the job profile are dangerously different.
- If the first offer is within the range, counter it with a figure approximately 15 percent higher.
- If your prior salary is brought into play, say that it was one of the reasons you started looking for another job.
- If a compromise is offered, ask for time to consider it, and move on to nonfinancial issues.
- If no compromise is offered, ask for a guaranteed early review and move on to nonfinancial issues.

Interviewing for a Career-Shift Job

5

STRATEGY

Most people are terribly afraid of interviews for jobs outside their own industry. They needn't be. The secret here is that if you've gotten an interview with a body outside of the human resources department, someone in the company—very likely the person you'll be meeting—has realized your experiences are relevant and applicable. This interview is an opportunity, not an obstacle. They think you could work out but aren't sure. They're giving you a chance to convince them. In other words, you don't need to change minds during the interview, only reinforce beliefs they already hold. Still, you should be prepared for a series of probes.

TACTICS

- **Attitude:** Be confident. If the interviewer couldn't see how your past experience applied to this position, you wouldn't have gotten the interview.
- **Preparation:** You need to do a great deal of research and study on both the industry in general and the company in particular. Learn the buzz words, jargon, and politics of the industry by reading a year's worth of trade magazines. Research the company's role in the industry by searching for mentions of it in the past five years of trade magazines. Learn about the competition. You want to demonstrate that you have the ability to gain and comprehend industry-specific knowledge very quickly.
- **Timing:** You'll have little control over when this meeting takes place, or over how long it lasts. That's why you need to make all your major points as early and as often as possible. If you get to the stage of the interview covered in this dialogue, you're a top candidate.
- **Behavior:** Don't get upset by questions about the applicability of your prior experience, or about how you'll deal with others' reactions to your shift of industries. These are understandable concerns. The interviewer will have to answer these questions from others—as will you—and may need the ammunition you'll provide.

5. Interviewing for a Career-Shift Job

General probe: *What makes you think you're qualified to fill this position even though you have no experience in this industry?*

General response: While I've never been in your industry, I've solved the same kinds of problems, met the same kinds of deadlines, managed the same kinds of people, and done the same kinds of marketing. Even though I come from a different industry, I possess the same skills and abilities you require. For example, *[cite specific examples]*.

Jargon/players probe: *That may be. But you're not familiar with the jargon we use, the language and culture of our industry [or] the players in the business, the people who make things happen.*

Jargon/players response: As a matter of fact, I've made a concerted effort to learn the industry's language *[or]* to familiarize myself with the players in the industry. I want to make sure this job isn't an experiment for either of us. I'm determined to bring with me the skills, abilities, and knowledge I'll need to succeed.

Underlings probe: *I'm confident about your skills, but how will you deal with underlings who have more experience in the industry than you?*

Underlings response: I'll deal with them just as I've dealt with staffs in the past. I'll learn from them when I can and take their suggestions if valid. But I'll also demonstrate to them, as I have to you, that my experience and knowledge is transferable to this industry.

Peers probe: *I'm afraid the other department managers may perceive you as a threat, or as a sign that massive changes are coming. After all, someone with your background being named to this position would be unprecedented for this company.*

Peers response: I think fear of change is natural to everyone. I saw the same kind of problems in other industries. I've discovered that once people show they can do the job, all those fears vanish.

Superiors probe: *You make a strong case for yourself. But you know, I may have a hard time selling you to the people upstairs. They're not as open-minded as I am.*

Superiors response: I understand. No matter how good an idea is, if it's new, it's tough to sell. Please let me know if there's anything I can do to help you with this. And also, please accept my gratitude for any efforts you can make on my behalf. No matter where I go in this industry I'll always be grateful.

ADAPTATIONS

This script can be modified to:

- Shift the direction of a career within an industry; for example, an actor who has done only comedy could use a modification of this script to solicit a dramatic role

KEY POINTS

- General probes should be met by general responses that reiterate how your skills and abilities, as demonstrated by your experience, are just as relevant to this industry as they were to the industry you came from. View this as a chance to make your case once again.

- Questions about your not knowing industry jargon, politics, or people should be answered with evidence that you've already started learning all three, showing you'll be up to speed in these areas very quickly.

- Questions about the reaction of underlings should be answered by explaining how this is simply a management issue like others you've dealt with in the past, and one that can be easily overcome.

- Questions about the reaction of peers should be answered by noting the universality of such reactions and stating that the best way to deal with them is simply to demonstrate the ability to get the job done.

- Questions about the difficulties of selling your hire to superiors are either veiled requests for help or subtle solicitations for gratitude that will extend into the future. In response, offer your help, gratitude, and future loyalty.

Responding to Tough Interview Questions

6

STRATEGY

In today's competitive job market, more and more personnel executives are using a technique called "the stress interview." Rather than trying to verify the claims on your résumé, which can be easily done with a few telephone calls, their goal is to see how you react when under pressure. Typically, the tough questions appear out of the blue and begin with a general probe about what you perceive to be your weaknesses. While the experience isn't pleasant, it can be turned to your advantage. Besides, getting a third degree like this means you're considered one of the top candidates.

TACTICS

- **Attitude:** The single most important thing you can do is not take these probes personally. In some organizations such stress interviews are now standard operating procedure. Look on these questions as a rite of passage rather than a torture session and you'll be fine.

- **Preparation:** The best way to prepare is to examine your résumé objectively and look for areas that could be probed. The three most common are: the frequency with which you've moved from job to job; your reasons for leaving your last job and why you may be without work at the moment; and the length of time you've spent either in one company or one position.

- **Timing:** In this situation you have little control over general timing. However, the best way to respond to these questions is to pause for one beat before launching into your defense. That shows you're not answering reflexively but that you're also quick on your feet.

- **Behavior:** The worst thing you can do is get angry. Instead, remain calm and try not to change either your body language or manner.

6. Responding to Tough Interview Questions

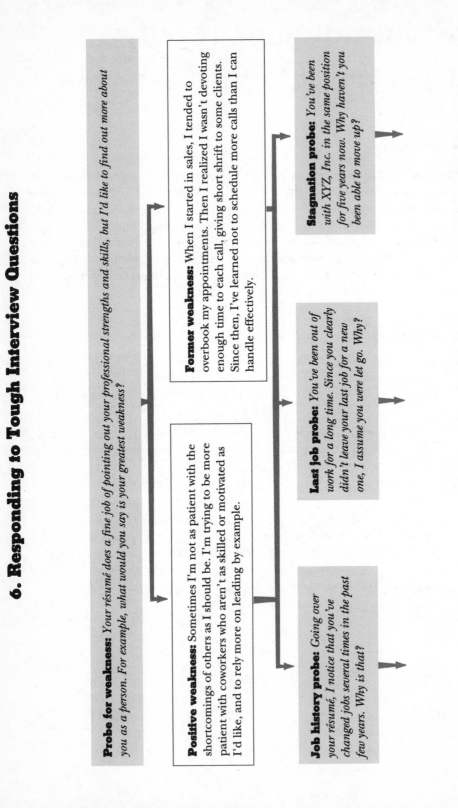

Probe for weakness: *Your résumé does a fine job of pointing out your professional strengths and skills, but I'd like to find out more about you as a person. For example, what would you say is your greatest weakness?*

Positive weakness: Sometimes I'm not as patient with the shortcomings of others as I should be. I'm trying to be more patient with coworkers who aren't as skilled or motivated as I'd like, and to rely more on leading by example.

Former weakness: When I started in sales, I tended to overbook my appointments. Then I realized I wasn't devoting enough time to each call, giving short shrift to some clients. Since then, I've learned not to schedule more calls than I can handle effectively.

Job history probe: *Going over your résumé, I notice that you've changed jobs several times in the past few years. Why is that?*

Last job probe: *You've been out of work for a long time. Since you clearly didn't leave your last job for a new one, I assume you were let go. Why?*

Stagnation probe: *You've been with XYZ, Inc. in the same position for five years now. Why haven't you been able to move up?*

Job history defense: As you can see, my job moves haven't been lateral; they've all led to positions of greater responsibility. Now that I've gained the experience, I'm looking to settle down with a company that will challenge me . . . . like this one.

→

Job history follow-up: *With your history of job-hopping, I'm not sure that you'd be content to stay in one place for long. Would you say you're the kind of person who gets bored easily?*

→

Closing job history defense: Not at all. But I do enjoy being challenged. In fact, what's been most exciting in my previous positions has been finding new ways to keep a product fresh in our customers' eyes. Am I right in thinking that's a crucial part of the job here?

Last job defense: Like so many places these days, my company was looking to cut payroll costs and wound up eliminating hundreds of jobs last year. I volunteered for the buyout program because I felt I'd reached the limit of what I could do there anyway.

→

Last job follow-up: *You've been looking for a new position for several months now, apparently without any luck. What seems to be the problem?*

→

Closing last job defense: I'm not looking for just another paycheck. My severance was generous enough to allow me to take the time to find a company that's right for me, where I can make a real contribution. Can you tell me more about precisely what this job entails?

Stagnation defense: The few positions that have opened up have gone to employees who have a lot more seniority than I do. That's why I'm looking for a company that offers a real opportunity to move up. What can you tell me about the possibilities for advancement here?

→

Stagnation follow-up: *Being in the same job at the same company for such a long time can make you stale. How will you cope with the challenge of a new job in a new organization?*

→

Closing stagnation defense: It's precisely because I don't want to get stale that I'm looking for new opportunities. From what I understand, your company offers just that. Can you tell me more about the kind of challenges I'd face in this job?

ADAPTATIONS

This script can be modified to:

- Deal with a co-op board or club screening committee
- Respond to probing informational interviews

KEY POINTS

- If asked about a general weakness, offer one that's either a "positive"—such as being a workaholic—or one that you had in the past which you've since corrected—such as overbooking.
- If your job history is probed, point out that your moves have been vertical rather than horizontal and that they've been part of a search for a position . . . coincidentally, like the one you're interviewing for.
- If your departure from your last job is probed, blame layoffs on the economy and long job hunts on your willingness to wait for the right position . . . coincidentally, like the one you're interviewing for.
- If you're accused of stagnation, blame seniority and explain that's why you're looking for a job that rewards merit and offers challenges . . . coincidentally, like the one you're interviewing for.
- The best way to deflect such probes is to constantly bring the discussion back to the job itself. The more specifically you do this, and the more diligently, the quicker the interviewer will back off the stress questions.

CHAPTER TWO

Lifescripts for Dealing with Superiors

Asking for a Salary Increase

7.

STRATEGY

While it has never been tougher to get a raise than today, it's still possible. The key is to realize there are only three acceptable reasons anymore: Your contributions to the company's bottom line have increased dramatically; your responsibilities have outgrown your job description; or (for professionals and upper-level managers) your income hasn't kept pace with your professional growth. Using and documenting one of these arguments, and forcing your supervisor to fall back on a poverty excuse, will at least result in your obtaining further nonfinancial compensation or a deferred promise. And sometimes, that's the best you can hope for.

TACTICS

- **Attitude:** Remember that your salary has nothing to do with your value as a human being. It is solely a reflection of what your supervisor or company is willing to pay for your services. It's an entirely economic issue.

- **Preparation:** It's essential to have irrefutable documentation that backs up whichever of the three arguments you're using. When it comes to documenting industrywide salary ranges, draw on trade magazine surveys, headhunters, and professional associations. All your information should be included in a memo, with appropriate attachments, that outlines your argument.

- **Timing:** The best times to ask are shortly after a positive evaluation, upon successful completion of an important project, or after receiving some third-party recognition, such as an award. Avoid Mondays and Fridays entirely. Ask for an appointment either before business hours or just after lunch. The former will offer fewer interruptions; the latter will find the other party more relaxed.

- **Behavior:** It's completely up to you to blow your own horn, so avoid humility and subservience. Don't project guilt—you're asking for what you deserve. This forthright attitude will come through if you maintain direct eye contact whenever listening or speaking. Only break eye contact when you're thinking. Avoid nodding reflexively. Your agreement is powerful, especially in this situation. Let the other party fill in gaps in the conversation. Chattiness will imply insecurity. Speak only when necessary and you'll convey strength and confidence.

7. Asking for a Salary Increase

Icebreaker: I'd like to thank you for the opportunity you and the company have given me. I recognize that you've been very influential in my growth and advancement. However, I have a problem that I need your help with.

Pitch #1: What has happened is that I've been concentrating solely on my professional growth and haven't been paying any attention to my stream of income. So I've done some research and found my peers in the industry are earning on average 15 percent more than my current compensation. I've drafted this memo that shows what I've found. It's logical for my compensation to keep pace with my growth. To do that, I'll need an increase of *[state increase]*.

Pitch #2: I think my salary no longer reflects my contribution to the company. In the past year I've helped the company save a great deal of money *[or]* bring in added revenue *[or]* trim quite a bit from the cost of operations. I've done some research and I've found that a salary of *[state salary]* would more accurately reflect my value. I've prepared a brief memo outlining my accomplishments and my request.

Pitch #3: I think my salary no longer matches my job responsibilities. During the past year I've moved from being an order taker to helping supervise the evening sales staff and helping draft the new selling scripts. I've done some research and I think a salary of *[state salary]* would more accurately reflect my responsibilities. I've prepared a brief memo outlining my increased responsibilities and my request.

Facts are wrong: *I can't believe you're underpaid. Let me take a look at your numbers. These figures come from companies larger than ours. If you check with companies the same size as ours you'll find you're making exactly what you should.*

Not enough time: *I won't argue your point. You've done an excellent job. But you simply haven't been here long enough [or] it simply hasn't been long enough since your last increase for you to merit a raise.*

Don't have the money: *I agree you've been doing a wonderful job. But, as you know, business has been slow. The company simply doesn't have the money for raises right now [or] doesn't have that kind of money right now.*

Wouldn't be fair: *I agree with you completely. We're very happy with your work. But we have a policy of . . . . How can I pay you more than Jean Smith, for instance, when she has worked here two years longer than you have?*

Solicit other sources: I don't want what I'm not entitled to. If my research is incomplete I'll be happy to do some more and come back to you with it, let's say, in two weeks. What companies would you consider comparable to ours?

Time is unfair measure: I really don't think you can fairly measure my contribution to the company by the amount of time I've been here [or] by how long it has been since my last raise. Let me go over the contributions I've outlined in my memo.

Seniority is unfair measure: I've always assumed that excellent performance and taking on added responsibility would be rewarded in this company. I don't think it's fair to deny rewarding me for my contributions because of my lack of seniority. Let me go over the contributions I've outlined in my memo.

Expand the discussion: I understand. You can't do the impossible. But perhaps we can agree to an increase that would take effect, let's say, in six months. Meanwhile, there are some nonfinancial areas I need to speak with you about. For instance, I'd like another five vacation days....

Refuses to expand: *I don't think either will be possible. The money may not be there in another six months, and adding to your vacation would be contrary to company policy. You'll have to wait.*

Won't offer sources: *I'd have to think about it. I'm really not sure. But I am sure you're not underpaid.*

Offers other sources: *Why don't you try looking at Smith & Jones and Pinnacle. They're both about our size. When you get numbers from them we'll talk again.*

Agrees to expand: *I can't guarantee the money will be there in another six months either. We'll have to see. But the added vacation days shouldn't be a problem.*

Ask for another meeting: I understand. But I need to leave here with a definite date for our next discussion. How about four months from today? Also, I'd appreciate your double checking about those vacation days. *[Start looking for another job.]*

Seize initiative: I'll look into it further, and take the companies you suggested into account. Then, I'll come back to you with more results. Meanwhile, let's nail down that meeting. How about two weeks from today?

ADAPTATIONS

This script can be modified to:

- Obtain consideration for a promotion to another department or get a title changed
- Get your employer to pay for continuing education

KEY POINTS

- Begin by stressing you love your job or company, but have a problem you need help with.
- Your argument is that your compensation doesn't match either your growth, contribution, or responsibilities.
- If your numbers are called into question, ask where you can get "correct" numbers. If none are offered, suggest some of your own and ask for a follow-up meeting.
- If the other party says insufficient time has passed from some other event, say time isn't relevant to your growth, contribution, or responsibilities.
- If fairness to others is cited, say that compensation based solely on seniority is also unfair.
- If the other party pleads poverty, ask for nonfinancial compensation and/or a future agreement.
- If you're stonewalled, force a future meeting and start looking for another job.

Asking for a Promotion

STRATEGY

Asking for a promotion is even more difficult than asking for a raise. That's because you have to demonstrate not only that you have the skills to handle the new position, but also that leaving your current job won't hurt either your boss or the company. The secret is to prepare two plans of action: one for the new position and one for your current job. Don't fall back on seniority or hierarchy to make your case—they don't hold water in today's business world. Focus on your proven ability to do the job and emphasize that you're ready to move up. One other essential: Make sure to present your case as soon as possible, preferably before an outside search has begun.

TACTICS

- **Attitude:** Look on this, not as something you're owed for past services, but as an opportunity you've shown you're ready for. There are no entitlements in today's workplace.

- **Preparation:** Draft two formal memos—one outlining what you'd do in the first 90 days in the new job and another explaining how you'd assist whoever takes over your current position. In addition, have in mind potential replacements for your position.

- **Timing:** It is absolutely essential to stake your claim to the job as soon as you hear it's available. Consider dropping hints and spreading the word informally if you can do it without looking pushy. The more time that passes, the less your chances of landing the job.

- **Behavior:** Accept compliments and constructive criticism gracefully, but don't hesitate to argue around these points by directing the conversation to your strengths rather than your weaknesses.

8. Asking for a Promotion

Icebreaker and pitch: I understand Keith is leaving. I'm hoping that you'll seriously consider me for his job. Since he and I have worked so closely together over the past year, I'm very familiar with the department and what's required. And when I've filled in for Keith, I think I've shown that I can manage the staff effectively.

You're not ready: *You've shown tremendous growth over the past year, but you don't have enough experience yet with customer service or with managing a staff to take on a job like Keith's.*

Have inside knowledge: I may not have been at it a long time, but I think I've shown a real flair for customer service. Even more important, I know how this department works, inside and out. You won't get that kind of experience if you go outside.

Need you where you are: *You've been doing an outstanding job in your position—that's exactly why I can't afford to move you right now. I need you where you are.*

Will help train: Thank you. I appreciate your confidence in me. But I'd be happy to work closely with my replacement until she's completely familiar with my system. In fact, I can suggest people in my department who would be great for the job.

Going outside: *I appreciate your interest in the position, but we've decided that we need a completely fresh approach. That's why we're looking outside the company for a replacement.*

Have fresh approach: I think I can offer a fresh approach—and at a much lower cost than if you go outside the company. I have a lot of ideas that I think could really reenergize the staff. And after four years in my current job I'm eager for a new challenge.

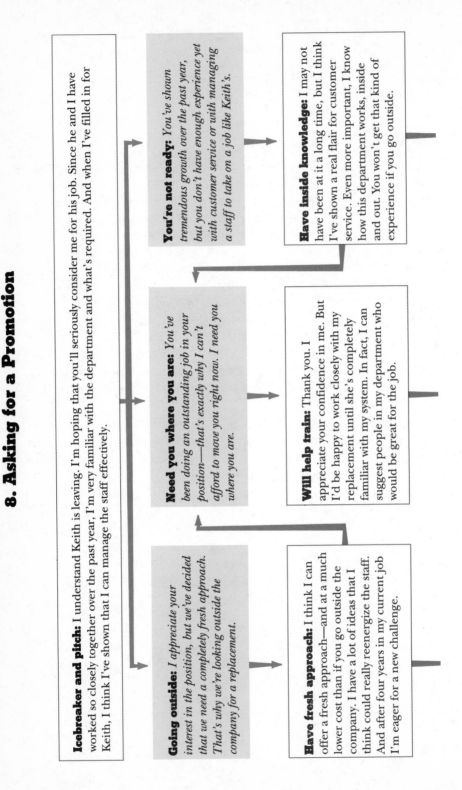

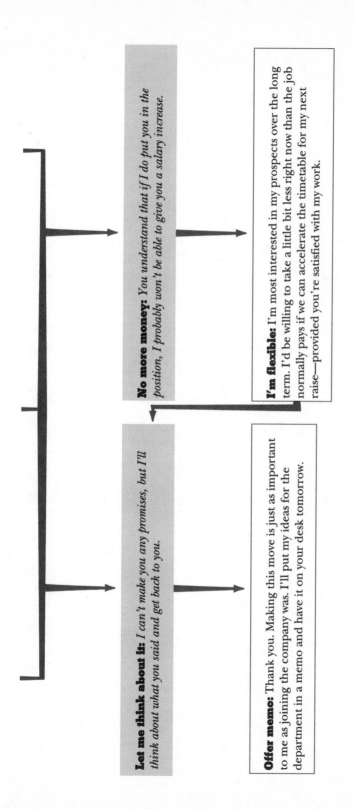

No more money: *You understand that if I do put you in the position, I probably won't be able to give you a salary increase.*

I'm flexible: I'm most interested in my prospects over the long term. I'd be willing to take a little bit less right now than the job normally pays if we can accelerate the timetable for my next raise—provided you're satisfied with my work.

Let me think about it: *I can't make you any promises, but I'll think about what you said and get back to you.*

Offer memo: Thank you. Making this move is just as important to me as joining the company was. I'll put my ideas for the department in a memo and have it on your desk tomorrow.

ADAPTATIONS

This script can be modified to:

- Request a transfer
- Move ahead in a political or social organization
- Broadcast your ambitions and willingness for more responsibility

KEY POINTS

- Acknowledge that you've heard there's an opening, state your qualifications, and directly ask to be considered for the job.
- Respond to arguments for going outside by demonstrating how you can bring a fresh approach . . . at a lower cost.
- Don't let your success be used against you. Offer to work closely with your own replacement.
- Claims that you don't have sufficient seniority can be met by showing how your time, while short, has been intensive and exactly what is necessary to do the job.
- Be prepared to forego a raise—at least until you've proven yourself.
- Have a memo ready outlining your plans.

Asking for Flextime

9

STRATEGY

One excellent solution to the child-care dilemma is for one or both parents to work out flexible hours, or "flextime," arrangements with their employers. While these are tough sells, especially to conservative employers, they can be accomplished. The secrets are to approach this as a rehire since, in effect, you're redefining your job status; to stress your commitment to the company especially in light of your being a parent; and to "yes" your employer to death, showing your willingness to assume every cost or burden yourself. Of course, the more valuable you are to the company, the more likely you are to get the schedule you want.

TACTICS

- **Attitude:** Realize that you're asking your employer to break company tradition as well as give up some control over you. That means it's essential to let her retain the feeling that she's still in charge.

- **Preparation:** First, ascertain your value to the company. Second, develop a plan that will let you accomplish as much, if not more, than before. Third, determine exactly what office or communications equipment you'll need to be able to do your job, and be ready to assume the cost. Fourth, think of every possible objection to your plan and have a solution ready—even if it means taking a temporary salary reduction. And fifth, draft a cogent, eloquent memo outlining your proposal.

- **Timing:** If you're already on parental leave, this meeting should take place before you actually return to work. If you haven't yet left on leave, postpone the meeting until you're ready to return. If you're not going on leave, have the meeting as soon as possible.

- **Behavior:** Express your gratitude to your supervisor and the company, but don't come off as a supplicant. Act as if you are on a job interview—confident and eager. Treat this as a business arrangement, not a favor. Sure, you're asking for something, but you're ready to make concessions in order to get it. If possible, let your supervisor have the last word—that will reaffirm her feeling of being in charge.

9. Asking for Flextime

Icebreaker: I wanted to tell you how much I've looked forward to coming back to work. Being away these past two months has reinforced how strongly I feel about my job here. That's why I wanted to meet with you today.

Pitch: I think I've figured out a way to balance my obligations to my family and my responsibilities on the job. By working at home on Mondays and Fridays I'll be able to resolve my child care problems and fulfill all my work duties. On Tuesdays, Wednesdays, and Thursdays I'll be able to attend staff meetings, sit in on planning sessions, and meet with clients and editors. Mondays and Fridays I'll concentrate on preparing press kits and releases and making follow-up calls to editors. I'll be able to accomplish as much as I did before, if not more, and I can guarantee the quality of my work won't suffer.

Feasibility objection: I know you feel strongly about your job—but you wouldn't be human if you didn't put your child first. I can't see how you're going to be able to concentrate on your work while you're at home with your son.

Explain your backup: I thought of that too. I spoke with my wife and she has agreed to care for our son in the morning and

Precedent objection: I don't doubt what you're saying. But if I make this kind of arrangement with you I'd have to do it with everyone else in the company who'd rather work at home. I'm sorry but I can't afford to set a precedent.

Make it an exception: This would let me continue to deliver the kind of performance you've praised me for in the past.

Salary objection: You may be able to do your job that way, but how am I going to justify your putting in less time here, while still making the same money? I know it's results that count, but the people upstairs and your coworkers watch the clock.

Make a concession: I also think it's productivity, not hours, that counts. But I know the kinds of pressures you're under.

Cost objection: I just don't see how you're going to be able to do your job from home without a tremendous amount of equipment. I don't think the company would be willing to foot the bill for what you'd need.

Assume the necessary cost: You're right. The equipment isn't cheap. But my wife and I decided it was a worthwhile

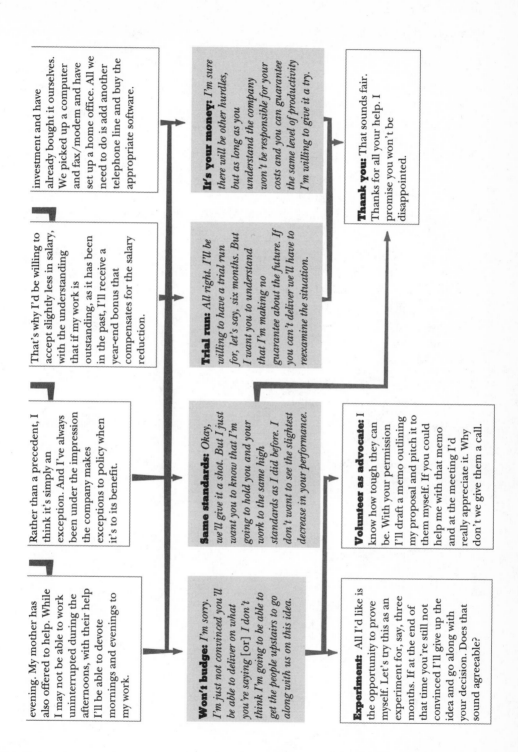

investment and have already bought it ourselves. We picked up a computer and fax/modem and have set up a home office. All we need to do is add another telephone line and buy the appropriate software.

That's why I'd be willing to accept slightly less in salary, with the understanding that if my work is outstanding, as it has been in the past, I'll receive a year-end bonus that compensates for the salary reduction.

Rather than a precedent, I think it's simply an exception. And I've always been under the impression the company makes exceptions to policy when it's to its benefit.

evening. My mother has also offered to help. While I may not be able to work uninterrupted during the afternoons, with their help I'll be able to devote mornings and evenings to my work.

It's your money: *I'm sure there will be other hurdles, but as long as you understand the company won't be responsible for your costs and you can guarantee the same level of productivity I'm willing to give it a try.*

Trial run: *All right. I'll be willing to have a trial run for, let's say, six months. But I want you to understand that I'm making no guarantee about the future. If you can't deliver we'll have to reexamine the situation.*

Same standards: *Okay, we'll give it a shot. But I just want you to know that I'm going to hold you and your work to the same high standards as I did before. I don't want to see the slightest decrease in your performance.*

Won't budge: *I'm sorry. I'm just not convinced you'll be able to deliver on what you're saying [or] I don't think I'm going to be able to get the people upstairs to go along with us on this idea.*

Thank you: That sounds fair. Thanks for all your help. I promise you won't be disappointed.

Volunteer as advocate: I know how tough they can be. With your permission I'll draft a memo outlining my proposal and pitch it to them myself. If you could help me with that memo and at the meeting I'd really appreciate it. Why don't we give them a call.

Experiment: All I'd like is the opportunity to prove myself. Let's try this as an experiment for, say, three months. If at the end of that time you're still not convinced I'll give up the idea and go along with your decision. Does that sound agreeable?

ADAPTATIONS

This script can be modified to:

- Obtain independent contractor status
- Obtain part-time status

KEY POINTS

- Stress that you love your job more than ever, now that you're a parent—that's why you're asking for the meeting.
- Your argument should be that you've figured out a way to balance your "obligations" to the job with your "responsibilities" to your child.
- If your supervisor reflexively says your plan isn't feasible, describe how your plan addresses every contingency.
- If your supervisor says she can't set a precedent, frame the arrangement as an exception, not a new rule.
- If your supervisor says she can't justify paying you the same as before, agree to a temporary salary concession, but ask for a year-end bonus if you maintain your productivity.
- If your supervisor objects to the cost, offer to assume it yourself.
- If your supervisor still refuses, ask for a short trial period.
- If your supervisor expresses fear of higher-ups, volunteer to present the proposal yourself.

Asking for Emergency Leave

10.

STRATEGY

Unless yours is a company with an established procedure for emergency leaves, you'll need to ask your supervisor directly for time off. Be forewarned that some supervisors, despite their protestations, will be much more concerned with the effect your absence will have on the bottom line than your personal problem. The secret to this dialogue is to make it clear you've no choice but to take the time off, but that your workload can be adequately handled either by others or through your remaining in constant touch with the office. While you may be able to fend off attempts to turn your emergency leave into your vacation, when push comes to shove you'll have to accept that unless your supervisor is both powerful and gracious, you may have to forgo salary while you're away. Your goal here is to get the time off and, if at all possible, to keep your vacation.

TACTICS

- **Attitude:** In your heart of hearts you must feel this is a true emergency—otherwise you won't convey the necessary sense of urgency to carry the day. You must be able to say honestly you've no choice.
- **Preparation:** Before having this conversation, make sure that you have plans—including detailed memos—in place to handle any workplace problems that could arise, and that your current projects are all in good shape.
- **Timing:** To the extent possible, have this conversation as early in the day and as early in the workweek as you can. Try contacting your staff or whoever will be filling in for you before working hours so contingency plans are already in place when it comes time to meet the boss.
- **Behavior:** The more concerned and determined you are to take a leave of absence, and the more willing you are to do whatever needs to be done to get the time off, the smoother this dialogue will go.

10. Asking for Emergency Leave

Icebreaker: I have a family problem and I need an emergency leave of absence. I'll need to be away for three weeks.

Ask for details: *Slow down. First tell me what's wrong. What happened?*

Explain situation: My uncle passed away unexpectedly and his affairs are in a shambles. He has no children and there's no one else in the family with the ability to handle it. I've already spoken to my assistant, Pat, about all pending matters. All our projects are in good shape and I'll be in touch daily by telephone, fax, and modem.

Use your vacation time: *Well, you do have two weeks vacation coming to you, although I'd prefer having had notice about when you'd be taking it. As for the third week, we'll work it out . . . maybe we can take it from next year's vacation.*

Gives grudging approval: *Well, as long as you're right and things are under control and you'll be in touch, I don't have a problem with it. Just try to be back as soon as possible.*

Not a vacation: I'd really rather not lose my vacation time for a family emergency. After all, it's not like I won't be working; and I will be in constant touch with the office. I was hoping the company wouldn't penalize me for the death of my uncle.

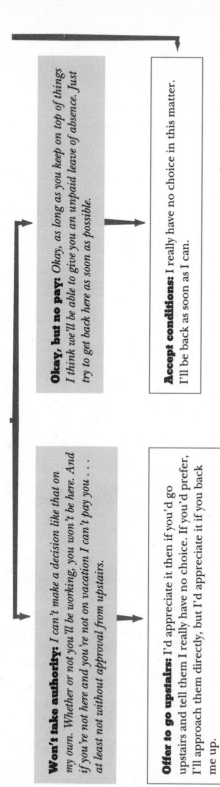

Won't take authority: *I can't make a decision like that on my own. Whether or not you'll be working, you won't be here. And if you're not here and you're not on vacation I can't pay you . . . at least not without approval from upstairs.*

Okay, but no pay: *Okay, as long as you keep on top of things I think we'll be able to give you an unpaid leave of absence. Just try to get back here as soon as possible.*

Offer to go upstairs: I'd appreciate it then if you'd go upstairs and tell them I really have no choice. If you'd prefer, I'll approach them directly, but I'd appreciate it if you back me up.

Accept conditions: I really have no choice in this matter. I'll be back as soon as I can.

ADAPTATIONS

This script can be modified to:

- Get partial time off to go to school
- Get an extended leave of absence to wind up family business
- Get a medical leave for elective surgery

KEY POINTS

- Present your request for time off prior to divulging the details of the emergency. This forces your boss to ask what's wrong, hopefully setting a humane tone for the meeting.
- Stress that all your work is under control and that you'll be available should any problems arise.
- Fend off any attempt to take away vacation time by suggesting that it would constitute unfair punishment for something that's beyond your control.
- If your boss claims she's powerless, offer to take your case to higher-ups, but ask for her support.
- If you're forced to go without pay, demonstrate the urgency of the matter by accepting the condition.

Asking for an Increased Budget

11.

STRATEGY

Asking for an increased budget is the ultimate uphill battle in today's lean business environment. Still, it can be done—as long as you frame it properly. The secret is to present the budget increase as a proactive effort to take advantage of an already existing opportunity, resulting in an improvement to the company's bottom line. That means it will boost revenues more than it will increase costs. It cannot be seen as a reaction to prior cuts, an attempt for more personal power, a totally new concept, an effort to save time, or a drain on the company's coffers. Be aware that asking for an increased budget carries risks, whether you get it or not. If you achieve your goal you'll be under increased scrutiny. If you don't achieve it, you may be marked as being out of step.

TACTICS

- **Attitude:** Whatever the real circumstances underlying your request, the attitude you bring to the meeting must be one of excitement and hope, rather than despair and exasperation.

- **Preparation:** Develop an ironclad business plan that documents how your proposed change will positively affect the bottom line. Make sure there are no loopholes or question marks. In addition, have a host of fall-back positions ready in case you're unable to overcome your superior's objections.

- **Timing:** Don't wait for budget time to present your plan. If you do, it will simply be seen as an effort to grab a bigger piece of the pie or to maintain what you've already got. Present your plan as soon as you've got all your documentation ready.

- **Behavior:** Act the same as in every other planning meeting you have with your supervisor. Remember: You're not asking for more money—you're demonstrating an opportunity to make more money and urging the company to take advantage of it. Refrain from suggesting cuts elsewhere, even if you're pushed. That will color your proposal as political.

11. Asking for an Increased Budget

Icebreaker: Thanks for seeing me. I think I've figured out a way for us to dramatically increase the net revenue generated by my department.

Pitch: By adding a sales position dedicated to classified sales, my figures show we can increase gross revenue by more than 40 percent with only a 10 percent increase in overhead. That translates into a substantial boost in our profitability. Take a look at this.

Attacks you: *Aren't you talking about something you should have done yourself? [or] Aren't you just trying to add to your power base?*

Too long-term: *Maybe you're right. But it looks like it could take a couple of years for it to pay off. We're not in the position to make any long-term investments right now.*

Don't have money: *You might be right. But we just don't have the money to gamble on something like this right now.*

Against grain: *Haven't you been reading the papers? The last thing anyone is doing these days is adding staff [or] increasing budgets. It's out of the question.*

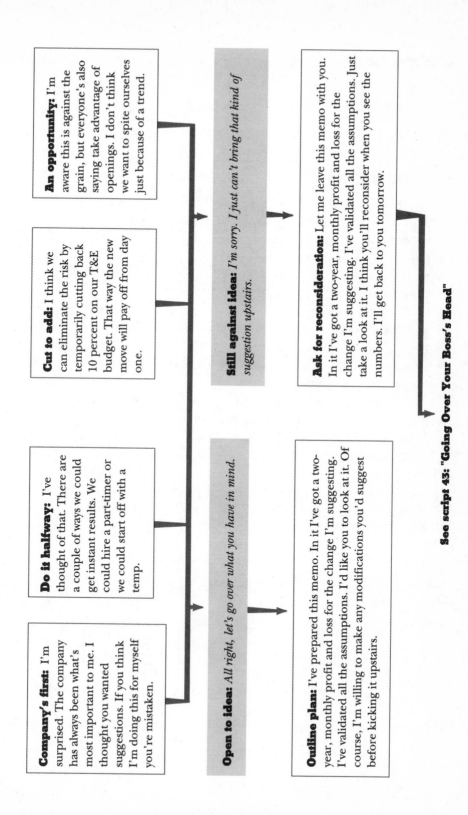

Company's first: I'm surprised. The company has always been what's most important to me. I thought you wanted suggestions. If you think I'm doing this for myself you're mistaken.

Do it halfway: I've thought of that. There are a couple of ways we could get instant results. We could hire a part-timer or we could start off with a temp.

Cut to add: I think we can eliminate the risk by temporarily cutting back 10 percent on our T&E budget. That way the new move will pay off from day one.

An opportunity: I'm aware this is against the grain, but everyone's also saying take advantage of openings. I don't think we want to spite ourselves just because of a trend.

Open to idea: *All right, let's go over what you have in mind.*

Still against idea: *I'm sorry. I just can't bring that kind of suggestion upstairs.*

Outline plan: I've prepared this memo. In it I've got a two-year, monthly profit and loss for the change I'm suggesting. I've validated all the assumptions. I'd like you to look at it. Of course, I'm willing to make any modifications you'd suggest before kicking it upstairs.

Ask for reconsideration: Let me leave this memo with you. In it I've got a two-year, monthly profit and loss for the change I'm suggesting. I've validated all the assumptions. Just take a look at it. I think you'll reconsider when you see the numbers. I'll get back to you tomorrow.

See script 43: "Going Over Your Boss's Head"

ADAPTATIONS

This script can be modified to:

- Ask for an assistant
- Ask for a new piece of equipment

KEY POINTS

- Frame your proposal as "an opportunity," explain that you've just "uncovered" it, and stress, as early in the conversation as possible, that it will boost net revenues.
- If your supervisor attacks you and suggests the proposal is self-serving, act surprised and hurt, but not angry, and stress you've always put the company first.
- If your supervisor objects to even a short-term negative impact on the bottom line, provide temporary options that will offer instant positive results.
- If your supervisor objects to any additional outlay, suggest temporary shifts in your own operations to compensate.
- If your supervisor says your idea is counter to current trends, show how it's really in line with today's business philosophy.
- If your supervisor remains hesitant, ask her to think about it and reconsider. Meanwhile, consider going over her head.

Breaking Bad News to a Boss

12.

STRATEGY

This is one of the most stressful and difficult dialogues you could have with a superior. Not only are you somewhat embarrassed by the failure—whether it was your fault or not—but you're also worried the setback could affect your standing in the organization. The key to fulfilling your obligations and minimizing any potential damage to you is to turn this meeting as quickly as possible into a discussion about what to do now, rather than a postmortem of what went wrong. The secrets of doing that are to make sure the news comes from you so you can control the spin; demonstrate that the situation was beyond your control, or accept the responsibility; and present a plan of action that mitigates the damage.

TACTICS

- **Attitude:** Approach this as an opportunity to prove you're resourceful and can take charge in a crisis. Be willing to accept the responsibility for what has happened, but not necessarily the blame. Finally, realize that your supervisor's anger may not be with you, but with the situation.

- **Preparation:** Have an explanation for why the problem has occurred. If there were any hints of trouble be ready to explain what you did in response. Most importantly, have a detailed written proposal that suggests a course of action.

- **Timing:** While you shouldn't burst into a closed-door meeting and blurt out the news, you must bring this to your supervisor's attention as soon as you can. It's essential the news come from you first.

- **Behavior:** Don't show contrition unless you were actually to blame. However, do show concern, not for yourself, but for the company. Use every possible chance to move beyond what happened to what to do now. Don't shy away from playing to your supervisor's ego . . . but try to be subtle. Sucking up won't take the place of accepting responsibility, but it can help deflect free-floating anger.

12. Breaking Bad News to a Boss

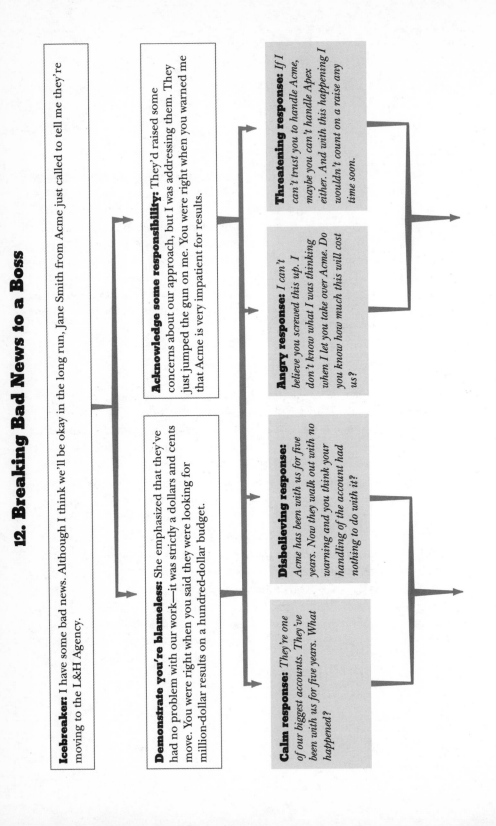

Icebreaker: I have some bad news. Although I think we'll be okay in the long run, Jane Smith from Acme just called to tell me they're moving to the L&H Agency.

Acknowledge some responsibility: They'd raised some concerns about our approach, but I was addressing them. They just jumped the gun on me. You were right when you warned me that Acme is very impatient for results.

Demonstrate you're blameless: She emphasized that they've had no problem with our work—it was strictly a dollars and cents move. You were right when you said they were looking for million-dollar results on a hundred-dollar budget.

Threatening response: *If I can't trust you to handle Acme, maybe you can't handle Apex either. And with this happening I wouldn't count on a raise any time soon.*

Angry response: *I can't believe you screwed this up. I don't know what I was thinking when I let you take over Acme. Do you know how much this will cost us?*

Disbelieving response: *Acme has been with us for five years. Now they walk out with no warning and you think your handling of the account had nothing to do with it?*

Calm response: *They're one of our biggest accounts. They've been with us for five years. What happened?*

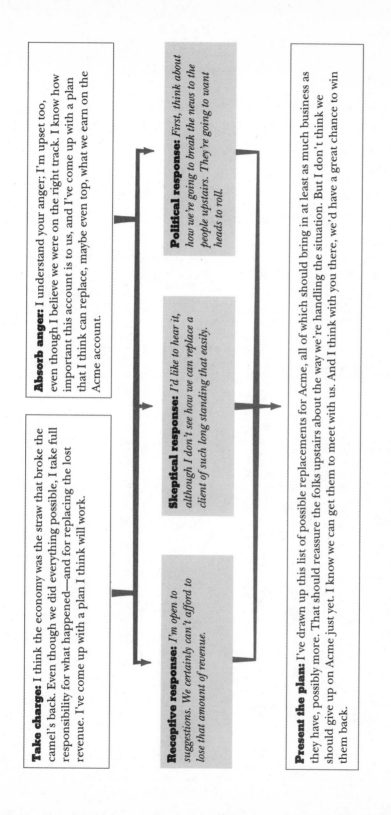

Take charge: I think the economy was the straw that broke the camel's back. Even though we did everything possible, I take full responsibility for what happened—and for replacing the lost revenue. I've come up with a plan I think will work.

Absorb anger: I understand your anger; I'm upset too, even though I believe we were on the right track. I know how important this account is to us, and I've come up with a plan that I think can replace, maybe even top, what we earn on the Acme account.

Political response: *First, think about how we're going to break the news to the people upstairs. They're going to want heads to roll.*

Skeptical response: *I'd like to hear it, although I don't see how we can replace a client of such long standing that easily.*

Receptive response: *I'm open to suggestions. We certainly can't afford to lose that amount of revenue.*

Present the plan: I've drawn up this list of possible replacements for Acme, all of which should bring in at least as much business as they have, possibly more. That should reassure the folks upstairs about the way we're handling the situation. But I don't think we should give up on Acme just yet. I know we can get them to meet with us. And I think with you there, we'd have a great chance to win them back.

ADAPTATIONS

This script can be modified to:

- Break bad news to parents, friends, spouses, teachers, etc.
- Deliver negative financial news to an investor or partner

KEY POINTS

- Be direct, but try to offer some hope as soon as possible.
- Immediately either demonstrate you're blameless or acknowledge your responsibility.
- If your supervisor takes the news well, or still questions your account, restate your position and move right on to your plan of action.
- If your supervisor gets angry or threatens you, try to get on her side by saying you're angry too, and then move on to what you think should be done now.
- Whatever the initial response to your plan, reaffirm your belief that it will work, add some flattery, and offer whatever help you can in overcoming the problem.

Maximizing a Performance Review

13.

STRATEGY

The key to getting the most from a positive performance review, or to minimizing the damage from a negative one, is to subtly take charge of the conversation by preempting the reviewer. If you expect a positive review, immediately launch into the new challenges you'd like to take on. If you expect a negative review, immediately describe your plan to improve. The idea is to get off negative issues as quickly as possible and turn this meeting into a positive and constructive discussion of your plan. If you don't succeed in taking control, push for a subsequent meeting and try again.

TACTICS

- **Attitude:** Look on this as a chance to take charge of your future, rather than a postmortem on your past.
- **Preparation:** Conduct a thorough self-analysis to determine whether your review will be primarily positive or negative. Then, develop a plan to either take advantage of the positive review or correct past mistakes and shortcomings.
- **Timing:** While you'll have little control over when this meeting takes place, be ready to postpone it should anything problematic occur during the conversation. For example, if you're in your supervisor's office discussing your performance and she gets a call that the company's largest customer has gone bankrupt, immediately suggest an adjournment.
- **Behavior:** When receiving constructive criticism or compliments, it's important to acknowledge them with more than just physical gestures. Rather than just nodding, say you understand. Take your supervisor's suggestions, put them in your own words, and repeat them. Offer sincere thanks for any input, positive or negative.

13. Maximizing a Performance Review

Icebreaker: I really enjoy my work, so I'm glad to have this opportunity to talk with you.

Expect positive review: I believe I've met most of last year's goals—I've brought in new clients and revamped our marketing strategy. So I've developed some new goals I'd like to shoot for.

Expect negative review: I know that I've had some difficulties this year and that some clients have complained. I've thought a lot about what happened and why, and about how I can improve.

Gives up control: *I've been very happy with your work, and I'm pleased that you took those goals so seriously. What do you have in mind for next year?*

Retains control: *In general, you've done a very good job this year, but there are a few areas I think you need to work on. [Explains specifics.]*

Retains control: *I have gotten negative feedback, and that has added to my own concerns. Let me tell you what I see as the major problems. [Explains specifics.]*

Gives up control: *I haven't been pleased with your performance, and I'm glad you realize that. Now tell me what you plan to do to turn things around.*

Your pitch: I've enjoyed working in marketing, but I think I'd be more useful if I had financial expertise too. So I'd like to take on budgeting.

Lead-in to pitch: *[After hearing specifics.]* I appreciate your suggestions, and I'll work hard on them. I'd also like to get your feedback on my idea.

Lead-in to defense: *[After hearing specifics.]* I understand completely, and I'll get right on it. In fact, I've already started to address some problems.

Defense: I think I was so focused on drumming up new business that I neglected some of our existing clients. So I've started taking clients out and mending fences.

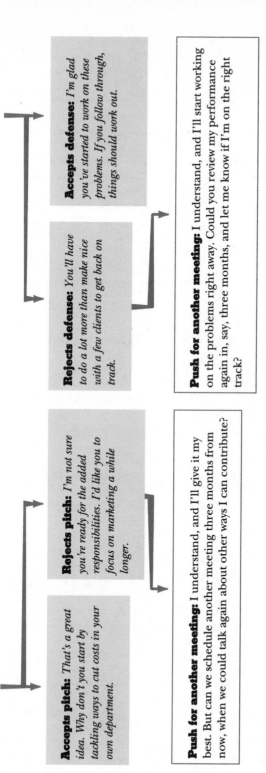

Accepts pitch: *That's a great idea. Why don't you start by tackling ways to cut costs in your own department.*

Rejects pitch: *I'm not sure you're ready for the added responsibilities. I'd like you to focus on marketing a while longer.*

Push for another meeting: I understand, and I'll give it my best. But can we schedule another meeting three months from now, when we could talk again about other ways I can contribute?

Rejects defense: *You'll have to do a lot more than make nice with a few clients to get back on track.*

Accepts defense: *I'm glad you've started to work on these problems. If you follow through, things should work out.*

Push for another meeting: I understand, and I'll start working on the problems right away. Could you review my performance again in, say, three months, and let me know if I'm on the right track?

ADAPTATIONS

This script can be modified to:

- Counter a problem that may arise when you're discussing a proposed raise or promotion
- Use as a segue into a discussion of a raise or promotion
- Handle a nonwork-related problem

KEY POINTS

- Stress how much you love your job and that you've looked forward to this meeting—whether or not it's true.
- If you expect a positive review, immediately launch into what you'd like to do in the coming year in order to set up raise or promotion discussions.
- If you expect a negative review, admit your problems and immediately launch into your plan for self-improvement.
- If your supervisor doesn't let you take charge of the conversation, segue into your plan after absorbing his comments.
- If your supervisor doesn't accept your plan, ask for another meeting at which you can try to take charge once again.

Asking for a Salary Advance

14

STRATEGY

Believe it or not, this is one of the most dangerous scripts in this book. While getting an advance on your salary may, in the short term, get you out of financial trouble, it carries a great many long-term risks. In order to maximize your chances for getting the advance, you're going to have to push your supervisor right to the edge—and then back off if necessary. That could change what has been a good relationship between you and your supervisor into an uncomfortable one. It could also change your supervisor's perception of you from a rising star to just your average Joe or Jane. Therefore, consider asking for an advance only as a last resort.

TACTICS

- **Attitude:** Realize you're asking for something out of the ordinary, but that you're really asking only for what already belongs to you. You're not a beggar or a borrower, but you are possibly asking to be treated like one.

- **Preparation:** Make sure that you've exhausted all your other options before going to your supervisor, and that the reason you need the money doesn't reflect an inability to manage your life or your finances. The best, in fact the only good, reason is that something unforeseen and beyond your control occurred to someone other than you.

- **Timing:** Lay the groundwork for the request by seeing your supervisor before business hours and asking for an appointment to discuss a personal matter. That conveys urgency but reassures your supervisor that it has nothing to do with business.

- **Behavior:** Stress that you're not asking for a loan. Instead, refer to this as a "draw" or an "advance" on future salary. Don't plead or beg, but showing some anxiety is okay—particularly if it's anxiety over what your supervisor will think of you.

14. Asking for a Salary Advance

Preliminary icebreaker: Excuse me, Susan, I need to speak with you sometime today about a personal matter. Would 2:00 P.M. be okay?

Later that day

Icebreaker: Thanks for seeing me. I need your help concerning an unforeseen financial responsibility. My uncle passed away last night, and since he left no money and there's no one else, I'm going to have to pick up the costs of the funeral and burial.

Pitch: My problem is that I'm not in a financial position to pay the bills right now. What I'd like is an advance on my future salary. I want to make it clear I'm not asking for a loan from you or the company.

No way: *I'm sorry about your uncle. However, the company has a policy against lending money to employees.*

Okay: *I'm sorry about your uncle. The company isn't crazy about issuing advances but I think I can swing it. How much do you need?*

Sneaky no: *I'm sorry about your uncle. We're not a bank but I'd like to help. Why don't you call Smith at our bank about a loan? I'll put in a good word for you.*

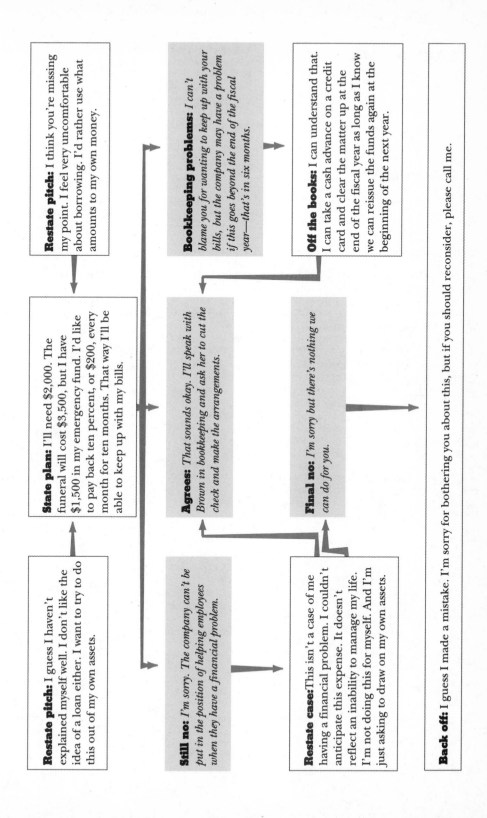

Restate pitch: I guess I haven't explained myself well. I don't like the idea of a loan either. I want to try to do this out of my own assets.

State plan: I'll need $2,000. The funeral will cost $3,500, but I have $1,500 in my emergency fund. I'd like to pay back ten percent, or $200, every month for ten months. That way I'll be able to keep up with my bills.

Restate pitch: I think you're missing my point. I feel very uncomfortable about borrowing. I'd rather use what amounts to my own money.

Bookkeeping problems: *I can't blame you for wanting to keep up with your bills, but the company may have a problem if this goes beyond the end of the fiscal year—that's in six months.*

Off the books: I can understand that. I can take a cash advance on a credit card and clear the matter up at the end of the fiscal year as long as I know we can reissue the funds again at the beginning of the next year.

Still no: *I'm sorry. The company can't be put in the position of helping employees when they have a financial problem.*

Agrees: *That sounds okay. I'll speak with Brown in bookkeeping and ask her to cut the check and make the arrangements.*

Final no: *I'm sorry but there's nothing we can do for you.*

Restate case: This isn't a case of me having a financial problem. I couldn't anticipate this expense. It doesn't reflect an inability to manage my life. I'm not doing this for myself. And I'm just asking to draw on my own assets.

Back off: I guess I made a mistake. I'm sorry for bothering you about this, but if you should reconsider, please call me.

ADAPTATIONS

This script can be modified to:

- Ask forbearance from a major creditor
- Ask for more after already receiving a major financial favor

KEY POINTS

- As early as possible, say you need an advance, not a loan, to help someone else, preferably a family member, out of an unforeseen and unavoidable problem.
- Make the point that this is actually drawing on your own assets.
- Reiterate your points until you feel your supervisor truly understands the situation, and either relents, or refuses outright to help.
- If your supervisor expresses bookkeeping concerns, offer to do whatever it takes to overcome the problem.
- If your supervisor refuses to help, back down, apologize for bothering her with a nonbusiness matter, but leave room for her to come back if she changes her mind.

Meeting a New Boss

15.

STRATEGY

Your first meeting with a new supervisor is vital since it often sets the tone for the entire relationship. Whether your new boss is coming in to clean up a troubled situation or to step into the shoes of a successful manager who has moved on, and whether she is coming from within or outside the company, you can count on one thing: She will want to put her own stamp on operations. That's why your goal in this first meeting should be to get a hint about her plans. In order to do that, make your first conversation seem spontaneous and casual—a simple welcome. Use whatever information you gain in this quick scouting mission to develop a full-fledged plan for a subsequent, in-depth, formal meeting.

TACTICS

- **Attitude:** Keep in mind this is only a scouting mission, but you still want to make a good first impression.
- **Preparation:** Learn as much as you can about your new boss's habits and history. Any specifics you learn can be used to make your subtle flattery more effective. Don't be concerned about actually using all your research.
- **Timing:** Timing is probably the key to pulling off this dialogue as planned. You must make sure to beat your new boss's secretary or assistant into the office, so you can just casually stick your head in the door and say hello. The secret is to make sure you're the first one in the office the day you've chosen for the meeting. This needs to be a speedy encounter.
- **Behavior:** Project warmth and good humor by smiling, making and maintaining eye contact, and offering a firm handshake. While this is supposed to be a casual conversation, don't forget to remain respectful and humble. If you can find a spot to offer some subtle flattery, feel free.

15. Meeting a New Boss

Icebreaker: Ms. Green? Hi. We haven't been formally introduced yet, but I didn't want to wait any longer to welcome you. I'm Sean Curtis, manager of the publicity department.

Gives the brushoff: *It's nice to meet you, Sean. I'd like to talk with you, but right now I'm very busy settling in. Why don't you stop by my office again later in the week.*

Wants to talk now: *I've been meaning to look you up, Sean. Come in, please, and sit down. Let's go over some of the issues I understand your department has been wrestling with.*

Probes for more: *Thanks for stopping by, Sean. I hear your department is one of the busiest in the company. Is this purely a social visit, or is there something specific you want to discuss?*

Float suggestion: Of course. For now, let me just quickly mention that I've been looking into ways to promote our image more aggressively and really get our name into the marketplace. I'll go into more detail once you've had a chance to catch your breath.

Elicit ideas: I don't want to tie you up with a long conversation now, but I was hoping to get a quick sense of your priorities for the department. I'll work specifically on those and be prepared when you have more time to talk.

Stall for time: I'm sorry, I have a client conference in a few minutes. Can you fill me in briefly on your priorities now? Then I'll be sure to bring the right information, along with some related ideas I've been developing, when we do talk.

Appreciates input: *That could be an interesting discussion. Why don't you run some numbers and outline the specifics to me in a memo.*

Remains noncommittal: *I'd prefer to hear from you first. After all, you're a lot more familiar with the agenda in your department than I am.*

Mentions a problem: *Frankly, I'm concerned about the size of our payroll, and I'd like you to take a really hard look at your staffing.*

Agree and set up meeting: I'd be happy to. I'll check with your assistant to set up a convenient time when we can talk in more detail. I think we can improve results. But for now, I just want to say welcome—we're happy to have you on board.

ADAPTATIONS

This script can be modified to:

- Introduce yourself to a newly elected official
- Welcome a new neighbor
- Introduce yourself to your child's new teacher
- Conduct a reconaissance before a major business meeting

KEY POINTS

- Start by simply introducing yourself and offering a welcome.
- If you're brushed off or have trouble getting a hint, float a suggestion in order to get a response.
- If the new boss probes to see if there's more to your sudden appearance, honestly say you'd like to get a sense of her priorities.
- If she wants to talk right then, beg off, blaming it on a client or customer. You don't want to take the chance of making a mistake due to your lack of knowledge and preparation.
- If she mentions a problem, don't get defensive. Instead, handle it the same as if she simply offered a topic for future discussion.

Justifying an
Expense Report

16.

STRATEGY

You need to tread very carefully if one of your expense reports is questioned by a supervisor. You can assume that if you're called into a face-to-face meeting the problem isn't one of documentation—that could be handled with a telephone call or a visit from an administrative assistant or bookkeeper. Therefore, this meeting is calling into question either your judgment or your honesty. It's even possible there's a hidden agenda—perhaps your supervisor is building a case for termination or a negative review. Whatever the situation, your goal is to immediately admit to the error, but turn it into one of omission rather than commission. Your mistake was not catching the error yourself or not preparing them for the unusual charge.

TACTICS

- **Attitude:** Take this as a very serious probe, even if it's for a small amount. You need to clearly demonstrate that this in no way reflects on your honesty or judgment.

- **Preparation:** Unless you're given advance notice of a problem with your report you'll have little or no time to prepare for this specific meeting. Instead, make it your business always to double- and triple-check your expense reports prior to submission and *never* to knowingly pad them.

- **Timing:** You'll also have no control over the timing of this meeting. The only element of timing you can control is to have an immediate answer ready for any questions: Either the questionable expense was a mistake or you forgot to provide advance warning.

- **Behavior:** Even though this may be a probe of your personal integrity, don't become defensive. And never, ever argue—no matter what the amount involved, the risk is too great. Anger is a defense mechanism. It could be seen as an admission of guilt and could turn the meeting into a fight rather than a conversation. Instead, be forthright, sincere, and if need be, apologetic.

16. Justifying an Expense Report

Opener: *I have a problem with your expense report for last week's trip to Las Vegas.*

Express puzzled concern: Is there a problem with my documentation?

You spent too much: *No, your documentation is fine. The problem is how much you spent. Don't you think $600 for a dinner for four is way out of line?*

Personal not business: *No, your documentation is fine. The problem is you've got about $100 here for in-room movies. It's not our obligation to pay for your entertainment when you're not out with clients.*

Not your choice: You're absolutely right . . . but I left the choice of restaurants up to them. Since I initiated the dinner, and they're such good clients, I felt I had no choice but to pick up the check. If you look at past reports, you'll see I usually take clients to Joe's, where the prices are more reasonable. I really felt dreadful for the company. I'm sorry—I should have attached a note explaining the situation.

It was a mistake: I'm sorry. I didn't realize that was on the bill. Normally I *[or]* my secretary audit the bills before submitting them, but I used the rapid checkout and didn't have a chance this time. I never intended for the company to have to pay those charges. I'll take care of it right away. It won't happen again.

Questions explanation: *That sounds like a reasonable explanation. But what if I hadn't gone over your bill so closely—what would've happened then?*

Reaffirm honesty: The minute I saw the mistake I would've reimbursed the company for the personal charges, whether or not they were discovered.

Wants more notice: *I understand. In the future, just remember I have to send these upstairs. I need some warning if there's anything unusual so I can offer my own explanation.*

Express thanks: Thanks for being so understanding. I appreciate it. It won't happen again.

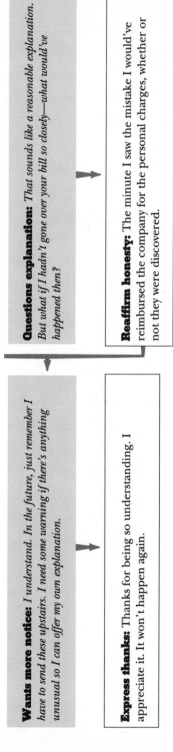

ADAPTATIONS

This script can be modified to:

- Explain a financial surprise to a spouse or partner
- Explain an error in an employment, loan, or credit application

KEY POINTS

- Even though you know it's not likely, ask if the problem is with your documentation. This shows you're feeling no guilt and were unaware of any potential problems.
- If you're accused of requesting reimbursement for personal expenses, immediately explain that the inclusion of the charges on your report was a mistake.
- If you're accused of spending too much, show how the cost was beyond your control and admit that it was a mistake not to provide forewarning of the unusually large charge.
- If your explanation is questioned, reaffirm your honesty as strongly as possible.
- Always express your thanks and stress the mistake won't happen again.

Pitching a Reluctant Supervisor

17

STRATEGY

There are some supervisors so insecure or fearful that they'll refuse to back up any ideas from subordinates (you) regardless of how potentially valuable they might be to the company. Pitching such an individual is an exercise in patience and preparation. Rather than approaching her with the germ of an idea, as you would a normal supervisor, you need to come with a fully developed proposal. That's because odds are you're not going to be able to convince her and you'll need to go over her head. Therefore, this dialogue can be a trial run for you, letting you see how your responses to objections are received. Your goal in this dialogue is to wear the reluctant supervisor down with answers to all her objections, until finally she relents and lets you put your idea forward to her superior.

TACTICS

- **Attitude:** You must have the company's best interests at heart, and hope that by helping the company you will help yourself. That's easiest to achieve if your idea is a solution to a problem or a way to boost the bottom line. If this is all about you and your ambition, it will be easy for a suspicious and fearful supervisor to block you.

- **Preparation:** Have answers to every possible objection, and include them in a well-written, thoroughly documented proposal memo. Be willing to share the credit.

- **Timing:** Make a formal appointment for either before business hours or just after lunch, when your supervisor is likely to be most relaxed. Don't hold the meeting shortly after or before performance review time—it will only add to your supervisor's suspicions and fears.

- **Behavior:** Don't belittle fears, no matter how petty or unrealistic. Instead, treat them as justified and show how you've answered them. Don't act as if it's a battle between you and your boss; it's an effort by you to help the company.

17. Pitching a Reluctant Supervisor

Icebreaker and pitch: Thanks for meeting with me. I know you're aware of the problem we've been having with very long lines forming at the checkouts twice a day. Customers are getting angry—I've even seen some walk out. I'm afraid if we don't address the problem soon we're going to lose customers for good. I'd like to propose a solution. I think we can solve the problem by instituting an automated checkout system and delivering the orders later in the day when we're not as busy.

Doesn't see problem : *Don't jump to conclusions. I don't think we've got a real problem here. After all, where are those customers going to go? I have more important problems to deal with. I can't waste time on this automated scheme of yours.*

Won't take any time: I know no one is busier than you are. That's why I've thoroughly tested this idea before coming to you with it. I can answer any questions the board might have. I've even drafted this memo with potential questions and our answers so you won't need to spend any time preparing for the presentation.

Gets defensive: *Listen, I've forgotten more about managing this operation than you'll ever know. Our problem is that your people aren't working hard enough. Crack the whip and those lines will disappear.*

Already done that: That was my first thought too. But I've developed incentive programs, had staff meetings, and even replaced someone, and the problem hasn't gone away. I think we have a customer problem, not a staff problem. I know customers can be fickle, but if we want to keep them I think we have to take this kind of step.

Financial objection: *Are you crazy? Something like that could end up costing us a fortune!*

Not that much money: I was concerned about the cost, too, so I made some calls and then did a cost/benefit analysis. An investment of $6,000 will yield $12,000 of additional profit each year by keeping customers who are now walking out.

Don't have the money: *Yes, but we don't have the $6,000 right now. Headquarters has been telling us to cut back. If we ask for additional funds, they'll blow their stacks.*

No money down: Instead of asking for a $6,000 outlay, we can spread the cost out by leasing the equipment. The monthly charges are so low that we'll be able to absorb them from our own budget.

Won't take a chance: *You make it sound foolproof, but I'm just not sure. The way business is right now, I'm not willing to go out on a limb and pitch something new, no matter how many good answers you've got prepared.*

Offer to assume responsibility: I can understand that. I wouldn't want you to take the blame if my idea doesn't pan out. I'll take full responsibility. I'd be glad to pitch upstairs if you'd prefer. If anyone's head will roll, it will be mine.

Agrees: *Okay. Run it by headquarters and let me know how it goes.*

Still refuses: *Saying that is one thing, but the buck still stops with me and I'm not willing to take the chance.*

See script 43: "Going Over Your Boss's Head"

ADAPTATIONS

This script can be modified to:

- Lay the foundation for an end run around your immediate superior
- Enhance your superior's perception of you

KEY POINTS

- Present your idea as something that can either solve a problem or boost the bottom line.
- Use mutual words like "we" and "our" until it becomes clear your supervisor wants nothing to do with the plan. At that point you can shift to words like "I" and "mine."
- If she gets angry, just absorb it and answer the actual objection rather than the emotional outburst.
- If she belittles the suggestion or complains of time constraints, offer to do all the work for her.
- If she objects on financial grounds, show how costs can be minimized and stress the long-term positive impact it will have on the bottom line.
- If she still won't support you, offer to pitch it to higher-ups and take all the blame if it fails (and therefore the credit if it works).

Refusing an Assignment

18

STRATEGY

The problem with refusing an assignment is there's no way to come out of it without some kind of loss. If you say it's a bad idea, you insult your supervisor who came up with it. If you say you don't have the time, your supervisor will think you're lazy. And if you say you don't have the skill to do it, your supervisor may lower her estimation of your abilities. Your goal should be to minimize the damage.

TACTICS

- **Attitude:** Realize that since you can't refuse outright or say it's a bad idea, you'll have to accept some damage to your image in order to get out of the assignment.

- **Preparation:** If you're going to claim lack of skill, have the name of someone else who has the skill. If you're asking for priorities to be set, prepare a complete list of the projects you're working on and the dates they're due.

- **Timing:** Never accept or decline an assignment immediately. Instead, say it's an interesting idea and you'd like some time to study it and prepare questions. Then, wait for your supervisor to bring it up again.

- **Behavior:** Express your disappointment at not being able to take on this wonderful assignment and your willingness, in fact, eagerness, to take on others in the future. Everything should be put in terms of what's best for the company.

18. Refusing an Assignment

The idea: *I was listening to the radio last night and I heard a story on a company that's selling compact discs in vending machines. I suddenly realized we could do the same thing with our books. We could put vending machines selling our line of books almost everywhere. Think of it! People could buy books at gas stations, at laundromats, at banks. I think this could revolutionize the way we do business. I want you to get on this right away. I need you to draft a report outlining how we can institute a vending-machine effort by this time next year. If this works out the way I hope, you could be in charge of our entire vending-machine effort. What do you think of that?*

Ask for time: I think you've come up with a fascinating idea, and I'm flattered you've brought it to me. I'll look into it right away, formulate some questions, and get back to you early next week. Thanks for thinking of me.

One week later

Icebreaker: I've finished reviewing the assignment we discussed last week. You were right to be excited. I think it's an extremely interesting idea. Ironically, that's why I'm not sure I'd be the best person for the job.

Pitch #1: This project is potentially extremely important, so I need to put my personal interests aside. While I think I'm our best financial *[or other discipline]* person, Meadows is our best marketer *[or other discipline]*. As much as I'd like to take it on, I think she's the most qualified person for this assignment.

Pitch #2: This project is so important it should be someone's top priority. As you know, I'm already devoting all my extra time to preparing the annual report. I'd love to tackle this project, but I would need you to help me reset my priorities and figure out a schedule.

Agrees to someone else: *You're right. I need the best for this assignment. I appreciate your honesty. Can you ask Meadows to come see me?*

Still wants you: *I don't think you want to turn this assignment down. It's very important to me and the company. I really want you to do it. How about it? Will you take it on?*

Won't set priority: *I thought you knew that to succeed in this company you've got to juggle more than one ball. I want you to do this and finish the annual report.*

Sets priority: *You're right. I forgot you're still working on the annual report. I suppose I'll have to give this new job to someone else, or put it on hold until you get the annual report done.*

Reinforce your expertise: Sure. I hate to pass this one up, but the company's interests do come first. I'll speak with Meadows and let her know that I'll be available if she needs my help with the financial projections *[or your area of expertise].*

Suggest committee formation: I appreciate the faith you have in me. Rest assured I'll give it 110 percent. Since it's so important to the company to do it efficiently, I'll need to set up a team of our best people and bring all our resources to bear on it.

Discuss future plans: I'll be finished with the annual report, and can take this on in about two weeks. I don't like to turn you down on an assignment—especially such a great opportunity—but if it's urgent I'd suggest assigning it to Meadows—she's an excellent marketer *[or other discipline].*

Demands you go solo: *By all means reach out for whatever help you need. But remember, it's your assignment. You're in charge. And you're responsible for its success or failure.*

Agrees to committee: *That's an excellent idea. This is an important project and I want our best people working on it.*

Accept with protective memo: I won't let the company down. I'll draft a memo that outlines the project, notes the high priority you've placed on it, and explains you've put me in charge of executing your idea.

Accept with outlining memo: We can do it. We've got a great team here. I'll draft a memo outlining how we're going to tackle the project and circulate it among the team.

ADAPTATIONS

This script can be modified to:

- Counter a request by a family member, friend, or officer of a club or organization
- Counter a request coming from your boss's boss

KEY POINTS

- Express gratitude for being considered, say the idea is interesting, and ask for time to study it and formulate questions.
- Stress that the project is so important it should either be done by an expert or be a top priority. Then say you're not an expert (but someone else is), or that you need help in setting priorities.
- If your suggestion of someone else is taken, reinforce your own expertise and future availability.
- If no priority is set or the assignment isn't shifted to someone else, ask to form a special ad hoc committee in order to dilute the potential fallout.
- If attempts at diluting responsibility fail, prepare a protective memo that subtly makes it clear the whole thing was your supervisor's idea.

Asking for a
Deadline Extension

19

STRATEGY

The secret to asking for a deadline extension is to make it clear that your only problem is time; nothing else is wrong. Rather than coming in to your supervisor with an apology and series of reasons why you're not going to be able to meet the established deadline, steer the discussion as quickly as possible to solutions. The schedule established was clearly unworkable, and now you need help in coming up with ways to deal with the situation. Offer alternatives, but make it clear that delivery as intended is impossible.

TACTICS

- **Attitude:** This is a time neither to fall on your own sword nor to assign blame to others. It's not important who or what is to blame. What's important is deciding the next step. The more you adopt this attitude, the more likely your supervisor will as well.

- **Preparation:** Don't waste time determining why you won't be able to deliver on time—invariably it's because the schedule was overly optimistic; there's nothing you can do about it now. Instead, come up with as many alternative solutions as you can. There are usually three variations: getting more time, hiring outside help to deliver on time, or submitting a draft on the due date with the final product to follow later. Be prepared to advocate one alternative over the others in case your supervisor is unwilling to take responsibility.

- **Timing:** It's essential you have this conversation as soon as you realize you're not going to meet your deadline. Procrastination can only hurt you since you don't know if there are other issues involved. The sooner you realize the deadline is unworkable and convey that to your supervisor, the better. The longer you wait, the more this will look like a failing on your part.

- **Behavior:** Remain objective and rational. Don't let anger put you on the defensive or fear get the better of you. You, your supervisor, the project, and the company will all be best served by your continuing to steer the conversation around to solutions rather than postmortems.

19. Asking for a Deadline Extension

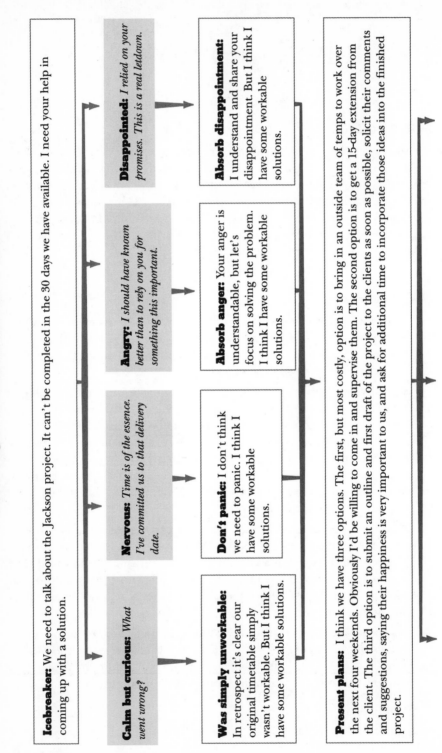

Icebreaker: We need to talk about the Jackson project. It can't be completed in the 30 days we have available. I need your help in coming up with a solution.

Calm but curious: *What went wrong?*

Nervous: *Time is of the essence. I've committed us to that delivery date.*

Angry: *I should have known better than to rely on you for something this important.*

Disappointed: *I relied on your promises. This is a real letdown.*

Was simply unworkable: In retrospect it's clear our original timetable simply wasn't workable. But I think I have some workable solutions.

Don't panic: I don't think we need to panic. I think I have some workable solutions.

Absorb anger: Your anger is understandable, but let's focus on solving the problem. I think I have some workable solutions.

Absorb disappointment: I understand and share your disappointment. But I think I have some workable solutions.

Present plans: I think we have three options. The first, but most costly, option is to bring in an outside team of temps to work over the next four weekends. Obviously I'd be willing to come in and supervise them. The second option is to get a 15-day extension from the client. The third option is to submit an outline and first draft of the project to the clients as soon as possible, solicit their comments and suggestions, saying their happiness is very important to us, and ask for additional time to incorporate those ideas into the finished project.

Still hesitant: *That's all very well, but you've left us in an awkward position with the client, not being able to deliver on time.*

Gives a cushion: *Okay. I'll take care of the client. You take another 15 days. Just make sure you deliver a first-class product.*

Needs time to choose: *Good thinking. Those are three viable options. Let me give it some thought and get back to you on which way we'll go.*

Suggest your choice: I've been thinking about that too. I've put together an outline and a first draft. I think you'll agree it's an excellent start. I think that once we incorporate your changes, we may be able to show this to them and mitigate the damage.

Express admiration: The way you've handled this situation just reaffirms my admiration for your management skills. Thanks for your help.

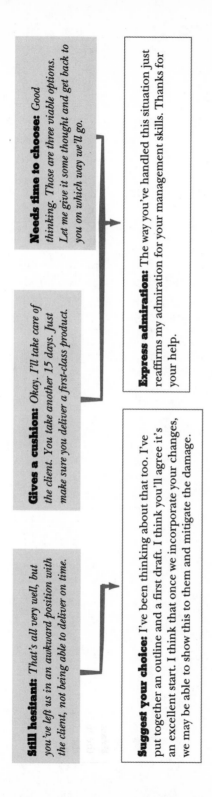

ADAPTATIONS

This script can be modified to:

- Mollify a client or customer
- Ask a client or customer for more time

KEY POINTS

- Present the failure to meet the deadline as a given and go directly to offering alternative solutions.
- If you're asked for a reason, just say the schedule was unworkable and launch into your suggestions.
- If your supervisor expresses anxiety, anger, or disappointment, say these feelings are understandable, but immediately shift the topic to solutions.
- Solutions generally involve either getting more time, bringing in outside help, or presenting an outline on time with the finished product to follow later.
- If your supervisor seems unwilling to select from your set of solutions, be prepared to advocate one approach.

Asking for Relief from an Assignment

20

STRATEGY

Trying to get relief from assignments that you either don't have the skill to accomplish or don't have the time to do well is an extremely delicate procedure—one that should never be entered into except when you have no other choice. Unless handled well, this could dramatically alter your superior's opinion of you for the worse. That's why it's essential you make sure you have a bona fide reason for the relief—saying you don't have the time simply won't do. The only way to come out of this with minimum damage to your reputation is to frame it as an objective problem for the company. It's not that "you" don't have the time, it's that the project can't be done well in the time allowed, or that your department doesn't have the skills necessary to do the job correctly. Expect resistance since such a reshuffling is going to cost the company money one way or another. The only way to counter bottom-line objections is to note that the alternatives are increased liability or decreased quality—both likely to be unacceptable. Deflect any personal attacks by saying you place the company's interests before your own. By the way, if your superior thinks you're bluffing, refuses your request, and says the increased liability or decreased quality is acceptable, prepare a memo for your files describing the meeting.

TACTICS

- **Attitude:** Realize this should be used only as a last resort to avoid disaster. At best it will hurt your reputation temporarily. At worst the damage will be permanent.
- **Preparation:** Determine whether the problem lies with your lack of skill or is specific to this project.
- **Timing:** Don't delay. While this won't be a pleasant meeting, it needs to take place as soon as possible.
- **Behavior:** One way or another you're going to have to eat some crow, so be humble from the beginning. Accepting criticism or hearing that you've disappointed is the price you'll pay for getting relief.

20. Asking for Relief from an Assignment

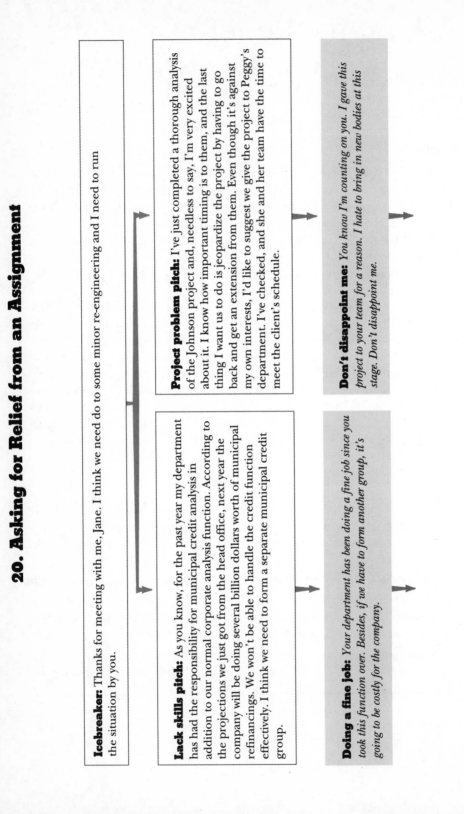

Icebreaker: Thanks for meeting with me, Jane. I think we need do to some minor re-engineering and I need to run the situation by you.

Lack skills pitch: As you know, for the past year my department has had the responsibility for municipal credit analysis in addition to our normal corporate analysis function. According to the projections we just got from the head office, next year the company will be doing several billion dollars worth of municipal refinancings. We won't be able to handle the credit function effectively. I think we need to form a separate municipal credit group.

Project problem pitch: I've just completed a thorough analysis of the Johnson project and, needless to say, I'm very excited about it. I know how important timing is to them, and the last thing I want us to do is jeopardize the project by having to go back and get an extension from them. Even though it's against my own interests, I'd like to suggest we give the project to Peggy's department. I've checked, and she and her team have the time to meet the client's schedule.

Doing a fine job: *Your department has been doing a fine job since you took this function over. Besides, if we have to form another group, it's going to be costly for the company.*

Don't disappoint me: *You know I'm counting on you. I gave this project to your team for a reason. I hate to bring in new bodies at this stage. Don't disappoint me.*

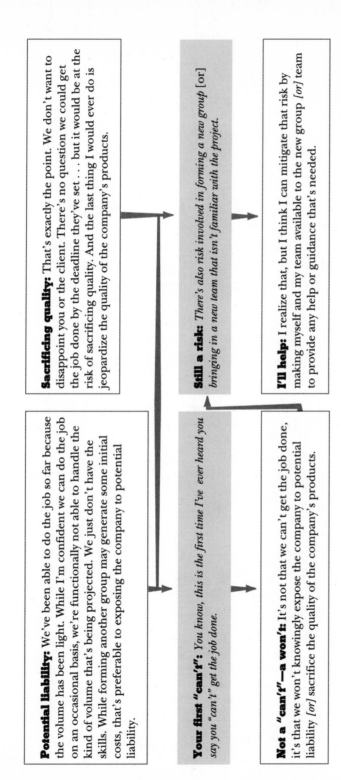

Potential liability: We've been able to do the job so far because the volume has been light. While I'm confident we can do the job on an occasional basis, we're functionally not able to handle the kind of volume that's being projected. We just don't have the skills. While forming another group may generate some initial costs, that's preferable to exposing the company to potential liability.

Sacrificing quality: That's exactly the point. We don't want to disappoint you or the client. There's no question we could get the job done by the deadline they've set . . . but it would be at the risk of sacrificing quality. And the last thing I would ever do is jeopardize the quality of the company's products.

Your first "can't": *You know, this is the first time I've ever heard you say you "can't" get the job done.*

Not a "can't"—a won't: It's not that we can't get the job done, it's that we won't knowingly expose the company to potential liability *[or]* sacrifice the quality of the company's products.

Still a risk: *There's also risk involved in forming a new group [or] bringing in a new team that isn't familiar with the project.*

I'll help: I realize that, but I think I can mitigate that risk by making myself and my team available to the new group *[or]* team to provide any help or guidance that's needed.

ADAPTATIONS

This script can be modified to:

- Get out of something you volunteered to do for the company, a friend, or a relative
- Get out of an office in an organization or association

KEY POINTS

- Present this as a problem brought on by your inherent lack of skill or the unique circumstances of the project.
- If your past ability to perform is cited, stress the differences of this situation and the potential liabilities.
- If your supervisor says he's disappointed, note that it's more important the client isn't disappointed.
- If your boss implies her opinion of you has dropped, state that the company's reputation is more important to you than your own.
- If she remains hesitant, offer to be of whatever assistance you can, short of carrying the ball yourself.

Asking Someone to Become Your Mentor

21.

STRATEGY

For mentor relationships to truly be of value, the protégé needs to select the mentor, looking for someone who's currently doing what the protégé would like to do in the future. However, it's human nature to want to pick your own protégé. That makes this dialogue a little tough. What makes it even harder is that a protégé really isn't offering anything in exchange for the mentor's guidance. That's why a key to winning someone over is flattery. Be wary of someone who readily accepts your request. She's probably the type who collects followers in an effort to boost her ego. She's likely not to offer you anything of real value. The best mentor is someone who doesn't have the time for such activities, and doesn't need the ego boost.

TACTICS

- **Attitude:** Realize that you're asking someone to do something entirely altruistic. You are basically in the position of a supplicant. You don't need to fall to your knees and beg, but you have to be willing to put your own ego aside for the duration of this conversation.

- **Preparation:** Look for someone who's in the position you want to grow into, or who has the reputation you would like to have in the future. Develop a brief description of that position or reputation and use it in your pitch.

- **Timing:** Set up this initial meeting for a time that's most convenient for your mentor candidate. That hints at your willingness to be flexible.

- **Behavior:** The keys are to act humble, offer some subtle flattery, and remain persistent. In effect, you're looking to flatter the person into taking you on as a protégé. Even if you're greeted with an outright "no," ask for reconsideration before looking for another potential mentor.

21. Asking Someone to Become Your Mentor

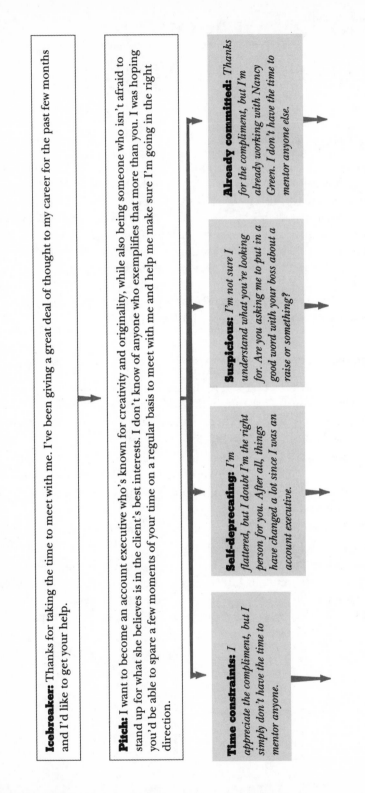

Icebreaker: Thanks for taking the time to meet with me. I've been giving a great deal of thought to my career for the past few months and I'd like to get your help.

Pitch: I want to become an account executive who's known for creativity and originality, while also being someone who isn't afraid to stand up for what she believes is in the client's best interests. I don't know of anyone who exemplifies that more than you. I was hoping you'd be able to spare a few moments of your time on a regular basis to meet with me and help me make sure I'm going in the right direction.

Time constraints: *I appreciate the compliment, but I simply don't have the time to mentor anyone.*

Self-deprecating: *I'm flattered, but I doubt I'm the right person for you. After all, things have changed a lot since I was an account executive.*

Suspicious: *I'm not sure I understand what you're looking for. Are you asking me to put in a good word with your boss about a raise or something?*

Already committed: *Thanks for the compliment, but I'm already working with Nancy Green. I don't have the time to mentor anyone else.*

Beg for moments: I'm not surprised. I know how busy you must be. The last thing I'd want to do is interfere with your schedule. I'd be happy with a just a few moments now and then. And I'm perfectly willing to work them around whatever time problems you might have.

Admire modesty: One of the things I admire most about you is your modesty. I don't think there's anyone in this industry whose advice and guidance could be more insightful and helpful. I wish you'd reconsider.

Allay fears: I'm sorry. I guess I didn't make myself clear. I wasn't talking about company politics. I was just hoping you could offer me general career guidance from time to time—serve as a mentor.

Offer to wait: I was afraid that might be the case. Nancy's very lucky to have your help. I know it's a lot to ask, but do you think you could also meet with me now and then, and, even if it's on a less regular basis and for less time?

Not interested: *I'm sorry. I'm really not interested in mentoring anyone [else] right now. I've just got too much of my own to do.*

Grudging acceptance: *Okay, but it really will have to be for only a few minutes a month at my convenience.*

Please reconsider: I understand. Thanks for meeting with me anyway. Would you mind if I give you a call back in a couple of weeks to see if you've reconsidered?

Express thanks: Thanks so much. I really appreciate your letting me draw on your knowledge and experience. Can we schedule our first meeting today?

ADAPTATIONS

This script can be modified to:

- Gather information for a career change
- Get an informational interview
- Conduct reconnaissance on a company for any reason

KEY POINTS

- Realize you're a supplicant and act accordingly.
- Explain why you've chosen to approach this person.
- If you're greeted with suspicions, allay them by making your request clearer.
- If the person acts humble, take it as an invitation for flattery.
- If she claims time constraints or a previous commitment, stress your flexibility and meager needs.
- If she still refuses, subtly ask her to reconsider.

Asking for a Lateral Reassignment

22.

STRATEGY

While employees are being told to broaden their skills base and experience to get ahead in today's workplace, it can be extremely difficult, even potentially risky. Not only will you need to go over your immediate supervisor's head—unless you're already heading up a department—but you may also need to risk your career in order to get the company to take a chance on someone they perceive to lack experience.

TACTICS

- **Attitude:** Once you've decided you need to transfer to move ahead, you must determine whether or not you're willing to risk your job to make the move. If you're not, either wait until you feel more daring or concentrate on finding a new job outside the company.

- **Preparation:** Make sure you're prepared to show that you do have experience in the area—even if it's in the past and hasn't been tested in the workplace. In addition, if you know there's an important project coming up soon, and you're committed to getting this position, work up a well-organized, comprehensive memo outlining your preliminary ideas for how to handle it. That may persuade the company to give you a shot.

- **Timing:** It's essential you make this approach as soon as you learn there's an opening. By offering yourself for the job before a search is launched, you can offer cost savings. In addition, you'll be judged independently on your past positive performance rather than be compared to more experienced candidates.

- **Behavior:** Be confident and determined, but understanding of the company's needs. Frame your growth in terms of how it will benefit the company. And by the way, don't even consider asking for a salary increase. Wait until you've succeeded in the new position before discussing salary.

22. Asking for a Lateral Reassignment

Phase I: Approaching your immediate supervisor

Icebreaker #1: I'd like to ask you for some career advice. I've heard there's an opening in the public relations department, and while I'm very happy here in direct marketing, I think I can become more valuable to the company by broadening my skill base. First, I'd like your permission to speak with Ms. Goodall. And second, I was hoping you could advise me how best to approach her.

Grudging help: *I'd hate to see you go, but I won't stand in the way of your improving your career and helping the company. We'll miss you if you get the spot. Let me think about it and get back to you with some ideas.*

Doesn't want to help: *I can't deny I'm disappointed. I certainly don't want to stand in your way, but I really need you here. I'd only be hurting myself if I helped you transfer. I'd rather you don't apply for the job. You have a future here, you know.*

Express thanks: Thanks so much for your support. I knew I could count on your help—you've always been a wonderful mentor to me.

Sorry, but I must: Thanks for the compliments. I'm sorry you can't back me up on this, but I really need to give this a shot. I think the best way to protect my future is to expand my skills.

Phase II: Approaching your boss's boss

Icebreaker #2: Thanks for meeting with me, Jane. I wanted to speak with you about my professional growth in the company. You've always said that to the extent we're valuable to the company, we'll move up, and I think the opening in public relations offers me a chance to increase my value. I really think by transferring over I could increase my contribution to the company.

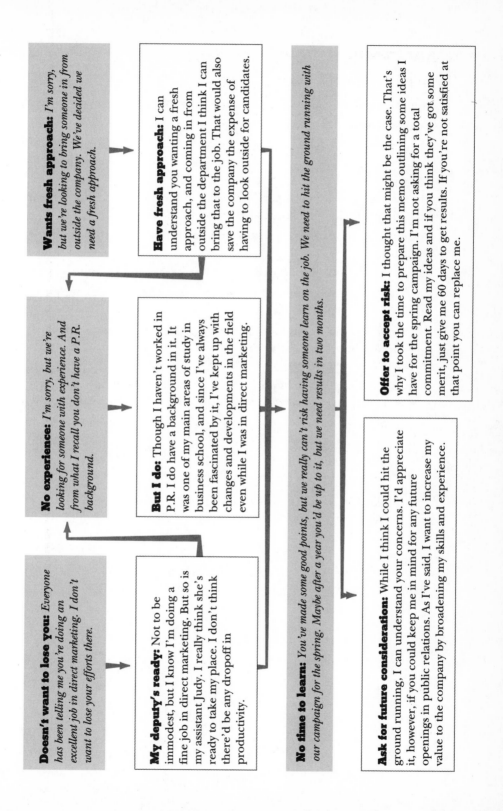

Doesn't want to lose you: *Everyone has been telling me you're doing an excellent job in direct marketing. I don't want to lose your efforts there.*

No experience: *I'm sorry, but we're looking for someone with experience. And from what I recall you don't have a P.R. background.*

Wants fresh approach: *I'm sorry, but we're looking to bring someone in from outside the company. We've decided we need a fresh approach.*

My deputy's ready: Not to be immodest, but I know I'm doing a fine job in direct marketing. But so is my assistant Judy. I really think she's ready to take my place. I don't think there'd be any dropoff in productivity.

But I do: Though I haven't worked in P.R. I do have a background in it. It was one of my main areas of study in business school, and since I've always been fascinated by it, I've kept up with changes and developments in the field even while I was in direct marketing.

Have fresh approach: I can understand you wanting a fresh approach, and coming in from outside the department I think I can bring that to the job. That would also save the company the expense of having to look outside for candidates.

No time to learn: *You've made some good points, but we really can't risk having someone learn on the job. We need to hit the ground running with our campaign for the spring. Maybe after a year you'd be up to it, but we need results in two months.*

Ask for future consideration: While I think I could hit the ground running, I can understand your concerns. I'd appreciate it, however, if you could keep me in mind for any future openings in public relations. As I've said, I want to increase my value to the company by broadening my skills and experience.

Offer to accept risk: I thought that might be the case. That's why I took the time to prepare this memo outlining some ideas I have for the spring campaign. I'm not asking for a total commitment. Read my ideas and if you think they've got some merit, just give me 60 days to get results. If you're not satisfied at that point you can replace me.

ADAPTATIONS

This script can be modified to:

- Switch specialties at an academic or media employer
- Get a similar type of position at a different type of firm

KEY POINTS

- Ask for your immediate supervisor's help in furthering your career, but be willing to go it alone if need be.
- Present your transfer as a way to increase your contribution to the company.
- Stress that your transfer won't hurt the department you're coming from.
- Offer whatever experience you can to counter the "no experience" excuse.
- Explain that coming from outside the department you can offer as fresh an approach as someone who comes from outside the company—and at the same time save the company money.
- If immediate success is important, either back off and ask for future consideration, or be ready to stake your future on producing results right away.

Warning Your Superior of Potential Client Problems

23

STRATEGY

Be cautious when delivering the news of a potential client problem. You need to tell your superiors you have a feeling, call it intuition, that Acme, Inc. may be preparing to pull its business. The fear is your superiors will react poorly and blame the messenger. Deliver the news and assume control of the meeting right away. If your superiors have a chance to vent anger, lay blame, or panic, the possibility of accomplishing something productive will be lost. Concentrate on moving the conversation forward and searching for a solution to the client problems. If you can demonstrate calm under fire, your superiors will think of you as a valuable employee. This is your chance to help the company avoid losing a client and make an effective impression. Devise a plan of action to share with your superiors during this potential crisis. Before they have time to point fingers, you can steer them toward a discussion about how to deal with the problem. Get them involved in the discussion, seek their opinions, and force them to comment on your thoughts and ideas for handling the client. Don't discuss who's at fault, but subtly prove you're not to blame for this situation. You're trying to help the company avoid a problem, not throwing yourself at the mercy of your superiors. By meeting with your superiors, you're taking a proactive stance and thus protecting yourself from future recrimination. If Acme pulls their business without any warning, you will be held accountable. If you warn your superiors of the potentially volatile situation, you will be recognized as a team player who is watching out for the well-being of the company.

TACTICS

- **Attitude:** Be quick and decisive. Seize control of the dialogue and make the group search for a solution. Force a discussion of potential defenses and counter maneuvers to the client problem.

- **Timing:** Meet with your superiors soon after you sense there's a problem. Don't race into a meeting half cocked. Meet with them as soon as you have control of your emotions and feel able to explain the situation in a clear and coherent fashion.

- **Preparation:** Organize your thoughts and prepare notes about the problem. Try to rehearse a quick and effective speech to begin the meeting. Formulate ideas for dealing with the situation and be ready to share your thoughts during the meeting.

23. Warning Your Superior of Potential Client Problems

Icebreaker: Thanks for meeting with me on short notice. I have a feeling that Acme may be preparing to pull their business. They haven't said anything directly, but I have a strong sense that something is wrong. Just to be on the safe side, I think we should discuss possible plans of action.

Remains calm: *Can you tell me why you have this feeling? If we can identify the problem, we'll have a better chance of rectifying the situation.*

Explain: As I said, it's nothing concrete, just a feeling. Still, I think we should prepare ourselves. I propose we meet with the partners of Acme. We can tell them we just want to review our working relationship.

You're paranoid: *I think you may be overreacting. You say you only have a sense. If they haven't said anything to indicate they're unhappy, then I don't think we should lose sleep over this.*

Cautious, not paranoid: I think it would be a big mistake to ignore this problem. It can't hurt to meet with the partners at Acme. At the very least, they will appreciate our personal attention and it will solidify our working relationship.

Panics: *If we lose Acme, we're in a heap of trouble. We need their business. What are we going to do about this? What did they tell you? What did they say?*

Soothe panic: If we react swiftly, we may not lose their business. We need to reevaluate our working relationship and address any problems. If we arrange a meeting with the partners at Acme, I think we can clear the air and get to the bottom of this.

Gets angry: *How the heck did this happen? What did your team do? Acme is an important client, and we can't afford to lose them. If we do, heads are going to roll.*

Redirect anger: I believe something is wrong at Acme. We need to find out what the problem is and address it head on. I propose we arrange a meeting with the partners of Acme to address any issues.

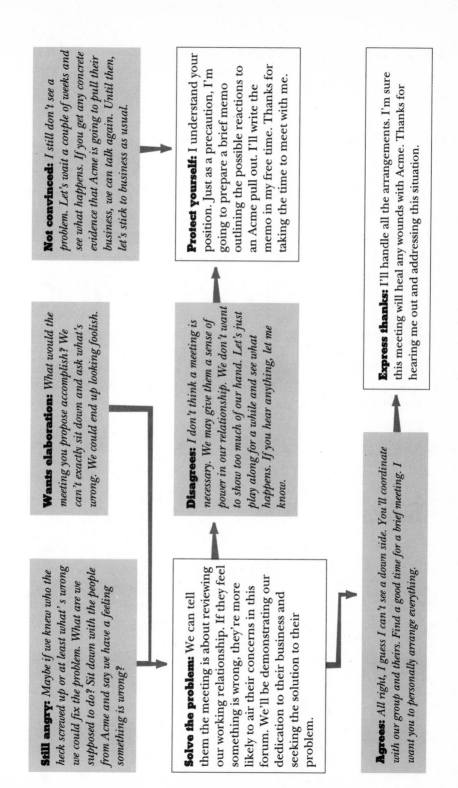

Still angry: *Maybe if we knew who the heck screwed up or at least what's wrong we could fix the problem. What are we supposed to do? Sit down with the people from Acme and say we have a feeling something is wrong?*

Wants elaboration: *What would the meeting you propose accomplish? We can't exactly sit down and ask what's wrong. We could end up looking foolish.*

Not convinced: *I still don't see a problem. Let's wait a couple of weeks and see what happens. If you get any concrete evidence that Acme is going to pull their business, we can talk again. Until then, let's stick to business as usual.*

Solve the problem: We can tell them the meeting is about reviewing our working relationship. If they feel something is wrong, they're more likely to air their concerns in this forum. We'll be demonstrating our dedication to their business and seeking the solution to their problem.

Disagrees: *I don't think a meeting is necessary. We may give them a sense of power in our relationship. We don't want to show too much of our hand. Let's just play along for a while and see what happens. If you hear anything, let me know.*

Protect yourself: I understand your position. Just as a precaution, I'm going to prepare a brief memo outlining the possible reactions to an Acme pull out. I'll write the memo in my free time. Thanks for taking the time to meet with me.

Agrees: *All right, I guess I can't see a down side. You'll coordinate with our group and theirs. Find a good time for a brief meeting. I want you to personally arrange everything.*

Express thanks: I'll handle all the arrangements. I'm sure this meeting will heal any wounds with Acme. Thanks for hearing me out and addressing this situation.

- **Behavior:** Be confidant. You are racing to the rescue of the company. Move the conversation swiftly and remind your superiors the most important thing to do is address the situation.

ADAPTATIONS

This script can be modified to:

- Protect yourself from a destructive peer

KEY POINTS

- Guide the conversation toward a solution. Don't let it degenerate into a finger–pointing melee.
- Don't accept blame for the situation. You have a feeling, but it's not your fault.
- Suggest meeting with the client and trying to get them to air any grievances. Even if they don't have a problem, the meeting will be a boost to your working relationship.
- If your superiors don't heed your warning, offer to prepare a memo outlining possible reactions to a client pullout. This will further protect you from recriminations.

Warning Your Superior of Potential Vendor Problems

24.

STRATEGY

If you learn a vendor your company relies on may be about to run into trouble either with their own operation or in servicing your company, you need to alert your superiors. However, you'll first need to take certain things into consideration. What's the likelihood that vendor service will be interrupted and how long will it be for that to happen? What are the alternative sources for the goods or services, and what are their relative strengths and weaknesses? Does the problem have to do with the workings of your own company or its relationship with the vendor? The reason for all this preliminary thought is that you want to provide some advice on a potential course of action. However, remember that the problems you foresee may not arise. If your company goes through a costly or time–consuming shift that wasn't necessary, you'll be blamed — just as if you hadn't noticed the problem at all.

TACTICS

- **Attitude:** You've noticed something that may be harmful, but because you've noticed it early, the company has the opportunity to proceed with caution. That means not rushing to judgment or taking action, although the more people you make aware of the problem the better.

- **Preparation:** Thoroughly analyze the problem and the potential solutions, coming up with a list of alternative responses, both now and in the future. Choose one response because you may be asked for a specific recommendation.

- **Timing:** Time may not be of the essence, but the longer you delay the less of an advantage your foresight will seem. Present the problem as soon as you've gathered all your facts and have formulated your own opinions. Don't schedule an emergency meeting or interrupt regular business — just ask for the next available time slot.

- **Behavior:** While this isn't good news, the fact that you saw the potential for it happening before it did gives your company a competitive advantage. Don't gloat, but don't shy away from credit. Try to walk the middle ground between alternatives unless the evidence clearly points to one solution or unless you're forced to choose.

24. Warning Your Superior of Potential Vendor Problems

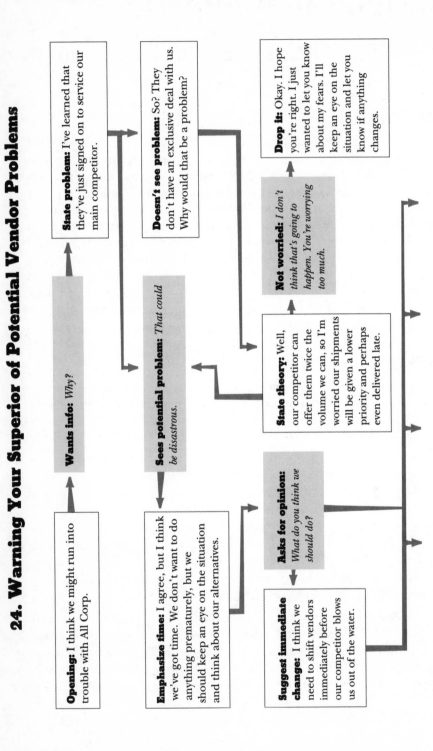

Opening: I think we might run into trouble with All Corp.

Wants info: *Why?*

State problem: I've learned that they've just signed on to service our main competitor.

Emphasize time: I agree, but I think we've got time. We don't want to do anything prematurely, but we should keep an eye on the situation and think about our alternatives.

Sees potential problem: *That could be disastrous.*

Doesn't see problem: So? They don't have an exclusive deal with us. Why would that be a problem?

Asks for opinion: *What do you think we should do?*

State theory: Well, our competitor can offer them twice the volume we can, so I'm worried our shipments will be given a lower priority and perhaps even delivered late.

Not worried: *I don't think that's going to happen. You're worrying too much.*

Suggest immediate change: I think we need to shift vendors immediately before our competitor blows us out of the water.

Drop it: Okay. I hope you're right. I just wanted to let you know about my fears. I'll keep an eye on the situation and let you know if anything changes.

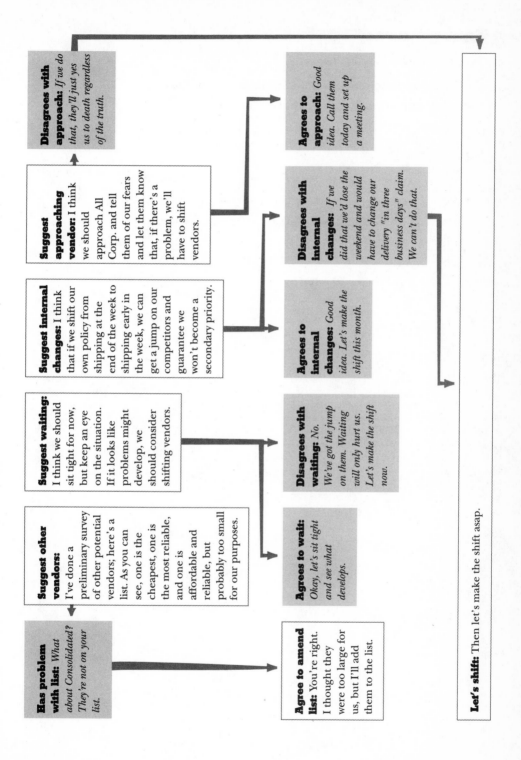

Has problem with list: *What about Consolidated? They're not on your list.*

Suggest other vendors: I've done a preliminary survey of other potential vendors; here's a list. As you can see, one is the cheapest, one is the most reliable, and one is affordable and reliable, but probably too small for our purposes.

Suggest waiting: I think we should sit tight for now, but keep an eye on the situation. If it looks like problems might develop, we should consider shifting vendors.

Suggest internal changes: I think that if we shift our own policy from shipping at the end of the week to shipping early in the week, we can get a jump on our competitors and guarantee we won't become a secondary priority.

Suggest approaching vendor: I think we should approach All Corp. and tell them of our fears and let them know that, if there's a problem, we'll have to shift vendors.

Disagrees with approach: *If we do that, they'll just yes us to death regardless of the truth.*

Agrees to approach: *Good idea. Call them today and set up a meeting.*

Agree to amend list: You're right. I thought they were too large for us, but I'll add them to the list.

Agrees to wait: *Okay, let's sit tight and see what develops.*

Disagrees with waiting: *No. We've got the jump on them. Waiting will only hurt us. Let's make the shift now.*

Agrees to internal changes: *Good idea. Let's make the shift this month.*

Disagrees with internal changes: *If we did that we'd lose the weekend and would have to change our delivery "in three business days" claim. We can't do that.*

Let's shift: Then let's make the shift asap.

ADAPTATIONS

This script can be modified to:

- Warn a superior about a potential personnel problem
- Warn a superior about a potential client problem

KEY POINTS

- Be prepared to present alternative responses to the problem.
- Recognize that time is an ally that shouldn't be ignored or relied on.
- Don't discount the possibility that the problem won't arise.
- Emphasize the advantage of taking the time to make the right choice, placing an even greater value on the time you've provided the company.

CHAPTER THREE

Lifescripts for Dealing with Subordinates

Criticizing a Subordinate's Work

STRATEGY

Delivering criticism requires a delicate touch. You need to present the problem strongly enough so the employee gets the message and hopefully changes his behavior, but not so strongly that you undermine his confidence or create lingering resentment. The best way to accomplish this is to start with positive comments before delivering the criticism. If the information is received openly, reaffirm your confidence and set up a future meeting. If the employee disputes your perception or gets angry, give him a chance to get over reflexive defensiveness by offering specifics. If that doesn't calm him down, stop pulling your punches and make it clear his future depends on improved performance.

TACTICS

- **Attitude:** Think of yourself as a teacher or mentor, not a judge and jury. And be willing to absorb a little anger without retaliating—it's not easy to take criticism submissively.

- **Preparation:** Make sure your list of criticisms is accurate and detailed— you don't want this to turn into a debate over facts. Have specific suggestions and advice ready to help the employee improve his performance.

- **Timing:** If this isn't a formal review, it should take place as soon as possible after a problem so it's fresh in everyone's mind. If you can, schedule it for early in the week so the employee has a chance to act on your advice right away and won't have to dwell on it over a weekend.

- **Behavior:** Lead off with positive comments so the meeting doesn't seem as if it's a one-sided attack. If the employee won't get past his initial anger or denial, forget subtlety and make it clear his future is at stake unless he cleans up his act.

25. Criticizing a Subordinate's Work

Icebreaker: I'm generally very pleased with your work—especially the way you're handling the arrangements for the sales conference. But there is one thing you need to work on. Maybe I haven't made it clear that you're also responsible for supervising all the promotional materials, but lately I've found quite a few mistakes and some sloppy work.

Gets angry: *I've been working overtime to get everything set for the sales conference. I can't believe you're complaining about this, given all I've accomplished here.*

Denies problem: *Really? I've been very careful about reviewing those pieces. I don't think there were any mistakes when they left my desk.*

Accepts criticism: *I'm really sorry. I didn't realize that I'd slipped up. I won't let it happen again*

Chance to defuse anger: I'm surprised by your reaction. I thought you'd be eager to improve your performance. Is there something else troubling you?

Chance to get past denial: Let me show you what I mean. Here are copies of the last three promotional pieces that you okayed. I've marked the problem areas.

Gets over anger: *I'm sorry that I got so defensive and snapped at you. It's just that I work very hard and really want to do the best job that I can.*

Remains angry: *I think you're being very unfair. On the whole, my work has been excellent, you're just nitpicking. You've been overly critical of me from day one.*

Still denies problem: *I'm not the only one whose job it is to check the promos. I can't believe that some of those mistakes weren't inserted after I signed off.*

Gets past denial: *I guess you're right. I didn't realize that all the time I was spending on the conference was affecting my other work. I'll be more careful from now on.*

Issue a warning: I have a real problem with your uncooperative attitude. If you want to make it in this company, you'll need to address this problem. Please come back to me in a day or so to discuss how you propose to handle it.

Schedule a meeting: I'm so glad to hear you say that, and I want to help you in any way I can. Let's schedule a meeting for a month from now to talk about how things are progressing.

ADAPTATIONS

This script can be modified to:

- Review a student's poor performance
- Discuss a partner's lack of effort
- Speak with a volunteer about lethargic efforts

KEY POINTS

- Soften initial criticism by suggesting that perhaps your instructions weren't clear, or maybe the employee has been overworked.
- If your criticism is denied, offer specifics without getting defensive.
- If the employee responds with anger, show surprise and ask if there's something else troubling him.
- If the employee accepts the criticism immediately, or after having a chance to blow off some steam, reiterate your desire to help, and schedule a subsequent meeting.
- If the employee refuses to get past his anger or denial, say you have a problem with his attitude, warn him it must change, and demand immediate action.

Turning Down a Raise Request

26

STRATEGY

In many situations it's easy to turn down a raise request: If a person's performance hasn't been up to expectations, that's a justifiable reason to maintain his salary level; if a person bases his request on what others are making, it's easy to explain that everyone is treated as an individual. The difficult dialogue is when you have to deny a request from someone who, in fact, merits an increase but can't get one because of the company's financial situation. The secret here is to hammer home that he is a valued employee, making a legitimate request that simply can't be met right now because of the company's financial situation. Every rational person realizes you can't get water from a stone. Temper his justifiable disappointment by stressing that you will come back to him with a raise, based on the argument he made in his request, as soon as the financial picture brightens.

TACTICS

- **Attitude:** Accept that in tough economic times, the needs of the company must come first. Simply maintaining staff is often a sacrifice for struggling companies.

- **Preparation:** You'll have little opportunity to prepare unless you're given advance warning of what the meeting will be about. In that unlikely case, documentation of the company's financial problems could help ease the pain.

- **Timing:** You'll have little or no control over when this meeting takes place since it will be instigated by the employee. Once asked, don't delay or stall.

- **Behavior:** Be compassionate, caring, and understanding. There's no need to apologize, however. It's just a fact of life that when a company's business is off, its employees will have to forgo raises.

26. Turning Down a Raise Request

Opener: *I need to thank you for the opportunity you and the company have given me. I recognize that you've been very influential in my growth and advancement. However, I have a problem that I need your help with.*

Show concern: I think you know that I'm always here if you need my help. What's the problem and what can I do?

Professional growth: *What has happened is that I've been concentrating solely on my professional growth and haven't been paying any attention to my stream of income. I've done some research and found my peers are earning on average 15 percent more than my current compensation. I've drafted this memo. It's logical for my compensation to keep pace with my growth. To do that I'll need an increase of . . .*

Contribution up: *I think my salary no longer reflects my contribution to the company. In the past year I've helped the company save a great deal of money [or] bring in added revenue [or] trim quite a bit from the cost of operations. I've done some research and I've found that a salary of . . . would more accurately reflect my value. I've prepared a brief memo outlining my accomplishments and my request.*

Responsibilities up: *I think my salary no longer matches my job responsibilities. During the past year I've moved from being an order taker to helping supervise the evening staff and helping draft the new sales scripts. I've done some research and I think a salary of . . . would more accurately reflect my responsibilities. I've prepared a brief memo outlining my increased responsibilities and my request.*

Anniversary raise: *I've come to ask you for a raise of 10 percent. It's been a year since my last increase, and in the past the company has had a policy of giving annual raises on the anniversary of our hiring date.*

Universal response: Although you may not be aware of it, I've been watching you carefully, and I've tried to help nurture your development. The company would never consciously be unfair to you, and neither would I. The company has always done its level best, consistent with its obligations to the stockholders [or] owners. I want you to know that we love having you here. I'm aware of everything that you've said [and] I'm sure your memo makes your case persuasively. But raises are out of the question right now. You do have an excellent future with this company if you continue on this track, and we do appreciate all you've been doing.

That's no help: *I'm glad to hear you say I have a future here, but my stream of income is important to me. While I'm flattered, your praise doesn't help me pay my daughter's college tuition.*

Not a partner: *I understand what you're saying. You're asking me to participate in the success or failure of the company, but I'm not an owner [or] a partner.*

You and the company linked: That's where you're wrong. To the extent the company succeeds financially, you will as well. And unfortunately, to the extent the company must sacrifice financially, you will have to also.

No commitment: *Are you saying you can't give me any kind of commitment about a raise in the near future?*

Personal commitment: I personally will give you a commitment that when things improve, I will come to you with an increase, based on the argument you made today. You won't have to come back to me again.

ADAPTATIONS

This script can be modified to:

- Deny requests for nonmonetary benefits that could create morale problems
- Deny requests from children for more spending money or an increase in their allowance

KEY POINTS

- Let the employee make his pitch without interruption or argument.
- If correct, accept his assertions and numbers openly.
- Respond to every request, regardless of which pitch is used, with the same answer: The money isn't there right now.
- Accept a certain amount of anger, sullenness, or annoyance—it's understandable.
- Make a personal commitment to come back with an increase as soon as it's possible.

Adding Responsibilities without Adding Pay

27.

STRATEGY

It's a fact of life today. Almost every manager will one day need to ask a subordinate to take on more work, without being able to offer him any more pay in compensation. The secret to making this a smooth discussion is to frame it as good news. Don't feel manipulative. Since the alternative is unemployment, it *is* good news. Astute employees will realize that and go along with your spin—at least superficially. Feel free to point out that the added responsibilities will increase their value—and marketability. Employees who aren't as swift or who take a piecework attitude toward their jobs will need to have it made clear to them that there's no alternative. If they're not willing to accept that, they are free to look elsewhere.

TACTICS

- **Attitude:** Realize that this really is good news. You could be telling this person he's terminated. Instead, you're telling him that he still has a job.
- **Preparation:** Give some thought to the employee's attitude toward his job. That will make his response less of a surprise.
- **Timing:** As soon as you're made aware of the new arrangements, tell your subordinates. You don't want them to hear it through the grapevine. If it comes from you first, you'll be able to put things in perspective.
- **Behavior:** Don't be gleeful about the situation, but on the other hand, there's no need to be glum either. This is a fact of life in today's workplace, so treat it as such.

27. Adding Responsibilities without Adding Pay

Icebreaker and pitch: I have some good news so I came right over to tell you. Your job is safe now. I was able to convince the people upstairs that our department could cut costs by becoming more efficient rather than by downsizing. They've decided to cut a position in international sales instead and pass some work on to us.

Workload objection: *Does that mean we're going to have to start staying later?* [or] *I'm already overloaded, I simply can't take on any additional work right now.*

Little price to pay: Yes, I suppose so. *[or]* I'm afraid you're going to have to. That's the price for holding on to our jobs in this kind of economy.

Grudging acceptance: *I suppose you're right . . . but I'm used to getting paid for the work I do.*

Financial objection: *I hope I'll be getting a pay raise to go along with the increase in my responsibilities and the change in my job description.*

Look long-term: No, I'm afraid not. But look at the long-term benefits. It's an opportunity to prove ourselves, increase our skills, and improve our job profiles. All of that will help in the future—either here or someplace else.

Piecework attitude: *Still, I expect to be paid for the work I do. If I do more, I expect to be paid more.*

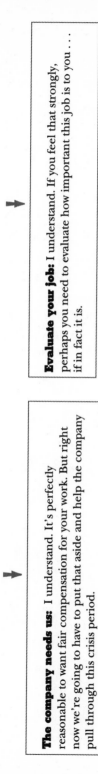

The company needs us: I understand. It's perfectly reasonable to want fair compensation for your work. But right now we're going to have to put that aside and help the company pull through this crisis period.

Evaluate your job: I understand. If you feel that strongly, perhaps you need to evaluate how important this job is to you . . . if in fact it is.

ADAPTATIONS

This script can be modified to:

- Give more tasks to a day worker without increasing their hours
- Get a contractor to increase the scope of his work without increasing his bid

KEY POINTS

- Present this as good news.
- If the employee objects to the increased workload, point out that he could have no work.
- If the employee objects on financial grounds, explain that in the long run, the added responsibilities will increase his value—here or elsewhere.
- If the employee still balks, and is a valuable member of your team, say this is something he will simply have to accept for the good of the company.
- If the employee still balks and isn't a key person, say he can leave if he doesn't like it.

Changing a Subordinate's Job Status to Part-Time

28.

STRATEGY

This dialog is easier than most people anticipate. While not good news, it isn't a termination. Obviously, the degree to which a company continues offering benefits to part-timers and promoting them will reduce complaints. In addition, part-time employees should be under no constraints about freelancing—and that should be made clear to them. All objections and even threats should be absorbed and answered if possible. All you have to offer is your understanding, so be liberal with it.

TACTICS

- **Attitude:** Try to be matter-of-fact. You're not bearing good news, but you're not terminating someone either. Treat this as just another part of doing business in the 1990s—albeit a part the employee isn't apt to be too happy about.

- **Preparation:** Give some thought to how the employee will react to the news, based on the likely responses outlined. Assume he will respond in character, but be ready for some anger or resentment. Have a plan in place to deal with his possible resignation.

- **Timing:** It's important that you give the employee as much time as possible to make whatever arrangements may be needed to make up for the decline in his stream of income. The more warning you give, the less likely that he'll become angry.

- **Behavior:** Stress that this is entirely a financial decision made necessary by dire circumstances. Reiterate that the company will provide whatever help possible, and stress whatever positive factors—continuing benefits, help with freelancing—you can.

28. Changing a Subordinate's Job Status to Part-Time

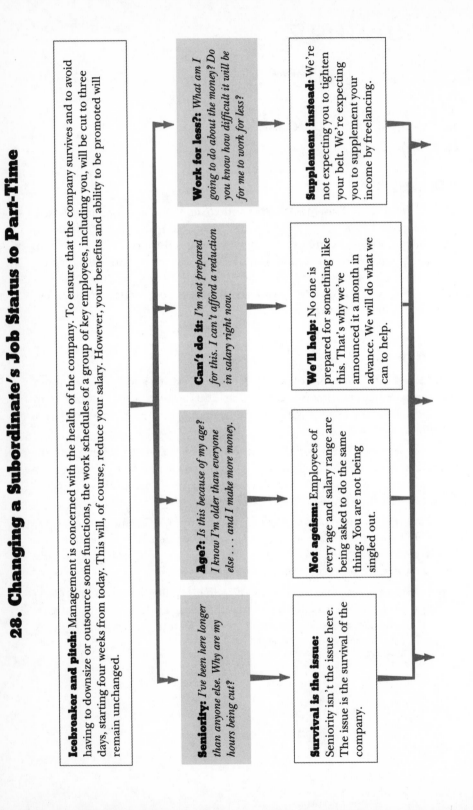

Icebreaker and pitch: Management is concerned with the health of the company. To ensure that the company survives and to avoid having to downsize or outsource some functions, the work schedules of a group of key employees, including you, will be cut to three days, starting four weeks from today. This will, of course, reduce your salary. However, your benefits and ability to be promoted will remain unchanged.

Seniority: *I've been here longer than anyone else. Why are my hours being cut?*

Age?: *Is this because of my age? I know I'm older than everyone else . . . and I make more money.*

Can't do it: *I'm not prepared for this. I can't afford a reduction in salary right now.*

Work for less?: *What am I going to do about the money? Do you know how difficult it will be for me to work for less?*

Survival is the issue: Seniority isn't the issue here. The issue is the survival of the company.

Not ageism: Employees of every age and salary range are being asked to do the same thing. You are not being singled out.

We'll help: No one is prepared for something like this. That's why we've announced it a month in advance. We will do what we can to help.

Supplement instead: We're not expecting you to tighten your belt. We're expecting you to supplement your income by freelancing.

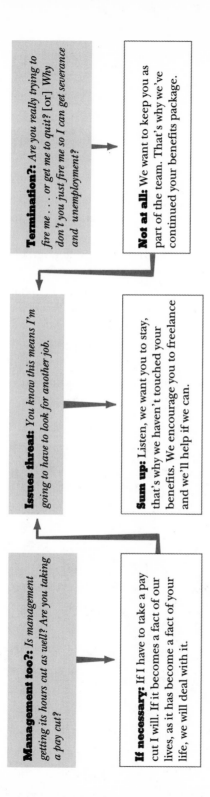

Management too?: *Is management getting its hours cut as well? Are you taking a pay cut?*

If necessary: If I have to take a pay cut I will. If it becomes a fact of our lives, as it has become a fact of your life, we will deal with it.

Issues threat: *You know this means I'm going to have to look for another job.*

Sum up: Listen, we want you to stay, that's why we haven't touched your benefits. We encourage you to freelance and we'll help if we can.

Termination?: *Are you really trying to fire me . . . or get me to quit? [or] Why don't you just fire me so I can get severance and unemployment?*

Not at all: We want to keep you as part of the team. That's why we've continued your benefits package.

ADAPTATIONS

This script can be modified to:

- Trim employee benefits
- Reduce the number of paid holidays
- Cut back on vacation time

KEY POINTS

- Stress this is strictly a financial decision that in no way reflects the company's feelings about the employee.
- If accused of ageism or of singling out the employee for any reason, absorb the anger and stress that the decision was based solely on finances.
- If the employee complains of financial hardship, commiserate, explain whatever positives there are in the situation, and offer to help in any way possible.
- If the employee asks if management will be doing the same, reply that it will, if it becomes necessary.
- If the employee threatens to leave, simply restate the company's position—they're not being unreasonable, and there's nothing you can do or say to stop them.

Announcing a Salary Reduction

29

STRATEGY

Here's one of the more difficult workplace dialogues in this book. Reducing salary is tough. The employee is bound to be very angry, so don't be glib or try to put too positive a spin on the situation. The great danger here is that he will take it as a sign that he isn't appreciated and will look elsewhere for a job. That's why it's essential you do everything you can to impress on him that you'd like to keep him. But at the same time you can't pull any punches. Don't imply it's only temporary if you know it's intended to be permanent, and don't promise to make it up to him in other areas if you can't. One secret is to go to the employee's office, rather than having him come to yours. That reduces some of the fear and also puts you more in the role of supplicant. Normally that's not appropriate, but in this case you *are* a supplicant. You're asking him to stick around even though you're cutting his pay.

TACTICS

- **Attitude:** Accept that you're asking the employee to give up a great deal, so a bit of fear and anger on his part is justifiable.
- **Preparation:** Make sure you understand the organization's rationale for the pay cut and can explain it succinctly. It's essential you use the same explanation with every person you speak with—mixed messages will imply a hidden agenda, and that will destroy the already battered morale.
- **Timing:** Present the news as soon as you know it's official, regardless of the time of day, day of week, or status of any other activities. This may require dramatic action on the part of employees, and they deserve as much lead time as you can give them.
- **Behavior:** Do all you can to reassure the employee that his job is safe and his future with the company secure. Absorb anger—it's a legitimate response to these circumstances. Be as compassionate as you can, but refrain from making promises you can't keep or sugar-coating the news.

29. Announcing a Salary Reduction

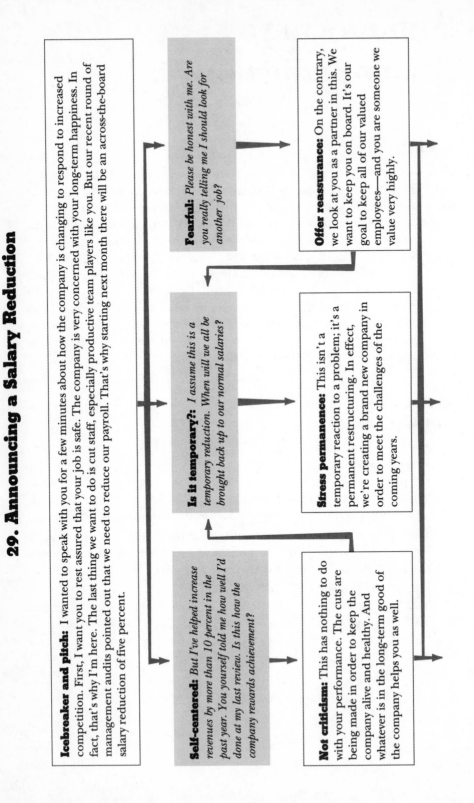

Icebreaker and pitch: I wanted to speak with you for a few minutes about how the company is changing to respond to increased competition. First, I want you to rest assured that your job is safe. The company is very concerned with your long-term happiness. In fact, that's why I'm here. The last thing we want to do is cut staff, especially productive team players like you. But our recent round of management audits pointed out that we need to reduce our payroll. That's why starting next month there will be an across-the-board salary reduction of five percent.

Fearful: *Please be honest with me. Are you really telling me I should look for another job?*

Offer reassurance: On the contrary, we look at you as a partner in this. We want to keep you on board. It's our goal to keep all of our valued employees —and you are someone we value very highly.

Is it temporary?: *I assume this is a temporary reduction. When will we all be brought back up to our normal salaries?*

Stress permanence: This isn't a temporary reaction to a problem; it's a permanent restructuring. In effect, we're creating a brand new company in order to meet the challenges of the coming years.

Self-centered: *But I've helped increase revenues by more than 10 percent in the past year. You yourself told me how well I'd done at my last review. Is this how the company rewards achievement?*

Not criticism: This has nothing to do with your performance. The cuts are being made in order to keep the company alive and healthy. And whatever is in the long-term good of the company helps you as well.

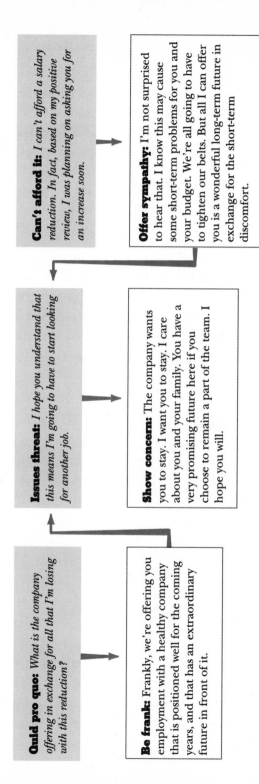

Quid pro quo: *What is the company offering in exchange for all that I'm losing with this reduction?*

Be frank: Frankly, we're offering you employment with a healthy company that is positioned well for the coming years, and that has an extraordinary future in front of it.

Issues threat: *I hope you understand that this means I'm going to have to start looking for another job.*

Show concern: The company wants you to stay. I want you to stay. I care about you and your family. You have a very promising future here if you choose to remain a part of the team. I hope you will.

Can't afford it: *I can't afford a salary reduction. In fact, based on my positive review, I was planning on asking you for an increase soon.*

Offer sympathy: I'm not surprised to hear that. I know this may cause some short-term problems for you and your budget. We're all going to have to tighten our belts. But all I can offer you is a wonderful long-term future in exchange for the short-term discomfort.

ADAPTATIONS

This script can be modified to:

- Reduce staff, benefits, or perquisites
- Increase employees' contribution toward a medical or pension plan
- Transfer an employee

KEY POINTS

- Be clear and direct, presenting this as an unavoidable and final decision that doesn't reflect on an employee's performance or standing in the organization.
- If the employee cites his own success in response, reiterate that the cut isn't linked to performance, it's across the board based on the company's needs.
- If the employee asks if it's temporary or asks what he'll be receiving in exchange, be honest.
- If the employee expresses fears about his position, reassure him that this isn't a question of performance.
- If the employee expresses fears about his finances, commiserate, but stress that there's no alternative.
- If the employee asks if you're taking a reduction, be truthful.
- If the employee threatens to look for another job, stress the company's desire to retain him, but accept that there's nothing you can do to stop him.

Warning a Subordinate to Stop Drinking

30

STRATEGY

In large organizations there are official policies for dealing with employee drug and alcohol problems and perhaps even individuals on staff trained in bringing such issues up with employees. But most small companies have no formal procedures or resources for these troubling matters. Instead, it often falls to a manager. If you're eager to retain the individual, you're going to need to impress on him the need to rehabilitate, or at the very least to clean up his act during working hours. Expect anger, denial, and projection, but reiterate that this is a workplace problem that needs to be addressed. Regardless of how the dialogue ends, offer whatever information about treatment you can. Then, keep your fingers crossed that the shock therapy works.

TACTICS

- **Attitude:** Be determined—employees' personal problems cannot be allowed to interfere with the workings of the company. An employee with a drinking problem is a danger to both you and the company.

- **Preparation:** Find out all you can about the company's health insurance coverage for such problems, and local programs or facilities.

- **Timing:** Do this as soon as possible after an incident where the employee's problem was obvious.

- **Behavior:** Hold this meeting in your office. Make sure it's entirely private and confidential. Be as businesslike as possible. It's not your role to explore the causes of the problem—leave that to a counselor. Your job is to make it clear that his behavior is affecting his work and you cannot allow that to continue.

30. Warning a Subordinate to Stop Drinking

Icebreaker: I called you in here to tell you that your job performance is not as good as it should be, and I think the reason is your drinking during business hours. You're not here to maintain potential. You're here to realize it.

Complete denial: *I don't know what you mean. I don't drink during business hours.*

It's the job's fault: *This is an awfully stressful job. I need a drink or two at lunch to be able to handle the stress.*

I'm still tops: *Listen, even after I have a couple of drinks at lunch, I'm still the best person you've got. Nobody does this job better than me.*

Angry: *You have no right to say that to me. My personal life is none of your business.*

No debate: I don't want to have a debate with you. Something is affecting your performance and whatever it is has to stop. When I hired you I looked forward to a long relationship. I still want that . . . if possible.

Less pressure?: When I hired you I saw someone who could handle pressure. No amount of drinking is going to make this job easier. If you want me to take some of the pressure off you, that could be arranged.

Needs your best: You're right. You do your job very well. But you're even better when you don't have a couple of drinks in you. The company, and you, need you to be the best you can be.

You're right but: You're right. Your personal life is none of my business. But this is affecting your work and that *is* my business. It could end up affecting how you earn your money.

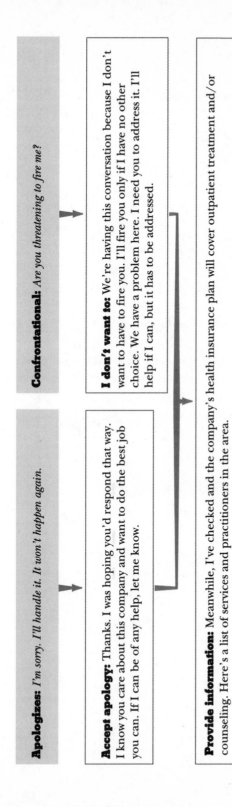

Apologizes: *I'm sorry. I'll handle it. It won't happen again.*

Confrontational: *Are you threatening to fire me?*

Accept apology: Thanks. I was hoping you'd respond that way. I know you care about this company and want to do the best job you can. If I can be of any help, let me know.

I don't want to: We're having this conversation because I don't want to have to fire you. I'll fire you only if I have no other choice. We have a problem here. I need you to address it. I'll help if I can, but it has to be addressed.

Provide information: Meanwhile, I've checked and the company's health insurance plan will cover outpatient treatment and/or counseling. Here's a list of services and practitioners in the area.

ADAPTATIONS

This script can be modified to:

- Stop an employee from proselytizing in the office
- Stop an employee from gossiping
- Curtail disruptive behavioral problems, such as loud radios

KEY POINTS

- Be businesslike, determined, clear, and direct. Remember this is a business discussion even though it revolves around a personal problem.
- If the employee denies he has a problem, refuse to get into a debate. Instead, stress there's a problem that must be corrected.
- If the employee blames job-related stress for his drinking, offer to help relieve some stress.
- If the employee claims his performance is still good, despite his drinking, say that it could be better yet.
- If the employee says his personal life is none of your business, agree, but note that when personal problems affect the workplace they become business problems.
- If the employee remains confrontational, say his job is in jeopardy.

Fixing a
Flextime Problem

31.

STRATEGY

Flextime arrangements often lead to problems for managers, even if they want them to work out. Whether the problem is with the employee or with the arrangement itself, recurring difficulties not only hurt day-to-day operations but can also damage morale and jeopardize future flextime deals for other staffers. The secret to resolving these kinds of problems is to take charge of the discussion from the outset. Immediately state that the current situation isn't working, cite your reasons, and then move on to your proposed solution. Don't get into a debate over whether or not the arrangement is working. Remain open to trial periods for workable compromises, however. An astute, dedicated employee is in the best position to come up with a solution. Finally, don't close the door on going back to the original arrangement if circumstances change—the problem could be a temporary one.

TACTICS

- **Attitude:** Be compassionate and caring, but also clear that there's a problem that must be addressed.
- **Preparation:** Gather examples of specific problems, and develop a solution of your own to resolve the matter.
- **Timing:** Do this as soon as possible after an incident where the problem came up.
- **Behavior:** Try to do this in person, and offer advance warning of the agenda so that the employee has time to draft a plan of his own.

31. Fixing a Flextime Problem

Icebreaker: Thanks for coming in, Jack. Unfortunately, your working only four days a week isn't going as smoothly as we'd hoped. While you're getting the basic work done, you're just not as accessible as I need you to be when unexpected problems crop up.

Becomes defensive: *What do you mean? Whenever you've left a message on my answering machine, I've returned your call before the end of the day.*

Becomes angry: *I think it's unfair of you to expect me to always be available on my agreed day off. I'm getting the work done—that should be enough.*

Becomes apologetic: *I'm sorry. I know I said I'd be available if you needed me on my day off, but I've been having problems with my sitter that make it difficult.*

Assert authority: That's not good enough. You know how important it is in this business to be able to get in touch at a moment's notice.

Document problems: Our agreement was that you would arrange for child care on that day so you'd be able to deal with matters that couldn't wait.

Accept apology: I thought that might be the problem. I know how hard it can be to find reliable child care. But your not being accessible really is a big problem for us.

Pitch: Rather than have you take the whole day off on Fridays, I'd like you to come in for half the day for the next two months. We can work the exact hours around your schedule.

Suggests compromise: *What if, instead of coming into the office for half the day, I get a beeper or a cellular phone? That way you'll always be able to reach me if something urgent comes up.*

Opposes suggestion: *That's going to be a real problem for me. With the commuting time and the extra child care involved, I might as well be working a full day at the office.*

Accepts suggestion: *Obviously, I prefer not to, but I understand the situation. Would you consider a different flextime arrangement down the line if I can come up with an idea that's better suited to the job?*

Offer trial period: That's an interesting idea. If you're willing to go to the expense, I'm willing to give it a try for a month. But if it doesn't work, I will need you to start coming in on Fridays.

Lay down law: I'm afraid the only alternative is to do away with a flextime arrangement altogether and go back to a regular work week. I need you to be accessible, and right now you're not.

Express thanks: Certainly. I know I can count on you to do what it takes to get the job done. If the situation changes and you think you can make the old arrangement work, I'd be willing to give it another try.

ADAPTATIONS

This script can be modified to:

- Change an employee's vacation schedule
- Curtail an employee's "clock-watching"
- Withdraw a time concession made for continuing education

KEY POINTS

- Be caring, but also businesslike and clearly in charge.
- If he becomes defensive, assert your authority and insist on a solution.
- If he becomes angry, document the problems.
- Offer a solution of your own.
- If he rejects your idea outright, insist that something must be done.
- If he offers a compromise, consider a trial period.

Turning Down a Promotion Request

32.

STRATEGY

Despite the changes in the workplace, most employees believe that positions should be filled from within by moving individuals up the chain of command. But today, such strict adherence to the hierarchy isn't the norm. Openings are usually filled on a case-by-case basis, or not at all. Sometimes people are moved laterally. Sometimes a replacement is brought in from outside. And sometimes people are indeed moved up the ladder. When an employee requests a promotion you cannot grant, the secret to breaking the bad news is to offer him praise and explain that his future lies elsewhere, to say he isn't quite ready for the job, or to suggest that the particular job description will be changed, making his experience—his major selling point—irrelevant. All three must be done gently, particularly if the person has a promising future in the company. Keep this discussion short and sweet. You're breaking the news of the decision, not engaging in another job interview. If the employee doesn't accept your primary rationale, be friendly but firm and note that he isn't the one who makes these decisions.

TACTICS

- **Attitude:** Think of yourself as a coach, inspiring a player to try again after falling short.
- **Preparation:** Decide prior to the meeting how important he will be to the company's future. If he does figure strongly in your plans, discuss these, vaguely, reassuring him of his value. If he's not likely to play an important role in the company's future, you can lean more toward his not being ready for the job.
- **Timing:** Do this as soon as you know he won't be getting the job. The last thing you want is for him to hear it through the grapevine before you've had a chance to add your spin to the message.
- **Behavior:** Be concise and businesslike. You're not passing a death sentence. Offer your best explanation, and then move on, refusing to engage in another job interview.

32. Turning Down a Promotion Request

Icebreaker: Jim, I've called you in here to let you know that you won't be taking Jack's place as manager of the department. I have other plans for you. I want to thank you for making yourself available for the job. Once again you've demonstrated how much you care for the company's success and we're excited about your future here.

Why not?: *I don't understand why I'm not getting Jack's job. I replaced him when he was on vacation. I'm the next in line. I've covered for him when he was sick. I know everything he does. Even he said I was the best man for the job.*

What plans?: *Naturally I'm disappointed. But I'm excited to hear you and the company have plans for me. If they're not for me to take Jack's place, what are they?*

Job changed: The job Jack did may no longer exist. We're reviewing the structure of the entire department and, in all likelihood, there will no longer be a manager's position. However, let me repeat that we admire your sense of urgency and your ambition, and there is a future for you here.

Not ready: You're not ready yet. Moving you into this kind of spot prematurely would do more harm than good to your long-term future. When you're more seasoned, you may well be moved into a more important position. Let me repeat, there's a future for you here—we don't want to see you self-destruct.

No specifics: Actually, we believe your progress in the company may not follow the traditional path. There's nothing specific just yet, but we're considering you in our long-term plans. You're part of a group that we'd like to play a major role in our future.

Hidden agenda?: *You make being turned down sound wonderful. But I've still been turned down. Is there some other agenda? Are you sending me a message about my career here?*

Close the Issue: Listen, we're happy with you. We want you to stay with us. I've said we think you're valuable and you have a future here. But we're not about to have you tell us how to run the company. You may get to that position one day . . . but you're not there yet.

ADAPTATIONS

This script can be modified to:

- Turn down a transfer request
- Turn down a request for an assistant
- Turn down a request for a change of title

KEY POINTS

- Be clear, direct, and concise, holding out the suggestion of a future with the company.
- Let him ask for a reason, since he may instead ask about your suggestion of an alternative future for him—that gets you into a more positive line of conversation.
- If he does ask for a reason, say he's either not ready or the job description will be changed.
- If he asks about his future, remain vague but hopeful.
- If he tries to engage in a further dialogue, cut him short, wielding your authority firmly but with good humor.

Giving a Negative
Performance Review

33

STRATEGY

Delivering criticism requires a delicate touch. You need to present the problem strongly enough so the employee gets the message and hopefully changes his behavior, but not so strongly that you undermine his confidence or create lingering resentment. The best way to accomplish this is to start with positive comments before delivering the criticism. If the information is received openly, reaffirm your confidence and set up a future meeting. If the employee disputes your perception or gets angry, give him a chance to get over reflexive defensiveness by offering specifics. If that doesn't calm him down, stop pulling your punches and make it clear his future depends on improved performance.

TACTICS

- **Attitude:** Think of yourself as a teacher or mentor, not a judge and jury. Be willing to absorb a little anger without retaliating — it's not easy to take criticism submissively.
- **Preparation:** Make sure your list of criticisms is accurate and detailed — you don't want this to turn into a debate over facts. Have specific suggestions and advice ready to help the employee improve his performance.
- **Timing:** If this isn't a formal review, it should take place as soon after a problem as possible so it's fresh in everyone's mind. If you can, schedule it for early in the week so the employee has a chance to act on your advice right away and won't have to dwell on it over a weekend.
- **Behavior:** Lead off with positive comments so the meeting doesn't seem like a one-sided attack. If the employee won't get past his initial anger or denial, forget subtlety and make it clear his future is at stake unless he cleans up his act.

33. Giving a Negative Performance Review

Icebreaker: I'm generally very pleased with your work—especially the way you're handling the arrangements for the sales conference—but there is one thing you need to work on. Maybe I haven't made it clear that you're also responsible for supervising all the promotional materials, because lately I've found quite a few mistakes and some sloppy work.

Accepts criticism: *I'm really sorry. I didn't realize that I'd slipped up. I won't let it happen again.*

Denies problem: *Really? I've been very careful about reviewing those pieces. I don't think there were any mistakes when they left my desk.*

Gets angry: *I've been working overtime to get everything set for the sales conference. I can't believe you're complaining about this given all I've accomplished here.*

Chance to get past denial: Let me show you what I mean. Here are copies of the last three promotional pieces that you okayed. I've marked the problem areas.

Gets past denial: *I guess you're right. I didn't realize that all the time I was spending on the conference was affecting my other work. I'll be more careful from now on.*

Still denies problem: *I'm not the only one whose job it is to check the promos. I can't believe that some of those mistakes weren't inserted after I signed off.*

Chance to diffuse anger: I'm surprised by your reaction. I thought you'd be eager to improve your performance. Is there something else troubling you?

Remains angry: *I think you're being very unfair. On the whole, my work has been excellent; you're just nitpicking. You've been overly critical of me from day one.*

Gets over anger: *I'm sorry that I got so defensive and snapped at you. It's just that I work very hard and really want to do the best job that I can.*

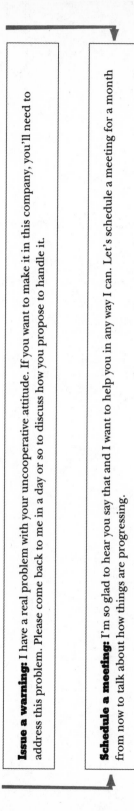

Issue a warning: I have a real problem with your uncooperative attitude. If you want to make it in this company, you'll need to address this problem. Please come back to me in a day or so to discuss how you propose to handle it.

Schedule a meeting: I'm so glad to hear you say that and I want to help you in any way I can. Let's schedule a meeting for a month from now to talk about how things are progressing.

ADAPTATIONS

This script can be modified to:

- Review a student's poor performance
- Discuss a partner's lack of effort
- Speak with a volunteer about lethargic efforts

KEY POINTS

- Soften initial criticism by suggesting that perhaps your instructions weren't clear or that the employee has been overworked.
- If your criticism is denied, offer specifics without getting defensive.
- If the employee responds with anger, show surprise and ask if there's something else troubling him.
- If the employee accepts the criticism immediately, or after having a chance to blow off some steam, reiterate your desire to help and schedule a subsequent meeting.
- If the employee refuses to get past his anger or denial, say you have a problem with his attitude, warn him it must change, and demand immediate action.

Correcting Repeated Mistakes by a Subordinate

34

STRATEGY

Managers are a haberdasher's delight: They have to wear so many hats. Some of these hats are comfortable and complimentary, while others are constraining and tight. Which should you choose to correct a subordinate who makes repeated mistakes? If the worker is new, a comfortable white hat of mentor supporting a fledgling employee is in order. If the subordinate is a veteran, a darker tone might be in order and a headache may loom on the horizon. That's because established workers may see attempts at corrective support as criticism of their performance. The potential for confrontation is ripe. The goal of this script is to help you no matter which hat you choose to wear. The key is your understanding and accepting that your primary role in all interactions with subordinates is supervising successful completion of assigned tasks. That's the head beneath every hat.

TACTICS

- **Attitude:** Your attitude should be confident and authoritative. You are carrying out your role as an effective supervisor. The expertise you share to help solve the problem establishes a position of supportive command.

- **Preparation:** Determine if the mistakes you've observed are random or recurring. Begin to document the mistakes being made. Self-evident mistakes are easy and quick to prove, while less obvious mistakes will take more time and effort to document. Write down the examples that you have seen and keep a record of complaints from others. Review your information to determine the pattern of mistakes. Finally, decide on solutions to correct the problems.

- **Timing:** Convene a meeting as soon as documentation and solutions are established to your satisfaction. However, be aware that a sudden stumble by a veteran employee can be signal of job unhappiness. You need to read this and act quickly.

- **Behavior:** Come out from behind the desk for this meeting and sit with your staff member. That will demonstrate you're interested in helping her solve a problem, not in chastising her for causing one. Clearly present your concerns and documentation and then offer solutions. Because the documentation can't lie, expect discomfort and excuses. The intensity of excuse making will be in direct proportion to seniority. A new person will work with you more quickly, but an experienced subordinate will ultimately come around as well.

34. Correcting Repeated Mistakes by a Subordinate

State problem: Pam, the past several weeks there have been similar mistakes in your weekly summaries. Let's take a look at them, see what the problem is, and see how we can fix it.

Embarrassed recognition: *I'm sorry. I've been trying so hard, I really have.*

Annoyed dismissal: *I've been preparing those summaries for two years and no one ever said anything about any mistakes.*

Emphasize concerns: I know. That's what is so puzzling. Here, take a look at what I'm talking about. [Review documentation.]

Reassurance: I know you have. We all make mistakes. Lets see what the problem might be and figure out how we can fix it. [Review documentation.]

Offers excuses: *Okay, I can see there are some mistakes here. There's a lot more work to do now than there used to be. Maybe I've been focusing too much on the new material and getting careless with the older routines.*

Recognizes problem: *I see what I did wrong. I guess I just wasn't concentrating. I was in too much of a hurry.*

Accept solutions: That could explain it. Maybe all you need to do is concentrate a bit more.

Accepts suggestion: *You're right. I'll pay more attention in the future.*

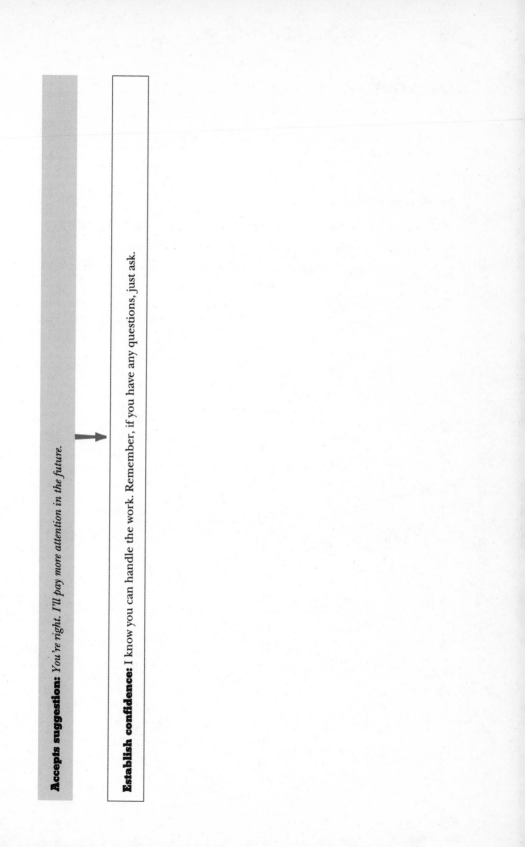

Establish confidence: I know you can handle the work. Remember, if you have any questions, just ask.

ADAPTATIONS

This script can be modified to:

- Correct a subordinate who repeatedly ignores required office protocol and procedures

KEY POINTS

- Approach the problem as a supportive supervisor, not a vindictive snoop.
- Gather documentation that exemplifies the mistakes being made.
- Be ready with solutions to solve the problem, but encourage the employee to come up with her own solution.
- Exhibit confidence in her ability to make corrections.
- Reaffirm your support by offering accessibility to help with future problems.

Turning down a Subordinate's Request for Time Off

35

STRATEGY

As a manager, you're no doubt aware the easiest way to earn a reputation as a bad guy is to say "no" to a subordinate without being able to give him a good, solid reason for your refusal. However, if you can legitimately back up your rejection, you've a chance of coming across as a human being while still maintaining managerial control of the office. When a valued, hard-working employee has already used up all his sick/personal time, you must be clear in your own mind as to what you and the company consider legitimate reasons for additional time off. For example, time off for a doctor's appointment or having to close on a home purchase might be acceptable: Both events must be scheduled during business hours and are important. On the other hand, time off for sports events or taking a son to look at a college shouldn't be acceptable because these are activities that easily can be taken care of on the weekend and aren't essential. If your subordinate's request is legitimate, the only reason you can give for turning him down is that his timing is bad: Things are simply too busy at work for you to let him have that day off . . . at least not without compensation time. If you feel his request is unacceptable, your tack will be to invoke precedent, as in, "If I let you have the day off to go to the Monster Truck Rally, before you know it I'll have everyone coming in here asking for days off." Just remember: Whatever your personal feelings about the employee and his request, the language of your refusal must pertain to business, period.

TACTICS

- **Attitude:** While your first instinct might be annoyance, try to keep an open mind and be fair. Let him state his case and then decide accordingly.

- **Preparation:** Although each request for time off must be handled individually, you can expedite the process greatly by knowing what you and the company consider valid reasons for time off and reasons that are beyond the pale.

35. Turning Down a Subordinate's Request for Time Off

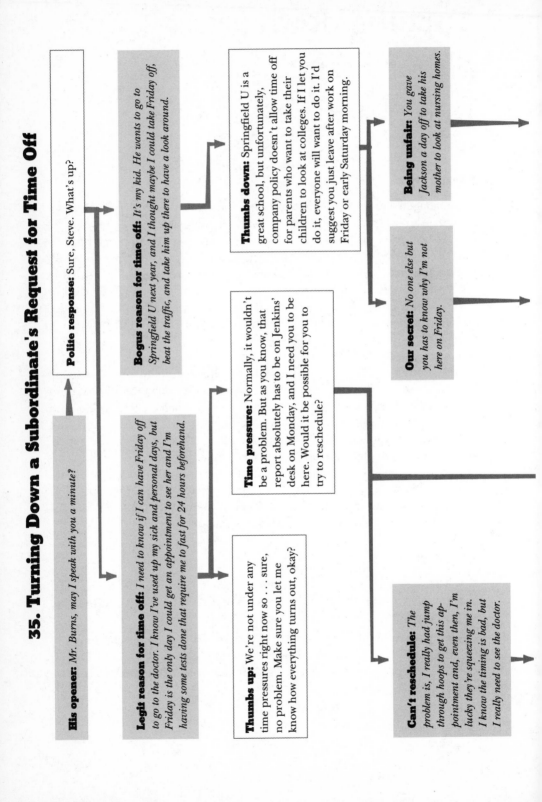

His opener: *Mr. Burns, may I speak with you a minute?*

Polite response: Sure, Steve. What's up?

Bogus reason for time off: *It's my kid. He wants to go to Springfield U next year, and I thought maybe I could take Friday off, beat the traffic, and take him up there to have a look around.*

Thumbs down: Springfield U is a great school, but unfortunately, company policy doesn't allow time off for parents who want to take their children to look at colleges. If I let you do it, everyone will want to do it. I'd suggest you just leave after work on Friday or early Saturday morning.

Being unfair: *You gave Jackson a day off to take his mother to look at nursing homes.*

Our secret: *No one else but you has to know why I'm not here on Friday.*

Legit reason for time off: *I need to know if I can have Friday off to go to the doctor. I know I've used up my sick and personal days, but Friday is the only day I could get an appointment to see her and I'm having some tests done that require me to fast for 24 hours beforehand.*

Time pressure: Normally, it wouldn't be a problem. But as you know, that report absolutely has to be on Jenkins' desk on Monday, and I need you to be here. Would it be possible for you to try to reschedule?

Thumbs up: We're not under any time pressures right now so . . . sure, no problem. Make sure you let me know how everything turns out, okay?

Can't reschedule: *The problem is, I really had jump through hoops to get this appointment and, even then, I'm lucky they're squeezing me in. I know the timing is bad, but I really need to see the doctor.*

Suggest comp time: If you can't reschedule, you could stay late on Thursday and come in on Saturday morning. I'd have no problem with you taking Friday off if you guarantee that report will be on Jenkins' desk first thing Monday morning.

Agrees: *I'll be here Thursday night and Saturday morning and the report will be on Jenkins' desk Monday morning. I promise. Thank you.*

Will try to reschedule: *I'll see what the doctor's office says about rescheduling and get back to you.*

Stick to your guns: I'll know why you're not here, and it's not my policy to lie for employees. How about this? If you can get your work done on time, you can leave an hour early. But there is no way I can give you the entire day or even half the day. There's simply too much to do.

Should have lied: *Are you saying I should have lied to you, maybe told you I had to go to the doctor?*

Not comparable: I gave Jackson the day off because that was an emergency situation that could not be rescheduled. You may not have known this, but Jackson stayed late three nights in a row to be able to take that day off.

Honesty is the rule: No, I'm saying there are valid reasons for taking time off and there are invalid reasons for taking time off, especially when you've run out of sick days and personal days. If you actually had a doctor's appointment, I've no doubt we could work something out. However, lying isn't the way to behave in the workplace.

- **Timing:** Unfortunately, this is one request you're likely to be blind-sided by: One minute you're sitting in your office working, the next you've got a subordinate poking his head around the door asking if he can have a word with you. If you can handle it there and then, great. However, if you can't, ask him to stop by after work or set up an appointment for the following day when he might speak to you in your office. If he corners you in the hallway, do the same.

- **Behavior:** Be polite, attentive, and sympathetic. Stop what you're doing when he makes his case and maintain eye contact. Don't interrupt. You're his boss, not the Grand Inquisitor, so avoid playing 20 questions. Whatever your personal feelings about the request, don't roll your eyes, sigh heavily, or chuckle. No one likes to be belittled.

ADAPTATIONS

This script can be modified to:

- Deal with a spouse or child seeking release from an obligation

KEY POINTS

- Before a conversation even takes place, have a clear sense of what you and the company consider legitimate as well as unacceptable reasons for time off.
- If the request is legitimate, but the timing is poor, simply tell him he can't have the time because he's needed at work.
- If the request is unacceptable, tell him you can't give him the time for that kind of reason and say it would set an unwanted company precedent.
- Be fair and open-minded about suggestions for compensation time.

CHAPTER FOUR

Lifescripts for Office
Politics and Behavior

Confronting a Backstabbing Peer

36

STRATEGY

The secret to confronting a backstabbing colleague is to show that the attacker, far from being constructive, is being unfair and personal. If the actions have been covert, deliver your message indirectly—that way the attacker can't simply deny involvement and end the conversation. If the attack was overt, or if the indirect approach doesn't work, deal directly. Ideally, you should conduct the discussion privately, which increases the chance of an honest exchange. But if that doesn't work, or if the attack is so damaging you must respond immediately, do it publicly. If all else fails, stress your willingness to take your dispute to a higher authority.

TACTICS

- **Attitude:** Don't feel defensive or uneasy. You are an aggrieved party looking for justice. You're coming from a position of honesty so you've a right to feel confident.

- **Preparation:** Jot down some notes about past attacks. For this script they'll simply serve as reminders. If need be, they'll help you prepare a memo if this dialogue doesn't work.

- **Timing:** If the incident demands an immediate public response, do so. If not, approach the attacker privately as soon as possible after the latest attack.

- **Behavior:** Hold this meeting in the attacker's office. Don't schedule it—simply arrive. If this is an indirect approach, you can sit down. If this is a direct approach, shut the door behind you and remain standing, keeping yourself between her and the door. In effect, this puts you in the dominant position, keeps her a captive in her office, and forces her to listen to you. As soon as you finish your script, turn your back on her and leave.

36. Confronting a Backstabbing Peer

Indirect private approach

Icebreaker: I've heard that someone has been complaining that I'm not pulling my weight. What do you think I should do?

Denial: *I can't believe someone would spread rumors maliciously. Maybe you misunderstood a comment that was meant to be helpful?*

Appeal for privacy: If that's the case, I would hope she or he would make any other comments to me directly—and in private. Then I would do the same.

Confrontation: *What do you expect? We all want to be promoted, but there's only one opening. It's every person for him or herself.*

Threat of action: That's not the way to go. If these attacks continue, I'm going to suggest to the boss that we have a staff meeting to air our feelings openly.

Rationalization: *The same thing happened to me last year. This place has become so political, don't you think?*

Appeal for unity: I agree—and it's really too bad. We'd all get a lot further if we worked together. And if we can't do that, at least we should stop cutting each other's throats.

Direct public response/Private approach

Direct public response: I can't understand why you'd want to slander me this way in public. I suggest you stop this public display and discuss any personal problems we may have in private. But right now, I suggest we get back to business.

Later that day

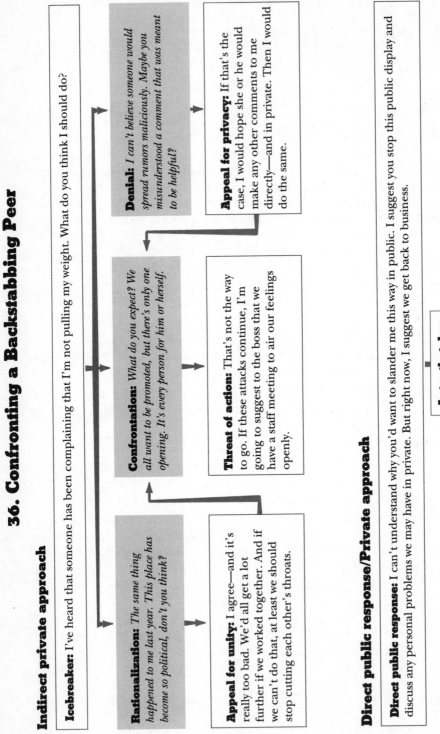

Icebreaker: What have I ever done to you to elicit this kind of behavior? I can't imagine why you're attacking me.

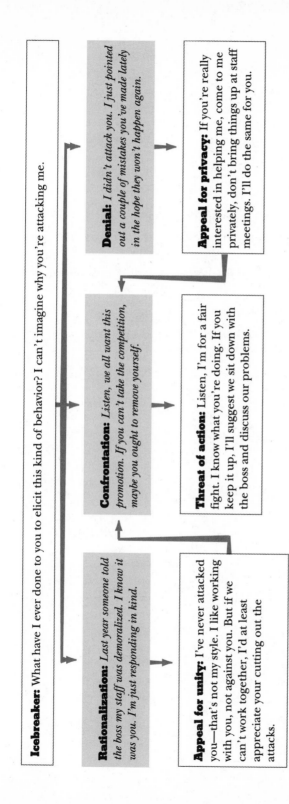

Denial: *I didn't attack you. I just pointed out a couple of mistakes you've made lately in the hope they won't happen again.*

Appeal for privacy: If you're really interested in helping me, come to me privately, don't bring things up at staff meetings. I'll do the same for you.

Confrontation: *Listen, we all want this promotion. If you can't take the competition, maybe you ought to remove yourself.*

Threat of action: Listen, I'm for a fair fight. I know what you're doing. If you keep it up, I'll suggest we sit down with the boss and discuss our problems.

Rationalization: *Last year someone told the boss my staff was demoralized. I know it was you. I'm just responding in kind.*

Appeal for unity: I've never attacked you—that's not my style. I like working with you, not against you. But if we can't work together, I'd at least appreciate your cutting out the attacks.

ADAPTATIONS

This script can be modified to:

- Confront a gossiping acquaintance or friend
- Dispel a rumor
- Handle an off-color joke

KEY POINTS

- Respond in kind: indirectly to covert attacks, directly to overt attacks.
- If need be, respond publicly and immediately. Otherewise, have the discussion in private.
- If the attacker denies either being the perpetrator, or that the attack was harmful, appeal for privacy.
- If the attacker rationalizes her action, appeal for unity.
- If the attacker is confrontational, threaten to bring the matter up with higher authorities or go public with it.

Ratting on
a Colleague

37

STRATEGY

Deciding whether to complain about a peer's performance is a tough call. Even if your gripes are entirely justified and your boss supports you, you can end up being viewed as a backstabber. So pick your fights carefully. If someone simply rubs you the wrong way, that's your problem. The only time it's worth entering these dangerous waters is when someone's sloppy work or procrastination is jeopardizing your ability to get your job done, and you've already tried, unsuccessfully, to set things right. Your goal in this script is to enlist your boss's direct intervention without incurring criticism yourself. You want to minimize any damage to your reputation and avoid being labeled the boss's spy. You can accomplish all this as long as you stress the connection to your own productivity and the company's goals. Make it clear that this is an unusual situation, not your common practice.

TACTICS

- **Attitude:** Your first loyalty must be to the company. It's by following this credo that you'll achieve your own success. You aren't putting someone down to boost yourself—you're helping the company achieve its goals.
- **Preparation:** Make sure you've established what you feel is the problem—quality or delay, for instance—and that you've tried on your own to resolve the situation.
- **Timing:** The timing here is tricky. You want to wait long enough so that action is vital, but not so long that it's a crisis beyond repair.
- **Behavior:** Show remorse at having to take this step, but offer no apologies. You have the company's goals at heart and there's no shame in that.

37. Ratting on a Colleague

Icebreaker: Excuse me, Sharon, but I need to speak with you. I'm afraid there's a problem with meeting our deadline for the Oxford proposal [or] I'm afraid the Oxford proposal just isn't going to meet our usual standards. I've asked several times, but Diane has yet to turn in her final sketches for the project [or] The sketches I've gotten from Diane just aren't up to par.

Wants to hear: *You know how important that project is. I'm not going to let anything keep us from delivering the kind of work we promised, and delivering it on time. What exactly is the problem?*

Upset at idea: *Listen, that project is crucial. I made you the lead person on it, and I don't want to hear any excuses or buck passing. Your job—and hers—is to get it done right, and on time.*

Not doing work: I know Diane is under a lot of pressure—we all are. But I'm not sure she's even begun the sketches I need from her. I've asked for them repeatedly, but she hasn't delivered. And we're running out of time.

Work not up to par: I know Diane is under a lot of pressure—we all are. But the sketches she's given me just aren't the quality we need. We've spoken about it repeatedly, but there's been no improvement. And we're running out of time.

Offer reassurance: I appreciate your concern, and I'm sure we'll meet the deadline if we solve this problem now. But I really need your help. Without it, I don't think I'll be able to get what we need out of Diane.

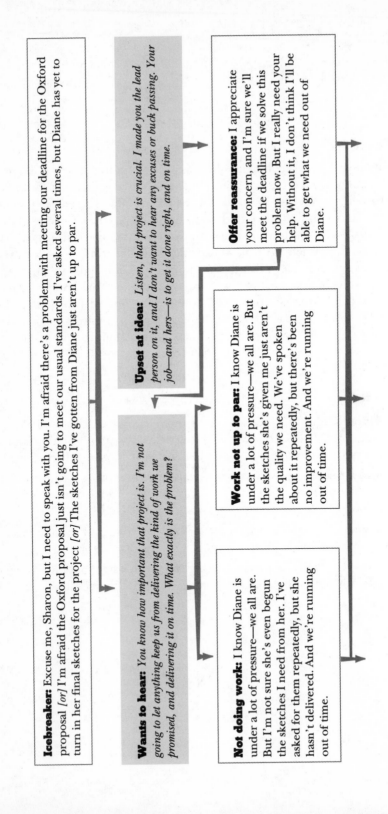

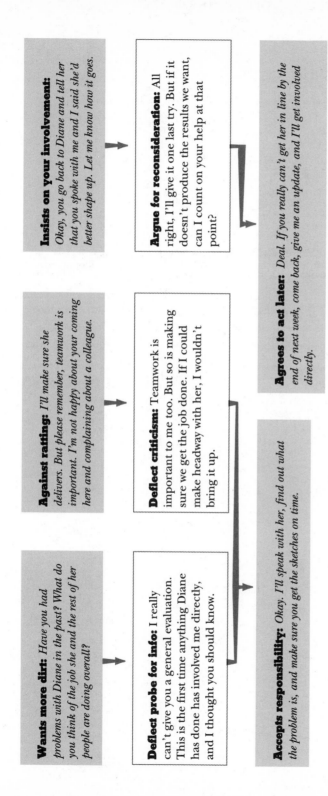

Wants more dirt: *Have you had problems with Diane in the past? What do you think of the job she and the rest of her people are doing overall?*

Deflect probe for info: I really can't give you a general evaluation. This is the first time anything Diane has done has involved me directly, and I thought you should know.

Accepts responsibility: *Okay. I'll speak with her, find out what the problem is, and make sure you get the sketches on time.*

Against ratting: *I'll make sure she delivers. But please remember, teamwork is important. I'm not happy about your coming here and complaining about a colleague.*

Deflect criticism: Teamwork is important to me too. But so is making sure we get the job done. If I could make headway with her, I wouldn't bring it up.

Insists on your involvement: *Okay, you go back to Diane and tell her that you spoke with me and I said she'd better shape up. Let me know how it goes.*

Argue for reconsideration: All right, I'll give it one last try. But if it doesn't produce the results we want, can I count on your help at that point?

Agrees to act later: *Deal. If you really can't get her in line by the end of next week, come back, give me an update, and I'll get involved directly.*

ADAPTATIONS

This script can be modified to:

- Speak to a customer or supplier about the behavior of one of its employees
- Speak to a partner at a professional firm you associate with about the behavior of another partner
- Speak to a store manager about a clerk's behavior
- Speak to a principal about your child's teacher

KEY POINTS

- Be clear about the problem and present it entirely in business terms.
- If your boss initially objects to getting involved, insist that you need her in order to get the job done.
- If your boss probes for more information on your colleague, stress that you have none to offer and that your concern is this project.
- If she insists on staying aloof, ask for a commitment that she'll get involved if you're once again unsuccessful.
- If she criticizes your coming to her with complaints about a peer, stress that you've only done it because the project was in jeopardy.

Complaining About an Immediate Superior's Behavior

38

STRATEGY

No one should have to put up with an insulting, abusive superior. If you've tried to speak to your immediate superior about her behavior and have gotten nowhere, the only solution is to make an end run and speak with her supervisor. Of course, this is one of the most dangerous political maneuvers you can make in an office environment. Not only could you appear to be a disloyal back-stabber to your boss's boss, but it's possible your relations to your immediate boss could get even worse if she learns of your actions. The best way to minimize the potential damage from such a conversation is to portray the situation as a rescue mission. Sure it's an end run, but it's not for your benefit, it's to help someone in trouble. This isn't about your problems with your boss's behavior—it's about *her* having a problem. Being an underling, you're probably in no postion to have such a conversation with her. You're asking her superior to speak to her about a problem (her behavior) that's affecting the company. Framed this way, there's little a manager can do but intervene.

TACTICS

- **Attitude:** Don't feel guilty about this end run. You're helping out someone in trouble whose inappropriate behavior or actions could be self-destructive and could bring harm to the company.

- **Preparation:** Try to commit to memory a list of your boss's inappropriate behavior. *Do not* put this in writing, however. Presenting such a memo, or even just reading from it, would imply premeditation and would have the appearance of back-stabbing.

- **Timing:** Do this either before or after normal business hours, if possible, reinforcing that it's a personal matter unfortunately affecting business.

- **Behavior:** Be concerned, caring, and compassionate. Show that your number one concern is that your boss is hurting herself and the company.

38. Complaining About an Immediate Superior's Behavior

Icebreaker: As you know, I have a great deal of respect for Sarah. I think she may have a serious problem, and although I'd like to help her on my own, I can't. That's why I'm here. I know how important she is to the company and that you respect her as well.

Takes the bait: *Okay, tell me what's going on.*

Concerned with hierarchy: *Does she know you've come to speak to me?*

Explain situation: In the past few weeks she has had a number of temper tantrums, launched into rages, become irrational, and even acted insulting in front of third parties. All this has led me to believe something personal is bothering her.

Not about business: No, but that's because this isn't job related. It's not about the chain of command, it's about someone who I think has a problem and may be in trouble.

Deal with it: *Listen, that's just Sarah. I know she's a pain, but she's also the best salesperson in the industry. I know she flies off the handle but she doesn't mean anything by it. You have to learn to let that kind of stuff go. Just do the best you can with her.*

Accepts responsibility: *Okay. Let me speak with her and see if there's something going on. Until then, just sit tight.*

Suspects intrigue: *Do you have another agenda here? You never got along with Sarah. Is this really about politics in the department?*

Not political: This isn't a question of whether or not I like Sarah. This is a question of a woman I think is in trouble. I wouldn't step on someone when she's down. I think she really needs help . . . help I can't give her.

Reaffirm concern: I hope you'll be able to help her out. I truly am worried about her. If there's anything I can do, please let me know.

Last resort: I've been trying to do just that. You're my last resort. This is becoming a regular pattern. I'm worried about her. I've spoken to her about it and gotten nowhere. I can't do my job and be her therapist too.

ADAPTATIONS

This script can be modified to:

- Discuss a problem child with his or her parent
- Complain about a municipal or governmental functionary

KEY POINTS

- This is your boss's problem, not yours. You're here to help her.
- If the chain of command is cited, explain that this is a personal, not a business issue.
- If the behavior is explained away or minimized, reiterate that this is a potentially self-destructive pattern that could damage the company as well.
- If your motives are called into question, stress that your concerns are for your boss and the company, not yourself.
- Reinforce your statements by expressing your willingness to help in any way you can.

Confronting a Sexual Harasser

39.

STRATEGY

Despite the trepidation and fear involved, if you're being sexually harassed you must deal with it immediately. If you don't put an end to the harassment, it will only escalate. The key to stopping harassment is to present a powerful, unequivocal objection, whatever the type of harassment and regardless of the harasser's motivations. An off-color joke should be treated with the same urgency as a pinch. Otherwise, your complaint won't be taken seriously. In many of these cases, power is as much an issue as sex. That's why you need to seize the power in this confrontation. You can do that by launching a direct assault.

TACTICS

- **Attitude:** All types of harassment are equal and require the same response—a powerful direct assault.
- **Preparation:** If you anticipate trouble, speak with a higher-up or the human resources department prior to the meeting.
- **Timing:** Deal with it as soon as possible. Delay will only empower the harasser and make you feel powerless.
- **Behavior:** Go to his office or workspace, position yourself between him and the door so he cannot leave, remain standing, maintain eye contact throughout, and walk out as soon as you're done, ensuring that you have the final word.

39. Confronting a Sexual Harasser

Icebreaker: I want you to stop working and listen very carefully to what I'm about to say.

Implied threat: Your behavior toward me is totally unacceptable and must stop right now.

You're overreacting: *Relax, you're overreacting. It was just a joke. Don't take everything so seriously! Why don't you cool off a bit and we'll forget all about it, okay?*

Your word against mine: *Ooh, I love it when you get mad. But seriously, babe, it's just your word against mine. And no one is going to believe you. So why don't you forget all about this and let's go out to lunch.*

Refuse to play games: This is my profession. Ours is a business relationship . . . period. I come here to work, not to play games.

I'm sorry: *I'm sorry. I didn't mean anything by it. I was just joking. I didn't realize it would offend you. Can't we just forget all about it?*

Beat him to punch: I thought you might respond this way, so I made sure to speak with personnel before I came here. They told me to speak to you prior to filing a formal complaint.

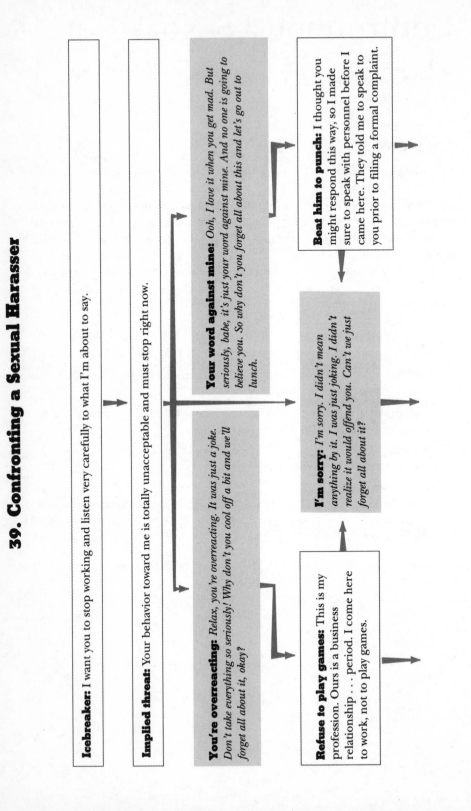

You're too sensitive: *Hold your horses. I said I didn't mean anything by it. You're exaggerating the importance of this. I really think you're being too sensitive.*

Put him on notice: I hear your apology, but there's no excuse for that kind of behavior. I've prepared a memo outlining what's happened, but I'll hold onto it for now. Maybe you'll be able to work things out.

You can't hurt me: *You don't scare me. I can make your life here miserable and destroy your future in this business. Go ahead. File your complaint. Nothing will happen to me.*

Imply legal action: That's not what my lawyer says.

ADAPTATIONS

This script can be modified to:

- Counter any type of on-the-job extortion
- Counter an announced threat to your position by a coworker

KEY POINTS

- Be as forceful as possible in your opening statement.
- Stress that there will be repercussions to continued harassment.
- If he says you're overreacting, state that this is a place of business, not a social club.
- If he says it's your word against his, explain that you've already gone to higher-ups.
- If he apologizes, say there's no excuse for his actions, but you'll hold off taking further action for now.
- If he says that you're too sensitive or that there's nothing you can do, say your lawyer disagrees.

Tactfully Suggesting Better Hygiene

40

STRATEGY

Having to tell someone that her breath or body odor is offensive may be one of the most awkward situations you'll ever face in the workplace. Yet sometimes it's essential to take action, not only for the comfort of you and other coworkers, but for the company and the person's future as well. Such problems are almost certain to undermine the image of the company if the offender comes in contact with clients. Hygiene problems will erode her standing in the company and will block any future progress in the organization. Begin with the assumption that she isn't conscious of the problem. Start off by subtly suggesting the same tools you use to avoid similar problems. If she takes the hint, let the matter drop. If your subtext isn't understood, you'll have to press further. With a subordinate you can be a bit more direct and demanding since this could be a business problem. With a peer you'll need to be more diplomatic.

TACTICS

- **Attitude:** Try not to be embarrassed. The other party will be embarrassed enough for both of you. Remember, you're doing this for her own good.
- **Preparation:** Buy some breath mints or look around for a nearby drug store.
- **Timing:** Do this immediately after lunch and privately. That way you minimize embarrassment and have an excuse for your actions.
- **Behavior:** Start off subtle, but if necessary, shift to sincere concern. There's no need to be apologetic since you're doing the person a favor.

40. Tactfully Suggesting Better Hygiene

To a peer

Bad breath: *[Show mints, pop one in your mouth.]* Would you like one? I don't know about you, but sometimes I really need these after lunch.

Body odor: You won't believe the sale I stumbled on. The drug store up the street was offering 50 percent off on perfumes and bath salts. You should check it out. If you want, I'll go over there with you after work.

Doesn't take hint: *No thanks. I never use those kinds of things.*

Gets angry: *Excuse me. Are you suggesting there's something wrong with me?*

Takes the hint: *Um . . . sure. I'll take one.* [or] *Oh, I never . . . uh . . . Thanks, I'll take you up on that.*

Strong hint: Are you sure? I always use them during the day when *my* breath gets stale. *[or]* I find they make *me* feel fresher throughout the day.

You're not alone: No. Not at all. We all have to watch ourselves. Working in such close quarters makes everyone a little sensitive.

None of your business: *I don't think my hygiene is any of your business. I think I take care of myself just fine, thank you.*

We're in this together: Under most circumstances I'd agree with you. But we work in very close quarters here. I'd expect you to do the same thing for me if the situation was reversed. We have to take care of each other.

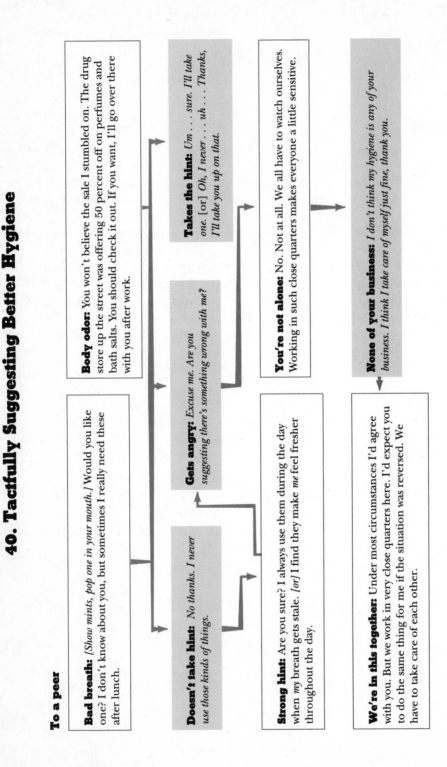

To a subordinate

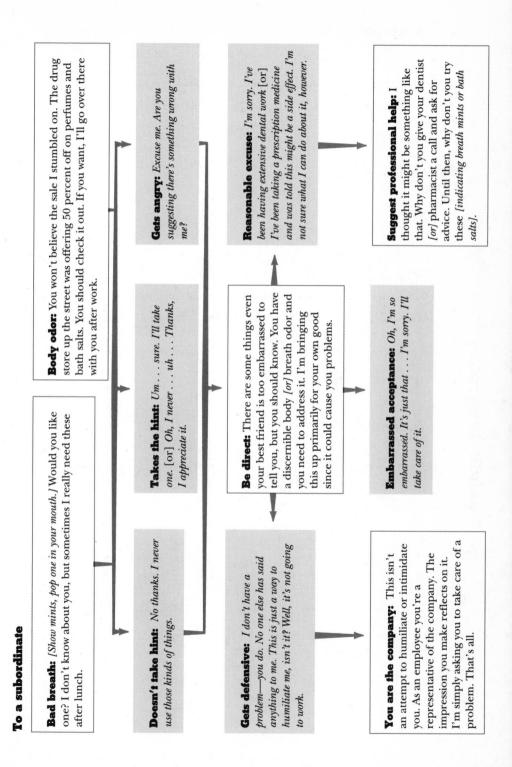

Bad breath: *[Show mints, pop one in your mouth.]* Would you like one? I don't know about you, but sometimes I really need these after lunch.

Body odor: You won't believe the sale I stumbled on. The drug store up the street was offering 50 percent off on perfumes and bath salts. You should check it out. If you want, I'll go over there with you after work.

Takes the hint: *Um . . . sure. I'll take one. [or] Oh, I never . . . uh . . . Thanks, I appreciate it.*

Doesn't take hint: *No thanks. I never use those kinds of things.*

Gets angry: *Excuse me. Are you suggesting there's something wrong with me?*

Be direct: There are some things even your best friend is too embarrassed to tell you, but you should know. You have a discernible body *[or]* breath odor and you need to address it. I'm bringing this up primarily for your own good since it could cause you problems.

Reasonable excuse: *I'm sorry. I've been having extensive dental work [or] I've been taking a prescription medicine and was told this might be a side effect. I'm not sure what I can do about it, however.*

Gets defensive: *I don't have a problem—you do. No one else has said anything to me. This is just a way to humiliate me, isn't it? Well, it's not going to work.*

Embarrassed acceptance: *Oh, I'm so embarrassed. It's just that . . . I'm sorry. I'll take care of it.*

Suggest professional help: I thought it might be something like that. Why don't you give your dentist *[or]* pharmacist a call and ask for advice. Until then, why don't you try these *[indicating breath mints or bath salts]*.

You are the company: This isn't an attempt to humiliate or intimidate you. As an employee you're a representative of the company. The impression you make reflects on it. I'm simply asking you to take care of a problem. That's all.

ADAPTATIONS

This script can be modified to:

- Discuss hygiene problems with a spouse
- Discuss hygiene problems or erratic behavior with a parent or older relative

KEY POINTS

- Start off subtly, but if necessary, be direct.
- If the person takes the hint, drop the issue.
- If a peer doesn't take the hint, make your case stronger.
- If a subordinate doesn't take the hint, be direct.
- If a peer gets angry, say it's a problem everyone there shares.
- If a subordinate gets angry, say it's a business problem too.
- If the person says it's none of your business, explain why it is something you need to be concerned with.

Suggesting No Further Drinking to a Peer

41

STRATEGY

It's always awkward to discuss drinking habits with a colleague, but never more so than at a sales conference or in some other out-of-the-office business/personal situation. Most large companies have established routines for identifying, warning, and assisting employees who show signs of chronic alcohol or drug abuse, but when a fellow sales rep blows a deal by getting drunk at a client dinner, there's no employee-assistance program around to intervene. There's probably little you can do at the time, short of making a scene—and she has probably already taken care of that; so your goal is to make sure it doesn't happen again. That means changing her behavior—at least in her business meetings with you.

TACTICS

- **Attitude:** Be direct, clear, and determined. You are doing this for her good, your good, and the company's good, so there's no reason for you to question your actions.

- **Preparation:** Expect efforts either to deny there's a problem or to shift the focus of the discussion from the issue of drinking. Consider "compromise solutions" short of abstinence.

- **Timing:** Do this as soon as possible after an incident where the problem was obvious. Breakfast the morning after a botched client dinner is fine—as long as she isn't too hung over.

- **Behavior:** Be compassionate, but keep the focus on business. Your goal is to keep from being embarrassed in the future, and make sure her problem doesn't hurt your career.

41. Suggesting No Further Drinking to a Peer

Icebreaker: I need to speak with you about something that's affecting the way we work together. I think you need to stop drinking when we're working together. It's hurting our chances to close deals. Drinking gives clients an excuse to drink more and lets them avoid making decisions. And to be honest, sometimes you're not careful about what you're saying.

None of your business: My drinking is my business. It's not like I'm getting drunk on the job. What I do outside the office is none of your business.

It is my business: It is. Your drinking in business situations affects the company and my livelihood.

You're exaggerating: I don't drink that much. I think you're exaggerating. Maybe I got a little buzzed when we were out with the people from Acme, but so did they.

I wish: I wish I were exaggerating, but I'm not the only person who has noticed it. You really should tone it down.

You're jealous: Listen, just because you have a hard time letting your hair down and don't know how to have a good time with clients doesn't mean I've got a drinking problem.

I'm on the job: I resent your implication. I'm not a robot, but when it comes to business I'm more concerned with closing the deal than having a good time. I think you should be too.

It works for me: I know it's not your style, but socializing with clients works for me. I think the people from Acme had a great time last night.

But no sale: It may have looked that way, but here we are this morning without a signed contract. We didn't do any business last night.

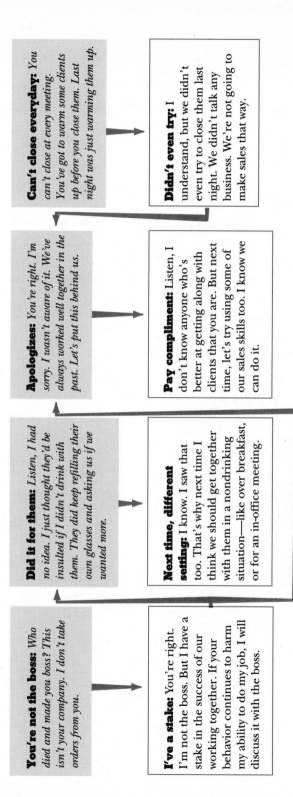

Can't close everyday: *You can't close at every meeting. You've got to warm some clients up before you close them. Last night was just warming them up.*

Didn't even try: I understand, but we didn't even try to close them last night. We didn't talk any business. We're not going to make sales that way.

Apologizes: *You're right. I'm sorry. I wasn't aware of it. We've always worked well together in the past. Let's put this behind us.*

Pay compliment: Listen, I don't know anyone who's better at getting along with clients that you are. But next time, let's try using some of our sales skills too. I know we can do it.

Did it for them: *Listen, I had no idea. I just thought they'd be insulted if I didn't drink with them. They did keep refilling their own glasses and asking us if we wanted more.*

Next time, different setting: I know. I saw that too. That's why next time I think we should get together with them in a nondrinking situation—like over breakfast, or for an in-office meeting.

You're not the boss: *Who died and made you boss? This isn't your company. I don't take orders from you.*

I've a stake: You're right. I'm not the boss. But I have a stake in the success of our working together. If your behavior continues to harm my ability to do my job, I will discuss it with the boss.

ADAPTATIONS

This script can be modified to:

- Address any form of antisocial behavior by a business peer
- Discuss the physical appearance of a business peer

KEY POINTS

- Be businesslike, determined, clear, and direct.
- If she says her drinking is none of your business, stress that when it happens in a work situation it is your business.
- If she says you're exaggerating, say other people have noticed too.
- If she says you're too uptight, say you're simply interested in getting your job done.
- If she blames the clients, suggest having meetings at nondrinking times or places.
- If she accuses you of acting superior, just reiterate your stake in the situation.

Dealing with a Sexual Harassment Charge between Subordinates

42.

STRATEGY

Surprisingly, it's easier to confront someone who's sexually harassing you personally than someone who's accused by a third party. That's because in the first instance you're certain of the facts and can have a one-on-one, person-to-person dialogue that transcends office hierarchy. On the other hand, when one subordinate complains to you about the actions of another, you can never be certain of the facts and must be just as concerned about the rights of the accused as the rights of the accuser. That said, it's vital you make some kind of prejudgment—based either on careful questioning of the accuser or on prior experience with the accused—about whether or not you believe the conduct in question was intentionally harassing. Treat an unintentional harasser harshly and you could be needlessly hurtful and jeopardize his future performance. Treat a malevolent harasser gently and you risk continuation of the behavior and incurring legal liability. Your judgment will probably be made clear by the accused's response to the situation. Whatever develops, the secret in this script is to focus attention, not on the actions or intent of the accused, but on the perceptions of the accuser.

TACTICS

- **Attitude:** Your goal is to make sure such a problem never happens again, so the facts of the situation aren't as important as putting your foot down—firmly.
- **Preparation:** Question the accuser closely and consider the accused's past record and actions. Then make a prejudgment on whether you believe the actions were intentionally harassing.
- **Timing:** Do this as soon as possible after the incident in question. Make sure to hold the conversation during business hours so the accused knows this is a business, not a personal, issue.
- **Behavior:** Hold this meeting in your office. Make sure it's just as private and confidential as your meeting with the accuser. Be as businesslike as possible. It's not your role to determine the facts of the case. It's your job to make sure it doesn't happen again.

42. Dealing with a Sexual Harassment Charge between Subordinates

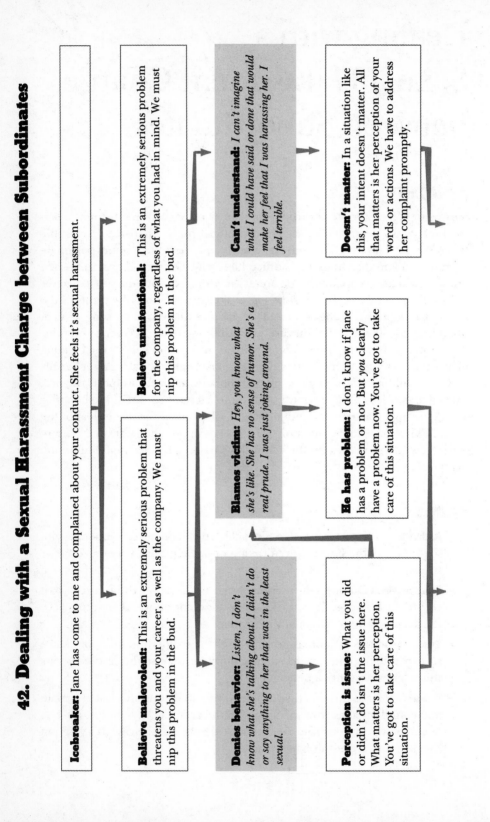

Icebreaker: Jane has come to me and complained about your conduct. She feels it's sexual harassment.

Believe malevolent: This is an extremely serious problem that threatens you and your career, as well as the company. We must nip this problem in the bud.

Believe unintentional: This is an extremely serious problem for the company, regardless of what you had in mind. We must nip this problem in the bud.

Can't understand: *I can't imagine what I could have said or done that would make her feel that I was harassing her. I feel terrible.*

Doesn't matter: In a situation like this, your intent doesn't matter. All that matters is her perception of your words or actions. We have to address her complaint promptly.

Denies behavior: *Listen, I don't know what she's talking about. I didn't do or say anything to her that was in the least sexual.*

Blames victim: *Hey, you know what she's like. She has no sense of humor. She's a real prude. I was just joking around.*

He has problem: I don't know if Jane has a problem or not. But *you* clearly have a problem now. You've got to take care of this situation.

Perception is issue: What you did or didn't do isn't the issue here. What matters is her perception. You've got to take care of this situation.

Clueless: *What do you want me to do about it?*

Forceful pitch: You are not to have any personal interaction with Jane, and you're to keep your business interaction with her to the absolute minimum required to get your job done . . . and try to have a third party present. I will convey your apologies to her. One other thing. I don't want to have to speak to you about this kind of situation ever again.

Wants to help: *Please tell me what I can do to clear this up.*

Pitch solution: Just stay as far away from her as you can. I will convey your apologies to her. Don't have any personal conversations with her. If you have to talk with her about business, keep it brief and to the point . . . and try to have a third party present. This is not a situation we want to see continue or escalate.

ADAPTATIONS

This script can be modified to:

- Question an employee about possible theft
- Question an employee about possibly phony expense reports

KEY POINTS

- If you suspect intent, stress the potential impact of this charge on the accused's career. Otherwise, stress the potential harm to the company.
- If he denies doing anything wrong, say his actions aren't the issue, her perceptions are.
- If he blames the victim, say she isn't in trouble, he is.
- If he doesn't seem to catch on to his problem, forcefully suggest a solution.
- If he seems eager to make amends, suggest a solution.

Going over
Your Boss's Head

43

STRATEGY

Taking a problem to your boss's boss is one of the biggest gambles in office politics. The payoff can be great, but you run the risk of becoming a pariah whose days in the company are numbered. That's why you should take this step only if you believe your future at the firm is at stake—because of a negative performance review, say, or because a vital project has been canceled. First, try to get permission for your end run. You may get the okay if you frame your request as a search for expert input. Even if your immediate boss objects, persevere. Asking to go over her head is as bad as actually doing it so you've nothing more to lose. When you do get upstairs, continue to frame your efforts as a search for advice. Resist the temptation to badmouth your boss. If you manage to win the top person over, you'll have gained a valuable ally—one who will most likely be able to protect you from recriminations. If you don't win Ms. Big to your side, start looking for another job.

TACTICS

- **Attitude:** Realize there's nothing your immediate boss can do to stop you, but you'd still like her permission.

- **Preparation:** Have your facts and arguments down cold—your future in the company will depend on your winning your boss's boss over to your side.

- **Timing:** While this should be done soon after either a negative review or the cancellation of an important project, your decision must be thought out, not reflexive. Give yourself at least a day or two to think things over.

- **Behavior:** Be forthright and determined. You must convey that you're bucking the system because of your extremely principled position and concern for justice.

43. Going over Your Boss's Head

Asking for permission

Project icebreaker: I understand your objections. Would you have a problem if I unofficially batted this around with Sharon? Maybe she can help us come up with a way to overcome your objections.

Personal icebreaker: Thank you for your time. I have one other request. I'd like permission to speak with Sharon about this issue.

No need: *I've already spoken to Sharon. She's in accord with me.*

New spin: I'd assumed you had, but I think I can put another spin on it that might change both of your minds.

Refuses: *I don't want you speaking to anyone else about this.*

Won't help: *This is my decision to make. Speaking to Sharon won't change my mind.*

No permission: *You can do whatever you want; but you don't have my permission.*

Am I forbidden?: Are you saying if the issue comes up I should say you've forbidden me to discuss it?

Still want to: That may be the case, but I don't want to do an end run. I'd like your permission to try.

Grudging permission: *If you want to waste your time, it's okay with me.*

Express thanks: Thank you. I appreciate it.

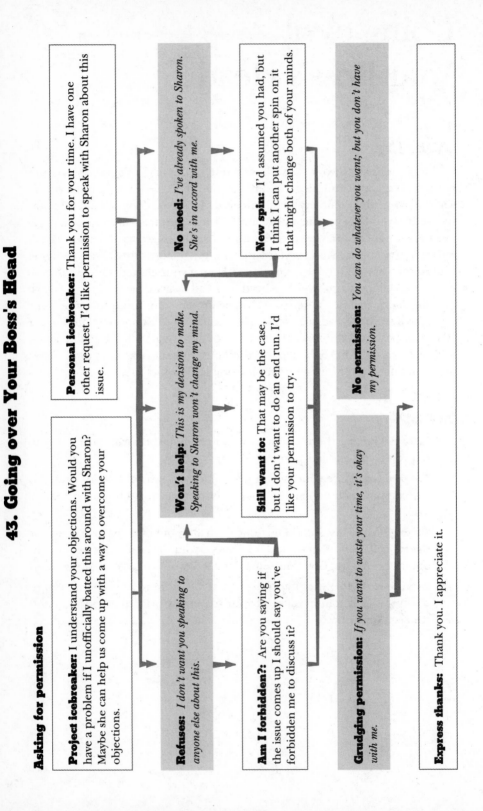

Explaining your actions

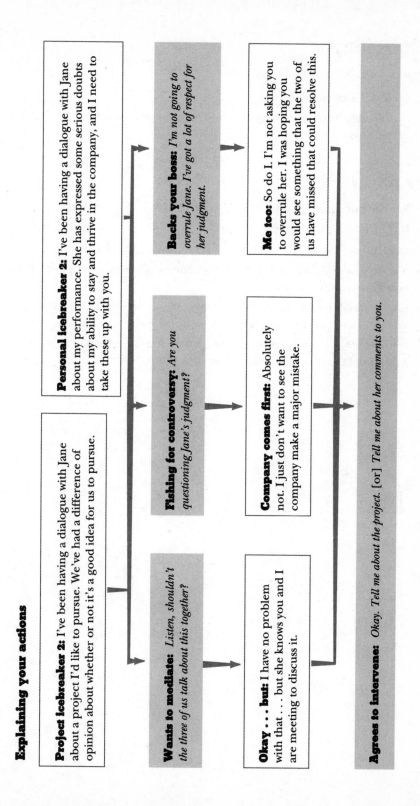

Project Icebreaker 2: I've been having a dialogue with Jane about a project I'd like to pursue. We've had a difference of opinion about whether or not it's a good idea for us to pursue.

Personal Icebreaker 2: I've been having a dialogue with Jane about my performance. She has expressed some serious doubts about my ability to stay and thrive in the company, and I need to take these up with you.

Wants to mediate: *Listen, shouldn't the three of us talk about this together?*

Fishing for controversy: *Are you questioning Jane's judgment?*

Backs your boss: *I'm not going to overrule Jane. I've got a lot of respect for her judgment.*

Okay . . . but: I have no problem with that . . . but she knows you and I are meeting to discuss it.

Company comes first: Absolutely not. I just don't want to see the company make a major mistake.

Me too: So do I. I'm not asking you to overrule her. I was hoping you would see something that the two of us have missed that could resolve this.

Agrees to intervene: *Okay. Tell me about the project.* [or] *Tell me about her comments to you.*

ADAPTATIONS

This script can be modified to:

- Appeal a loan rejection
- Correct detrimental or incorrect information your boss has passed along to her boss

KEY POINTS

- Frame your jumping the ladder as a search for expert advice.
- If your immediate boss objects, persist.
- Regardless of your immediate boss's conclusion, thank her.
- If your boss's boss wants to serve as mediator, explain that your immediate boss knows of this meeting.
- If your boss's boss fishes for controversy, stress that your concern is first and foremost for the company.
- If your boss's boss refuses to overrule a decision, stress you're looking for a potential compromise, not a reversal.

Demanding Better Work 44. Habits from a Subordinate

STRATEGY

Time really is money. The time-shaving employee — late in, early out — is stealing from you and the company. You are paying a full-time salary for less than full-time service. The longer the problem is ignored, the more comfortable the offender feels in continuing and adding to this behavior. By dealing effectively with this one individual, you'll also help insure others don't emulate his behavior. Even though you'll be confronting the subordinate's actual behavior, expect a torrent of excuses as to why the behavior took place. Stress that *what* has happened is the issue, not *why* it has happened. Focus on what has taken place and the effect it is having on both cost and job effectiveness. Stick to this tack, and the individual will ultimately acknowledge his destructive behavior. After he does, be clear about the outcome if the abuse continues. Only then should you consider ending the meeting on a practical, humanistic note by offering advice to help the employee deal with the "whys" of his problem.

TACTICS

- **Attitude:** Be totally confident and at ease. You hold all the cards going in. You'll be citing a problem easily observed and documented. A vacant work station is a red flag. And, if there's a time clock, you have ironclad evidence. The actual time shaving and the cost in money and job effectiveness are undeniable. Be confident and indignant that such obvious and blatant behavior is taking place.

- **Preparation:** At the point you realize there's a pattern of neglect, start writing down dates and times the employee is away from the job. Documenting these specifics is the most critical part of your preparation. Create a "memorandum for the record" indicating what you're doing and why. This becomes part of the documentation. Clearly, if the subordinate's actions hadn't prompted it, there would be no such memo. Time sheets or cards are obvious support to be gathered. Comments from other managers who have experienced similar behavior aren't necessary, but could augment your evidence.

44. Demanding Better Work Habits from a Subordinate

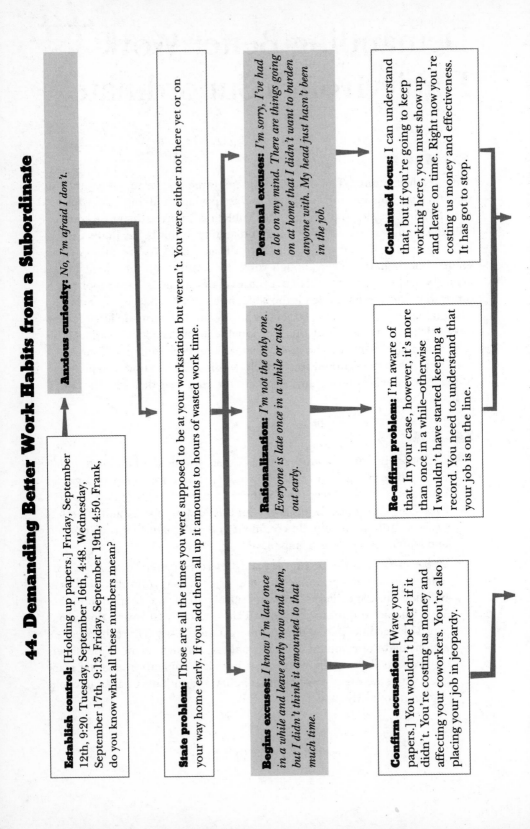

Establish control: [Holding up papers.] Friday, September 12th, 9:20. Tuesday, September 16th, 4:48. Wednesday, September 17th, 9:13. Friday, September 19th, 4:50. Frank, do you know what all these numbers mean?

Anxious curiosity: *No, I'm afraid I don't.*

State problem: Those are all the times you were supposed to be at your workstation but weren't. You were either not here yet or on your way home early. If you add them all up it amounts to hours of wasted work time.

Personal excuses: *I'm sorry, I've had a lot on my mind. There are things going on at home that I didn't want to burden anyone with. My head just hasn't been in the job.*

Continued focus: I can understand that, but if you're going to keep working here, you must show up and leave on time. Right now you're costing us money and effectiveness. It has got to stop.

Rationalization: *I'm not the only one. Everyone is late once in a while or cuts out early.*

Re-affirm problem: I'm aware of that. In your case, however, it's more than once in a while—otherwise I wouldn't have started keeping a record. You need to understand that your job is on the line.

Begins excuses: *I know I'm late once in a while and leave early now and then, but I didn't think it amounted to that much time.*

Confirm accusation: [Wave your papers.] You wouldn't be here if it didn't. You're costing us money and affecting your coworkers. You're also placing your job in jeopardy.

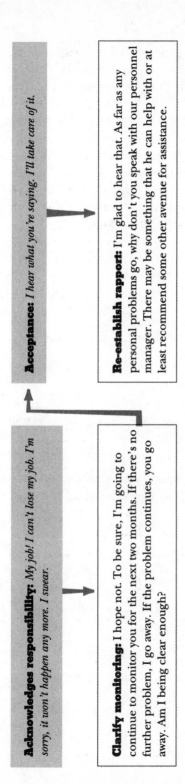

Acknowledges responsibility: *My job! I can't lose my job. I'm sorry, it won't happen any more. I swear.*

Clarify monitoring: I hope not. To be sure, I'm going to continue to monitor you for the next two months. If there's no further problem, I go away. If the problem continues, you go away. Am I being clear enough?

Acceptance: *I hear what you're saying. I'll take care of it.*

Re-establish rapport: I'm glad to hear that. As far as any personal problems go, why don't you speak with our personnel manager. There may be something that he can help with or at least recommend some other avenue for assistance.

- **Timing:** After you've observed an abusive pattern — a week, several weeks, a month — move quickly as soon as the behavior occurs again. Publicly ask the employee to come into your office just as he eases back to his work station. You'll have seized control of the dialogue as well as the attention of the other workers who know perfectly well what is going on.

- **Behavior:** Be conspicuous in the work area at a time when the latecomer should be there. As soon as he returns to his desk and sits down, announce you want to meet — right now. Don't wait for a response, just move directly to your office. When he enters, silently gesture him to a seat while you remain engrossed in an open folder of documents clearly visible on your desk. When you're ready to speak, hold the documents up.

ADAPTATIONS

This script can be modified to:

- Deal with the subordinate who wastes time on the job or who is chronically absent, absent on particular days, or late for meetings and deadlines

KEY POINTS

- When you believe a pattern of behavior is in place, document dates and times.
- Call for your meeting in front of other workers.
- Use physical evidence as a means of reinforcing your position.
- Stay focused on what the behavior has been and its effect on the workplace.
- Do not get side-tracked into debating why the behavior has occurred.
- Be clear about future actions and outcomes.

Asking a Subordinate to Improve Her Appearance

STRATEGY

There's no second chance to make a first impression. Even when a business may have a good track record, prospective clients are still greatly influenced by the "what you see is what you get" attitude. A staff that projects a professional appearance can only help build client confidence. A subordinate who doesn't reinforce a "dressed for success" image can only hurt your chances of securing and maintaining clients.

The goal of this script is to help you bring any sartorially challenged members of your staff to the high standard of appearance required as a norm in the world of business. Errant subordinates will try to make this an issue of personal taste because it's really the only argument they can muster. If you're dealing with staff members of the opposite sex, they may even try to lead you into the minefield of gender harassment. That's why you should consider having a fellow supervisor of the same gender as the offender present in your office when you deal with an opposite gender subordinate. This reinforces the professional tone of your position, safeguards potential future misreporting of events or comments, and serves as a role model for proper dress.

Though not absolutely necessary, refer to any print materials distributed previously to employees regarding dress. Don't waiver from your responsibility for maintaining the highest professional standards in the workplace. All possible arguments to justify personal dress shatter against this brick wall position.

TACTICS

- **Attitude:** This problem is visually obvious to any and all, so be confident in confronting it. Given this, project an air of disbelief and disappointment: How could anyone not know how to dress for work! Project this attitude in a clear, matter-of-fact presentation of the problem and the solution. This will underline that your concern is professional, not personal.

45. Asking a Subordinate to Improve Her Appearance

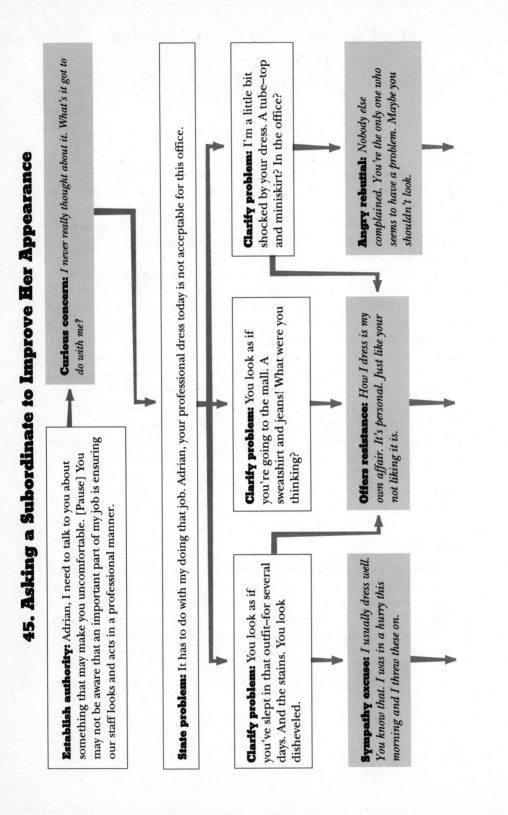

Establish authority: Adrian, I need to talk to you about something that may make you uncomfortable. [Pause] You may not be aware that an important part of my job is ensuring our staff looks and acts in a professional manner.

Curious concern: *I never really thought about it. What's it got to do with me?*

State problem: It has to do with my doing that job. Adrian, your professional dress today is not acceptable for this office.

Clarify problem: You look as if you've slept in that outfit–for several days. And the stains. You look disheveled.

Sympathy excuse: *I usually dress well. You know that. I was in a hurry this morning and I threw these on.*

Clarify problem: You look as if you're going to the mall. A sweatshirt and jeans! What were you thinking?

Offers resistance: *How I dress is my own affair. It's personal. Just like your not liking it is.*

Clarify problem: I'm a little bit shocked by your dress. A tube-top and miniskirt? In the office?

Angry rebuttal: *Nobody else complained. You're the only one who seems to have a problem. Maybe you shouldn't look.*

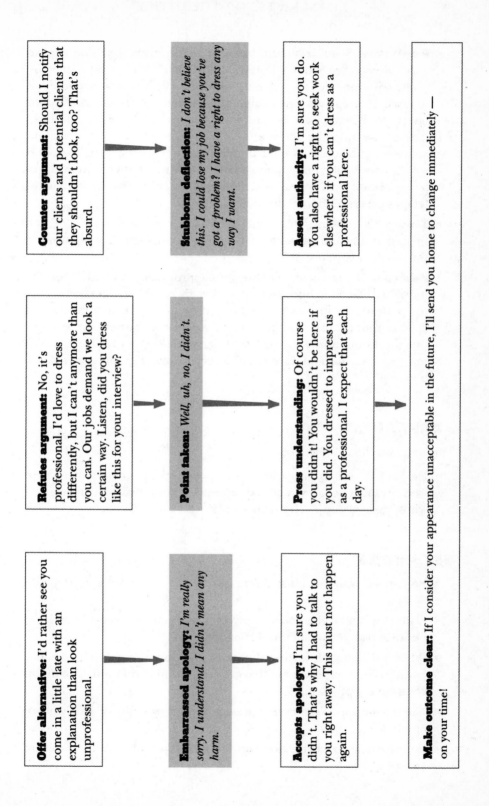

Offer alternative: I'd rather see you come in a little late with an explanation than look unprofessional.

Embarrassed apology: *I'm really sorry. I understand. I didn't mean any harm.*

Accepts apology: I'm sure you didn't. That's why I had to talk to you right away. This must not happen again.

Refutes argument: No, it's professional. I'd love to dress differently, but I can't anymore than you can. Our jobs demand we look a certain way. Listen, did you dress like this for your interview?

Point taken: *Well, uh, no, I didn't.*

Press understanding: Of course you didn't! You wouldn't be here if you did. You dressed to impress us as a professional. I expect that each day.

Counter argument: Should I notify our clients and potential clients that they shouldn't look, too? That's absurd.

Stubborn deflection: *I don't believe this. I could lose my job because you've got a problem? I have a right to dress any way I want.*

Assert authority: I'm sure you do. You also have a right to seek work elsewhere if you can't dress as a professional here.

Make outcome clear: If I consider your appearance unacceptable in the future, I'll send you home to change immediately — on your time!

- **Preparation:** See if your firm has anything in print regarding appearance: an employee handbook, new employee hand-outs, or recent memos. Check with interviewers to see if they discuss appearance when hiring. Also see if you can get information on how your transgressor dressed for interviews. When you assumed supervisory responsibility of the individual, did you say anything about attire? Make note of all the information concerning the obligation for professional dress in the workplace. This supports your point that appearance is not a matter of any one individual's personal taste but a professional requirement. The proper appearance of fellow workers reinforces this view.
- **Timing:** The instant you see inappropriate dress, move on it. The first time should be the last time. Moving rapidly highlights the importance the problem requires.
- **Behavior:** The moment you observe inappropriate dress, ask to see the individual. Be straightforward in stating the problem. Emphasize that the professional appearance of the staff influences client attitudes and actions. Your concern is, therefore, not a personal one but a professional one that could touch any staff member who does not realize this. You must stick to this and wave your banner throughout: professional not personal!

ADAPTATIONS

This script can be modified to:

- Deal with the subordinate who displays poor hygiene, a subordinate whose work area may be slovenly or inappropriately decorated, or a subordinate whose make-up or jewelry is out of place

KEY POINTS

- Be familiar with any information given to staff regarding appropriate attire.
- State clearly that the concern involves professional decorum and not personal taste. Maintain this throughout.
- When dealing with a subordinate of the opposite gender, consider having a fellow supervisor of that gender present in your office when you confront the problem.
- Use the individual's interview dress as the key example of what you are after.
- Be specific as to what action you will take if you observe the problem again.

Handling a Subordinate's Personal Use of Equipment 46.

STRATEGY

Some employees consider office supplies and the machines required for their work as available for their personal use. If paper-clip pilfering adds up, imagine the hidden costs for the worker who thinks "job ownership" means personal use of the firm's copiers, computers, postal machines, telephones, and anything else that plugs into an outlet. When the employee is a highly valued and productive subordinate, some managers look the other way, but this only encourages more of the same. Eventually, personal use of equipment may become so rampant orders will come down from above to crack down hard. That's why it's essential to stop such problems before they attract attention from upstairs.

TACTICS

- **Attitude:** You'll be dealing with behavior you've observed so you can be confident. Be understanding in your approach because the issue is one workers easily rationalize as a job perk, not a problem.

- **Preparation:** The essential element of preparation is validating that abusive behavior is taking place. Your first–hand observations are often enough. But the more effectively you can corroborate those observations with tangible evidence, the more confident you can be of controlling the dialogue and ending the problem.

- **Timing:** Gathering tangible evidence will mean a stronger case, but also more time. When ready, meet at the end of the day. This provides a night of thoughtful reflection and eliminates the potential for day-long gripe sessions with other employees.

- **Behavior:** Project confidence and authority from behind your desk. Have any back-up materials clearly visible and peruse them before speaking. Be authoritative and direct, but not necessarily angry. You don't want to alienate a productive subordinate, but you can't ignore his behavior either.

46. Handling a Subordinate's Personal Use of Equipment

Capture attention: Glen, I'm concerned about a problem I've observed over the last few weeks. You feel perfectly at ease using any of our machines for your own personal needs. [Pointing to papers on desk] If it were just occasional I would say so, but these logs and records show use far beyond what is required for the job. Plus, I've seen it with my own eyes. It's costing us money and must stop.

Singled out: *Why are you singling me out? Everyone does this.*

No big deal: *I make the company a lot of money. I don't think a few copies is a big deal.*

Own fault: It's the facts that singled you out [hold up papers]. According to these records, you're the biggest offender. I'll speak with others separately, but right now I'm speaking with you. If you don't stop, this behavior will be noticed upstairs. It must stop now.

Bottom line counts: You know it's the bottom line that counts. This isn't a charity. Your actions are costing the company money and encouraging others to do the same. Eventually, they'll come to the attention of the people upstairs. This has to stop now.

Emphasize confidence: I'm glad to hear that. You're much too savvy a worker to get into more hot water over something like this.

Acceptance: *Fair enough. I'm sorry. It won't happen again.*

ADAPTATIONS

This script can be modified to:

- Deal with the worker who borrows personal and professional materials from fellow workers

KEY POINTS

- Be prepared to cite specific incidents based on observation and documentation.
- Do not link the problem to the worker's job performance unless it applies.
- Stay focused on the behavior as a cost factor.
- Be exact in regard to how the problem will be monitored.
- Be clear what the result will be if the problem persists.

CHAPTER FIVE

Lifescripts
for Terminations

Giving Two Weeks' Notice to Your Boss

STRATEGY

Giving notice can be dangerous, even when you already have another job. It's conceivable an angry boss could fire you on the spot, forcing you to lose at least two weeks' pay. If you give too much notice you could end up getting fired as soon as you've wrapped up your work or your replacement is selected. The solution is to give the two weeks that have become customary, and to be prepared to deflect attempts to fire you. The best way to do that is to practice a subtle form of workplace extortion. Your obligation to conclude short-term projects and prepare memos on your long-term projects should be implicit with your being given two weeks to wrap things up. By the way, it makes sense to hold off actually preparing and presenting those memos as long as possible since they're your only leverage to ensure you get your final paycheck.

TACTICS

- **Attitude:** Be direct, businesslike, and confident. The only thing he can do to you is fire you—and you're leaving for another job anyway.
- **Preparation:** In this script it's actually more a matter of not preparing. State what you'll do during your two weeks as a lame duck, but don't actually do it until you've gotten his agreement that you'll be employed for those two weeks.
- **Timing:** Do this as soon as possible after learning you've been hired and have cleaned up your files. Do it as early in the day and as early in the week as possible so the company has a chance to react right away.
- **Behavior:** Remain calm, even in the face of anger or threats. Don't simply absorb abuse, however. Make it clear that your being fired will not only hurt the company and the staff, but will send a clear message to other staffers that they should simply quit rather than give notice.

47. Giving Two Weeks' Notice to Your Boss

Icebreaker: I've received an irresistible job offer from Acme, Inc. which I've accepted effective two weeks from today. I've gone over everything that I'm working on here, and I believe that I'll be able to complete all of my short-term projects without incident or additional expense within two weeks. I'll prepare memos for those who take over my long-term projects.

Accepts inevitable: *I hate to see you go, but that's part of business. Just make sure you finish your projects and get those memos to me as soon as possible.*

Thanks: Thank you. I'll get those memos to you right away. Incidentally, working for you has been a wonderful experience for me and I'm grateful.

Not enough time: *Two weeks notice is like quitting on the spot. If that's all you can give me, you might as well leave today.*

As much as possible: I honestly have considered your needs very carefully. As I said, I'll wrap up my short-term projects and prepare memos on my long-term assignments. I'll also do whatever I can to help you find a replacement for me. Finally, if necessary, I'll be available on weekends and evenings to help out my replacement, even after I make the shift. However, if you prefer that I leave today, I will.

Gets angry: *You ungrateful SOB. We don't need your help. Pack up your stuff and get out of here today. And don't even try to take any of our customers. I'm going to call security right now and have them watch while you empty out your desk.*

Notice a mistake?: Was it a mistake to give you notice? Would you have preferred that I just leave? Is that how you want this company to operate? It's your choice. I've told everyone in my department that I'm leaving and that I'll help them with the transition. But if you want me to leave today without helping them, and you want everyone in the company to see it's a mistake to give you any notice at all, that's fine too.

Backs off . . . some: *No, you can spend the next two weeks tying up loose ends. I should have realized I couldn't count on you. Get me those memos as soon as possible.*

Backs off: *No. I was just worried about the workload. I'd appreciate your doing everything possible to get your work done. And get me those memos as soon as you can.*

ADAPTATIONS

This script can be modified to:

- Terminate a nonbusiness relationship

KEY POINTS

- Be confident, direct, and determined. The die has been cast so be forceful.
- If he gets angry and threatens to fire you, say that will hurt the company and give the wrong message to employees.
- If he says two weeks isn't enough, tell him you'll do everything possible to help, but insist it's the best you can do.
- Unless he accepts the situation gracefully, give him the last word—it will help assuage his bruised ego.

Negotiating for More Severance

48

STRATEGY

Severance packages are more negotiable than you may think. Treat them as preliminary offers, not done deals, and use whatever leverage you have. Do not sign a release—or even a statement acknowledging that you've been terminated—at the initial meeting, when you receive the news. Insist on postponing all decisions to a subsequent meeting with both your immediate supervisor and someone from personnel. Say you need the time to digest the news or even that you feel too emotional to continue. Most reasonable employers will agree. If yours doesn't, simply say you're not feeling well, you'll be back to finish the discussion first thing tomorrow, and then stand up and leave. What can they do?—they've already fired you. Use the time before your subsequent meeting to determine your needs in terms of money and other benefits. Draft a memo outlining your dream severance package, listing a reason for each request. If you're a member of a protected minority contact an employment lawyer. Put aside hurt and anger at your second meeting, and instead treat it like a business negotiation. Be firm in your demand for more, but flexible in what that constitutes. Know your bottom line. Keep in mind that both you and they want this wrapped up as soon as possible. If they try to stonewall you, ask for another adjournment to speak with an attorney. The threat may break their resolve. If not, come back with another proposal the next day, either directly, or through an attorney if you have legal leverage.

TACTICS

- **Attitude:** Don't be fearful, you have nothing to lose. Be willing to use personal and legal leverage.
- **Preparation:** Analyze your needs and draft a memo outlining them. Speak with a lawyer if you are a member of a protected minority.
- **Timing:** Do not sign anything until you've agreed on a package, and don't do that until a second meeting takes place.
- **Behavior:** Try to get beyond your anger and be as businesslike as possible. Roll up your sleeves and get down to serious horse trading—you want the deal done at this meeting.

48. Negotiating for More Severance

Deflect closing: I'm afraid I'm in no condition right now to sign anything or make any decisions. I need some time. I'd like to continue this discussion tomorrow afternoon instead.

The next day

Icebreaker and pitch: First, I'd like to thank you very much for agreeing to meet with me today. I've had a chance to go over your offer and I'd like to present my own proposal in response. I've seen that there's nothing out there in the job market, and it will take at least a year for me to find another position. Severance is supposed to bridge the gap between jobs, and what you're offering falls far short. I've taken the liberty of drafting a brief memo outlining my requests and the reasons for them. For example: I'd like one month's pay for each year I've been with the company. I'd like the company to continue to pay for my health insurance until I'm covered by a new employer. I'd like use of my office for another two weeks. And I'd like the company to provide at least four outplacement counseling sessions.

Against policy: *I'm sorry, but the package you were offered the other day is our only offer. Our policy is not to negotiate severance packages.*

Open to negotiation: *I'm willing to discuss your severance package, but I can't possibly provide all the things you've asked for in this memo.*

Wouldn't be fair: *I'm sorry, but the package you were offered the other day is our only offer. Negotiating with you wouldn't be fair to the others who were laid off.*

Exception to the rule: I understand your need to follow policy, but I believe my case is exceptional. I was recruited by you from another company and came here with the understanding I wouldn't lose the seniority I had at my prior job.

Willing to compromise: I understand the constraints you're under. Why don't we just go over the items in my memo line by line. I'm not inflexible. I'm sure we can reach an agreement.

Special circumstances: I understand your need to be fair to all those who have been laid off, but I believe there are special circumstances in my case. Even though I have only been here for six months, I was recruited to come here from a job which I held for more than 10 years.

Still unwilling to negotiate: *I'm sorry. Whatever the facts of your case are, I simply cannot negotiate the severance package. That's our only [best] offer.*

Imply legal action: I'm sorry as well. If that's the case, I must ask to adjourn this meeting in order to consult with my attorney. Either he or I will be back in touch with you shortly. Good day.

KEY POINTS

- Put your anger aside and get down to business.
- If he cites policy, say you're an exception to the rule.
- If he cites the need for fairness, say yours is a special case.
- If he's open to negotiation, be ready to compromise.
- If he stonewalls, ask for another adjournment to speak with your lawyer or formulate another package.

Firing an Employee

49.

STRATEGY

Ever since the recession of the late 1980s, companies have been using layoffs as a cost-cutting strategy. But even though firing employees is an all-too-common part of their duties these days, few managers handle the process well. That's because, whatever the facts of the dismissal, most managers feel bad about letting someone go. Ironically, expressing those feelings of remorse can be cruel because they give the employee false hope. Instead, the best way to deal with a termination is to make it a quick, unambiguous act. Spell out exactly why you are letting the employee go, state clearly that the decision is final, and explain the details of the company's severance policy. Then ask the employee to sign a letter of acknowledgment and agreement which will make it more difficult for him to reopen the discussion or sue. Resist all attempts to turn the discussion into an argument or debate. The decision has been made and it's final.

TACTICS

- **Attitude:** Whatever your feelings, be dispassionate and businesslike—it's actually in the employee's best interests.
- **Preparation:** Have documentation of poor performance, if any, on hand. Also have details of the severance package written into a termination letter that can be signed at this meeting. Have severance checks written out and signed prior to the meeting.
- **Timing:** Do this as early in the week and as early in the day as possible so that the individual can apply for unemployment benefits and start looking for a job immediately.
- **Behavior:** Hold this meeting in your office. If possible have a third party on hand to deter anger. Offer immediate severance payment in exchange for immediate signing of the termination memo. Absorb anger, deflect guilt, and acknowledge the employee's right to legal representation. Resist efforts to negotiate more severance or a second chance.

49. Firing an Employee

Icebreaker: I have bad news for you. I'm afraid your employment here is being terminated. The company has already cut a check for one month's severance pay, and prepared a reference letter for you. I can give you both now.

Fired for poor performance: I must stress this decision is final. It was based on your inability to rebound from two unsatisfactory performance reviews. However, because we know you've tried, if asked, the company will say you were laid off for economic reasons. If you sign this letter that says you understand our discussion, we can put this behind us.

Laid off for economic reasons: I'm sorry but this decision is final. It was based on the company's bottom line profitability and has nothing to do with your performance. If asked, the company will say it was your decision to leave, and I'll be happy to add my personal recommendation. If you sign this letter that outlines what I've just said, we can get this unhappy business over with.

Gets angry: *I expected something like this to happen. You've had it in for me from day one. You're just using me as a scapegoat for your own mistakes.*

Gets personal: *How could you do this to me? We've been friends. I've had you over to my home for dinner. Isn't there something you can do?*

Defends professional record: *I have to take exception to your singling me out. I think I've performed as well as anyone else in the department. I've never had anyone call my skills and abilities into question before.*

Absorb anger: I'm sorry you feel that way. Everyone here, especially me, wanted to see your relationship with the company work out. Unfortunately it simply hasn't. Why don't you look at this letter and then sign it.

Deflect guilt: I feel terrible about this, but it's strictly a business decision. I can't let my personal feelings get in the way of the company's bottom line. I hope you understand. As your friend, I'll be happy to do everything I can to help you land another job. For now, though, I need you to take a look at this letter and then sign it.

Deflect defense: As I mentioned before, this is purely an economic decision having nothing to do with your abilities. You were simply the last hired. *[or]* We're not questioning your skills and abilities. We've simply decided that you're not as productive as we need you to be. That's something we warned you about in two prior reviews.

Demands more severance: *I'm not going to sign anything until we've had a chance to talk about this severance package. I've worked here for two years, and with the job market the way it is, this simply isn't enough.*

Threatens legal action: *I'm not going to sign anything until I speak with my attorney. I think there are some issues I need to get a legal opinion on.*

Asks for another chance: *Isn't there something I can do? I need this job. I promise my work will improve. All I need is another chance.*

Not negotiable: I'm afraid my hands are tied when it comes to the severance offer. You can speak with the chairman if you'd like, but I must tell you that he is aware of, and approved, the offer. Please sign this and I can give you your check and reference letter.

State rights: You have every right to speak with your attorney if you'd like. I'll hold onto the check and paperwork until I hear from you. *[Stand up.]* Good day.

Stress finality: I'm terribly sorry but the decision really is final. Please sign this and I can give you your check and reference letter.

ADAPTATIONS

This script can be modified to:

- Terminate a professional
- Terminate an independent contractor

KEY POINTS

- Be dispassionate, efficient, and businesslike.
- If he gets angry, absorb the outburst and push for closure.
- If he gets defensive, deflect the effort and push for closure.
- If he gets personal, deflect the guilt, stress this is business, and push for closure.
- Deny requests for more severance or a second chance.
- If he threatens legal action, acknowledge his right to representation.

II

Lifescripts

FOR BUSINESS

CHAPTER SIX

Lifescripts for Customers and Clients

Cold Calling a
Potential Client

STRATEGY

There are few things more frustrating and daunting than making cold calls for new clients or customers. But in many businesses it's a necessity. First, don't try to sell anything in your initial conversation. You'll increase your success rate by simply pushing for a meeting rather than trying to close a sale. Second, have good retorts to the two most common responses—generally, those are a vague "not interested" or a cost objection. Third, don't waste your efforts and push more than twice. That will only lead to anger and be a waste of both parties' time. It's better to move on to another prospect. Assume you'll get appointments with, at best, 25 percent of those you call, and you'll only close deals with, at best, 20 percent of those you actually meet. This is a matter of volume so your dialogue is necessarily short.

TACTICS

- **Attitude:** Be enthusiastic, interested, and optimistic. You have to feel that you are truly offering her an opportunity—so never apologize for calling.
- **Preparation:** Have a written script prepared prior to making your calls.
- **Timing:** Since you'll be working on volume, you're apt to make these calls whenever you have free time. Consider saving your best prospects for the hours just before office hours begin or end.
- **Behavior:** Don't be antagonistic or condescending. Try to sound spontaneous, even though you're working from a script. Use the other person's name as often as possible. Ask questions as a way of trying to direct the conversation. Keep the dialogue short—save your sales pitch for in-person meetings.

50. Cold Calling a Potential Client

Icebreaker and pitch: Good afternoon, Ms. Jackson. This is Sheila Sterling from Zenith Communications here in Topeka. Ms. Jackson, the reason I'm calling you today is to introduce you to our new marketing consulting program which can dramatically increase the effectiveness of your marketing efforts. Ms. Jackson, are you interested in boosting the effectiveness of your marketing?

Don't need it: *I'm really not interested, Sheila. We don't need any help with our marketing program right now.*

Financial objection: *I'm sorry, Sheila, we really can't afford to spend money on outside consulting services right now.*

Heard that before: Ms. Jackson, I've heard that before from other people in your industry before I had a chance to explain our program. But after hearing about it they decided to enlist our help. I wonder if we could get together to talk about it. Is first thing Thursday morning good for you?

Cost not a problem: Ms. Jackson, if it's a question of cost that's an issue, we usually have no problem overcoming it. As a matter of fact, Tekno, Inc., which I believe is up the street from you, had the same initial concern until we had a chance to sit down with them. How about 9 A.M. on Thursday?

Relent: *You know what Sheila, that sounds interesting. But Thursdays are no good; we'll be tied up all day with deadlines.*

Still not interested: *I'm sorry, I'm really not interested in your service.*

Propose another time: I have an opening on Tuesday at 2:00 P.M. Would that be convenient?

Give up: I'm sorry to hear that, Ms. Jackson. If you do need a service like ours in the future, please don't hesitate to call us. Thank you for your time, and have a good day.

ADAPTATIONS

This script can be modified to:

- Request charitable donations
- Solicit political support

KEY POINTS

- Be friendly, caring, enthusiastic, and above all, concise.
- In response to general objections, say that others said the same thing until they heard about the product or service.
- In response to cost objections, say that's not an insurmountable problem—implying fees are negotiable—and cite another organization that was able to overcome price objections.
- If you're turned down twice, give up and move on to another prospect.

Explaining an Overcharge to a Client

51.

STRATEGY

If you discover that you've overcharged a client, you need to correct the situation immediately. That's because if clients discover the overcharge first, they will probably assume the mistake was intentional. They'll be much more forgiving and quicker to forget the mistake if you bring it to their attention. Of course, that's not always going to happen. Sometimes they'll be the ones who spot a mistake, or what's perceived to be a mistake. Unless you have a very good reason to disagree with their assessment, in almost every case you should simply thank them for bringing it to your attention, accept their number, and send a corrected bill. If you're in the personal service business you must accept that the customer is always right and that you must do everything possible to keep her happy. If the problem is that the client is surprised by the size of the bill, the best response is to ask her what she thinks a fair price would be, or what she anticipated. Most people will be fair because your flexibility will have disarmed them. If the price suggested covers your costs, accept it. If it doesn't, ask her to pay your costs. In either case, insist that fees be spelled out more clearly in the future. And if you expect you are being taken advantage of intentionally, don't work for the client again.

TACTICS

- **Attitude:** The customer is always right when it comes to objective facts. If it's a subjective matter, the customer is always right as long as she covers your costs.

- **Preparation:** Since you're apt to be surprised by this dialogue, your only preparation is to have a policy in place that provides for these situations.

- **Timing:** If you spot the mistake, contact the client as soon as possible—day or night, weekday or weekend.

- **Behavior:** Don't get angry. Show that your concern is your client's welfare. However, be determined to at least recoup your costs.

51. Explaining an Overcharge to a Client

If you discover the overcharge

Icebreaker: We've just discovered there was an error on your bill not in your favor. We're sending out another bill to rectify it. Please disregard the earlier bill. Thank you.

If the client discovers the overcharge

Complaint intro: *I have a problem with the bill you just sent me.*

Didn't get it: *You billed me for something I didn't receive.*

Math wrong: *The addition is wrong. You've overcharged me by $24.*

Wrong discount: *You didn't give me the usual 10 percent discount.*

Wrong price: *You had advertised a price $10 less.*

Wrong price: *This wasn't the price we had negotiated.*

More than I thought: *I was shocked. This was for much more than I expected.*

Bite the bullet: Thank you for calling it to our attention. Please disregard the bill you've received. We'll send a correct bill out right away.

Ask for value estimate: I'm terribly sorry to hear that. How much do you think would be fair to charge for coming up with your marketing budget, developing a program, implementing it, and tracking the results?

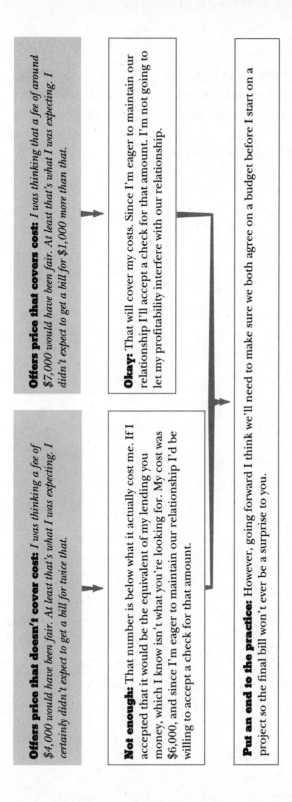

Offers price that doesn't cover cost: *I was thinking a fee of $4,000 would have been fair. At least that's what I was expecting. I certainly didn't expect to get a bill for twice that.*

Offers price that covers cost: *I was thinking that a fee of around $7,000 would have been fair. At least that's what I was expecting. I didn't expect to get a bill for $1,000 more than that.*

Not enough: That number is below what it actually cost me. If I accepted that it would be the equivalent of my lending you money, which I know isn't what you're looking for. My cost was $6,000, and since I'm eager to maintain our relationship I'd be willing to accept a check for that amount.

Okay: That will cover my costs. Since I'm eager to maintain our relationship I'll accept a check for that amount. I'm not going to let my profitability interfere with our relationship.

Put an end to the practice: However, going forward I think we'll need to make sure we both agree on a budget before I start on a project so the final bill won't ever be a surprise to you.

KEY POINTS

- Be eager to please the customer, as long as it doesn't cost you anything.
- If the client has an objective problem with your price, accept her claim.
- If the client says she was surprised, negotiate a price that covers your costs.
- Insist on clear pricing for all future projects.

Breaking Bad News to a Client

52

STRATEGY

Being the bearer of bad news is never easy. It's even harder if you're being paid by the other party, and the bad news directly or indirectly reflects on your abilities. But potential disaster can be averted. The actual language you use depends on who is to blame for the problem. (If you truly are to blame, see script 49, "Apologizing to a Client.") Remember, however, that in the final analysis you are responsible for your client's problems, whether or not you were culpable. That's why it's essential to express your regret and take responsibility, even if there was absolutely nothing you could do about the situation. From your first words, paint the situation as an obstacle that can be overcome rather than a disaster, and the sin as one of omission rather than commission. Then, offer your head, or a third party's head, on a platter to your client, along with your plan of action, in the hope that your mea culpa and solution will be enough. If it was the client's own fault, you should refrain from pointing that out directly, and just imply that that was the problem. Your goal is to explain the situation, offer a solution, and keep the client.

TACTICS

- **Attitude:** Be apologetic and contrite, but don't grovel or beg for forgiveness.
- **Preparation:** Make sure you know all the facts and can relay them concisely, and have a plan of action that requires only client approval to be set into motion.
- **Timing:** For your own sake the news must come from you so have the conversation as soon as possible.
- **Behavior:** Holding this dialogue over the telephone implies urgency and also protects you somewhat from anger. Put emotions in personal rather than business terms. Let the client vent—interrupting will only increase her anger.

52. Breaking Bad News to a Client

Icebreaker: I need to speak with you about an extraordinary situation that has come up. We've hit a roadblock, but together, I think we can overcome it.

Third party's fault: I'm afraid Acme Production has let us down. I just got off the phone with them, and they told me they're not going to be able to deliver the spot on time. I've never had a problem with them before—in fact, they were my best vendor. That's why I chose them to work on your project. I feel just awful. I've found another production house, Zenith Studios, who can take on the job, and who will absolutely guarantee delivery by the end of next week. I hold myself responsible. What upsets me most is that I've let a friend down. I'm terribly sorry.

Client's own fault: I'm afraid the television spot we farmed out to Acme Production isn't going to be completed on time, at least not without a big cost overrun. There's no point in assigning blame or fault. What's done is done. I was worried about all those special effects we asked for. I had a feeling they couldn't deliver them for the price they quoted. But what's important is to move on from here, learn from the mistake, and make sure we work together more closely in the future. I suggest we speak with Zenith Studios about taking over the project.

No one's fault: I'm afraid the television spot isn't going to come in on time. I just got off the phone with Acme Production, and they told me their facility was destroyed by a hurricane over the weekend. They saved the preliminary tapes but there's no way they can keep to schedule. I've spoken with Zenith Studios and they're willing to take over the project, but I feel just terrible about this. You're the last person I'd want to let down this way. I keep asking myself, could I have done something, should I have planned for such a disaster?

Accepting: It's not your fault. You can't control your vendors. Just make sure we get the project back on schedule.

Angry: Sorry won't cut it. You might not be to blame but you're responsible. I'm out time and money and your feeling bad won't make those losses go away.

Accepting: Don't be ridiculous. How could you plan for a hurricane? There's no reason to blame yourself.

Angry: I don't know if you should have thought about the weather or not. All I know is my spot is going to be late and I'm out big bucks.

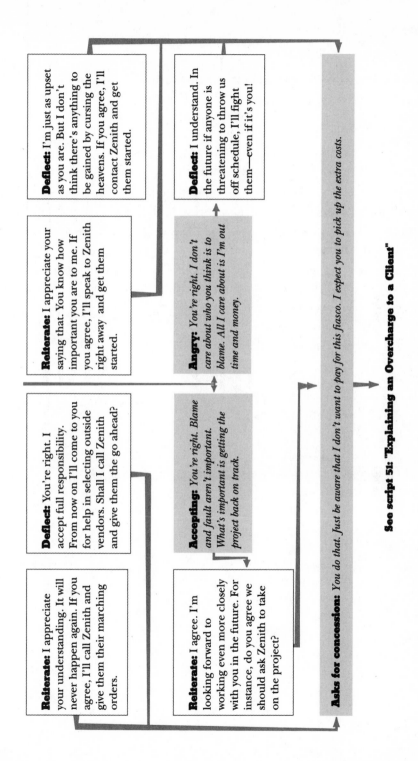

Reiterate: I appreciate your understanding. It will never happen again. If you agree, I'll call Zenith and give them their marching orders.

Deflect: You're right. I accept full responsibility. From now on I'll come to you for help in selecting outside vendors. Shall I call Zenith and give them the go ahead?

Reiterate: I appreciate your saying that. You know how important you are to me. If you agree, I'll speak to Zenith right away and get them started.

Deflect: I'm just as upset as you are. But I don't think there's anything to be gained by cursing the heavens. If you agree, I'll contact Zenith and get them started.

Reiterate: I agree. I'm looking forward to working even more closely with you in the future. For instance, do you agree we should ask Zenith to take on the project?

Accepting: *You're right. Blame and fault aren't important. What's important is getting the project back on track.*

Angry: *You're right. I don't care about who you think is to blame. All I care about is I'm out time and money.*

Deflect: I understand. In the future if anyone is threatening to throw us off schedule, I'll fight them—even if it's you!

Asks for concession: *You do that. Just be aware that I don't want to pay for this fiasco. I expect you to pick up the extra costs.*

See script 51: "Explaining an Overcharge to a Client"

ADAPTATIONS

This script can be modified to:

- Revise the terms of an agreement due to unanticipated events out of your control

KEY POINTS

- Use words like "obstacle" or "hurdle" rather than "problem" or "disaster."
- If it's clearly no one's fault, ask if it was your fault.
- If it's a third party's fault, say so, accept responsibility, and offer a plan.
- If it's the client's own fault, say you need to work more closely in the future, and offer a plan.
- If the client gets angry, deflect the anger by saying you understand the response, but urge moving on.
- If the client accepts the situation, reiterate your plan.

Refusing a Client's Request

53

STRATEGY

The business world has its share of unethical members. On occasion you may be unfortunate enough to have one of them as a client. Or perhaps you have a client who wants to use you to do something unethical in order to shield her. In either case, if you don't want or need to keep the client, you can simply refuse and tell her to find another professional. But if you need to retain the client, you face a dilemma. The solution is to offer an alternative, ethical course of action which, while it may not lead to the same results, will achieve some of the results without the potential side effects.

TACTICS

- **Attitude:** You are not a judge and jury, nor a board of ethics. You are simply trying to keep your client from harming herself—and you.
- **Preparation:** Understand, and be prepared to discuss, the ramifications of the proposed actions. At the same time, have the groundwork in place for an alternative course. Even if you complete the planning, don't say so. You want the client to have time to think over what you're saying in this dialogue and maybe become involved in the planning.
- **Timing:** Do this only after making sure that the request is indeed unethical or clearly improper. Once you've convinced yourself of that, have the dialogue as soon as possible.
- **Behavior:** This dialogue can be held either over the telephone or in person. But in either case refrain from being condescending and accusatory. Be specific, perhaps alluding to similar experiences you have had.

53. Refusing a Client's Request

Icebreaker: I've been thinking about your suggestion. The possible effects have been weighing on my mind. I've been thinking about how it should be handled, if at all. I need to know when you can spend as much time as possible to talk about it.

Receptive: *Right now is fine. I'm all ears. What's going on?*

Unreceptive: *Aren't you overreacting? I didn't think what I suggested was that significant.*

Not what you planned: I've been doing some research, and I've discovered that the ramifications of what you asked me to do could be significant, and not at all what you want to achieve. *[Explain situation.]*

Still willing: *That may or may not be the case. But I'm willing to take the risk so I suggest you go ahead.*

Do your job: *Correct me if I'm wrong, but isn't it your job to protect me from any possible side effects?*

It's my job to protect: You hired me, not only to do a competent professional job, but to protect you and your family. I can't let you commit financial *[or]* professional *[or]* legal suicide.

That's what I'm doing: That's exactly what I'm doing by having this conversation with you. My job is to keep you and your family from getting into potentially dangerous situations.

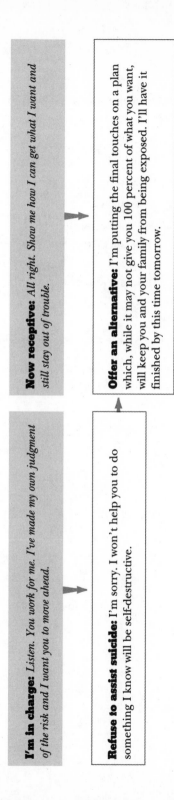

I'm in charge: Listen. You work for me. I've made my own judgment of the risk and I want you to move ahead.

Now receptive: All right. Show me how I can get what I want and still stay out of trouble.

Refuse to assist suicide: I'm sorry. I won't help you to do something I know will be self-destructive.

Offer an alternative: I'm putting the final touches on a plan which, while it may not give you 100 percent of what you want, will keep you and your family from being exposed. I'll have it finished by this time tomorrow.

ADAPTATIONS

This script can be modified to:

- Dissuade a family member, friend, or coworker who wants your help in committing some questionable act

KEY POINTS

- Be professional, not condescending or accusatory.
- Explain the potential ramifications of the proposed action.
- If the client is still willing to go ahead, say it's your job to stop her.
- If the client insists you just do your job, say that's exactly what you're doing.
- If the client demands compliance, say you can't and won't assist in her suicide.
- Close by suggesting another course of action.
- If the client insists on the original course, say you'll have to withdraw from the project/case.

Resurrecting a Former Client

54.

STRATEGY

Too many business people stand on ceremony and foolish pride and never try to resurrect former clients. That's a mistake. It's far easier to get back together with a client you've lost or had no contact with than to get a new client—just take a look at script 42, "Cold Calling a Potential Client." Your goal in this script should be limited: to get a meeting with the former client at which you can pitch to become part of her life once again. The secret to achieving this is to play, as much as possible, on any personal relationship or event the two of you shared. Assuming there was a problem that caused your falling out, the former client may still be angry. Your response should be to absorb her anger and simply ask for the chance to tell your side of the story and make amends. To do either of those, you'll need a meeting.

TACTICS

- **Attitude:** Be cordial, humble, and if necessary, persistent.
- **Preparation:** Before the call, gather as much personal data about the former client and her family as you can, if you don't remember names and ages. Be prepared to call back since your sudden reappearance may put her off balance initially.
- **Timing:** Try to call either early—before 9 A.M.—or late—after 5 P.M.—in the work day.
- **Behavior:** Don't call the former client at home, or on the weekend. You'll get the most civil responses during normal working hours when she is at the office. Be prepared to absorb residual anger. If possible, imply that your request is a modest one.

54. Resurrecting a Former Client

Icebreaker: How are you? I ran into our mutual friend Jim Jackson yesterday and it got me thinking about you. I'm just calling to patch things up and see how you and your family are doing. I hope I'm not calling at a time when you can't be bothered with a call like this.

It's a good time: *Uh . . . no, it's not a bother at all. We're all doing fine. How are you?*

Miss relationship: I'm okay. But I think about you often. Even though we no longer have a business relationship, I've always wanted to call and chat and see how you're doing.

Over anger: *Listen. I'm over the problem we had. I know you did your best. It just wasn't good enough.*

Make amends: That's another reason for this call. I'd like to make amends and work for you again. What happened could never happen again. I think I could really be of help.

It's a bad time: *Actually, it is a bad time. I'm very busy at the moment.*

Say you'll call back: Oh, I'm terribly sorry. I'll give you a call back later this week.

Still angry: *I think about you too . . . every time I look at that boarded-up storefront and the bills I still have to pay.*

Absorb anger: I understand your anger. I hope one day you'll be able to sit down with me over a cup of coffee and hear my side of the story. I'm sorry for troubling you.

Open to possibility: *Hey, I don't harbor grudges. I'd be happy to speak with you.*

Ask for meeting: I'd like to come down and show you what I've been doing and how it might help your business. I'd really like to resume our friendship—it meant a lot to me.

Not open to possibility: *I'm sorry, but you can't turn the clock back. I'm not interested.*

Meet for coffee: Why don't we just meet for a cup of coffee then. I miss our personal relationship and would really like to see you again—it meant a lot to me.

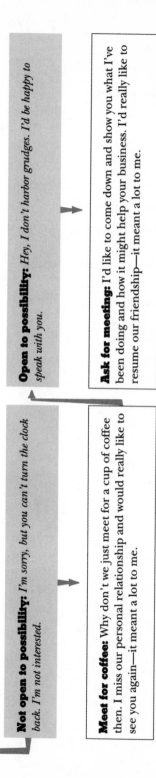

ADAPTATIONS

This script can be modified to:

- Rekindle a dormant relationship for networking purposes
- Tell a former customer about a new product or service you're offering

KEY POINTS

- Be contrite, humble, and personable—this is initially a personal call.
- Explain that you miss the relationship and would like to renew it.
- If the former client is still angry, absorb the anger and imply your request is too modest to justify such anger.
- If the former client is no longer angry, but hasn't forgotten the matter, ask for a chance to make amends.
- If the former client isn't open to renewing the relationship, push for a personal meeting over coffee.
- If the former client appears willing to renew the relationship, ask for a more formal meeting.

Dealing with a Client Who Is Angry with Your Staff

55.

STRATEGY

When a client calls to tell you that she is upset with one of your staff members, there's really very little you can do. Your goal is to keep the anger at the individual from being extended to you and your company. Whether or not you know about the situation, it's best to act as if this is the first you've heard of it. The best response is simply to allow the client to vent. **Don't apologize for someone else**—that will allow the anger to be shifted to you. And don't offer a defense. That will only turn the conversation into a debate. Instead, show personal concern, express your regrets over the whole situation, ask if you can bring the matter to the staff member's attention, and then offer to make amends. In most cases, all the client needed to do was to express her anger. By accepting her anger, without accepting blame or rising to your staffer's defense, you should be able to resolve the situation quickly and painlessly.

TACTICS

- **Attitude:** Be concerned and regretful—not reflexively defensive or apologetic.
- **Preparation:** You'll have little or no time to prepare for specific situations, so put a continuing policy in place for dealing with such issues.
- **Timing:** You'll have no control over the timing of this dialogue.
- **Behavior:** Moderation is the key. If you're too responsive, you'll open yourself up for blame. If you're unresponsive, you won't give the client a chance to vent. Listen, show you care, offer to do what you can, and leave it at that.

55. Dealing with a Client Who Is Angry with Your Staff

Makes complaint: *I'm very upset with your office. I just found out your paralegal insulted my mother when she came to your office to notarize the wills. You know, my mother isn't well, and being upset doesn't help her health. I'm very concerned with the way your staff treated her.*

→

Show concern: First, and most importantly, how is your mother feeling? Is she okay?

→

Restates softened complaint: *She's as well as could be expected. Thank you for asking. I know she's hard of hearing and obstinate at times, but that's no excuse for how she was treated.*

→

Offer amends: Thank you for bringing this to my attention. I feel terrible that you had to make this call. May I mention this to my paralegal to make sure it never happens again to your mother or to anyone else? Meanwhile, if there's any way I can make amends, please let me know.

→

Final venting: *By all means talk to her. There's no way to make up for it, just make sure it doesn't happen again.*

ADAPTATIONS

This script can be modified to:

- Derail criticism from someone important to you about someone important to you

KEY POINTS

- Show concern.
- Don't apologize or rise to a defense.
- Offer to make amends.

Correcting a Client's Behavior

56

STRATEGY

In most cases, accepting a client's boorish behavior is just part of being a business person. The old maxim is true: The customer is always right. You're not going to be able to change someone who you have no leverage over. But what if the client's behavior or manner is threatening to derail a project? It's in your interest and your client's interest to get her under control. The best way to do that is to throw the blame on a third party and to enlist the client in an effort to sway her by playacting. In effect, you're asking the client to act a certain way, not because her current behavior is inappropriate but because her new behavior will get what you both want from a third party.

TACTICS

- **Attitude:** This is one instance where you need to be willing to assume the role of spin master.
- **Preparation:** Give some thought to exactly what it is about the client's behavior that is problematic, and then develop a plan that will offset the behavior.
- **Timing:** Do this as soon as you realize your client's behavior is likely to get in the way of achieving your common goals.
- **Behavior:** Hold this meeting alone and in person, if possible. That lends the conspiratorial air to the conversation that will back up your spin. Do all you can to deflect suspicion and absorb anger.

56. Correcting a Client's Behavior

Icebreaker: I need your help in restrategizing the way we approach this whole negotiation. Our meetings with the bank have been too angry and there's too much facesaving going on. In order for us to put some humility into the meetings, I think we're going to have to show them by example, and I'm going to need your help with that.

Angry: *Listen. Don't tell me about your problems. I'm paying you to take care of this, so just do your job.*

Absorb anger: One of the reasons I love working for you is that you can offer excellent input. In this transaction I need to draw on your interpersonal skills and experience in order to keep it moving forward.

Open to new approach: *Hey, I just want to get what I need from them. I'll do whatever it takes. What did you have in mind?*

Offer plan: At the next meeting let's have them do most of the talking. We also need to make them feel like they're very important to us and that we want to maintain our relationship with them. You can do that much better than I could.

Realizes implication: *What are you saying? Are you telling me you don't like the way I'm acting at the meetings?*

Deflect suspicion: No, not at all. You've been acting like yourself. It's the transaction and the bank's people that I have a problem with.

ADAPTATIONS

This script can be modified to:

- Eliminate aggressive behavior, inappropriate language, or a pompous attitude that is having a negative impact on a third party in an office or social setting

KEY POINTS

- Blame a third party for the problems and enlist the client as your accomplice in an effort to overcome the difficulty.
- If the client realizes that you're actually criticizing her behavior, deflect the suspicion and focus matters on the third party.
- If the client gets angry, just absorb the anger and directly ask for help in overcoming the problem.
- If the client is open to taking a new approach, offer your plan with a dash of flattery.

Apologizing to a Client for Your Own Mistake

57.

STRATEGY

When you've made a mistake that affects a client, financially or otherwise, you're obligated to apologize. If you want to keep the client, you'll need to come clean and offer a plan for addressing the situation. That said, you'll have to make an individual judgment on how far you're willing to go to keep the client. Remember: Words cost you nothing other than pride, so I'd suggest you go pretty far verbally. On the other hand, lowering your fee probably isn't a good idea since it will cut into any future work you do for the client. A compromise solution is to pick up some, but not all, of the costs of cleaning up the problem you created. How much of the cost you absorb is a matter for negotiation.

TACTICS

- **Attitude:** Be contrite, honest, and apologetic. But move on to the solution as quickly as possible.
- **Preparation:** Do a thorough postmortem so you can completely yet concisely explain what went wrong and why. Have a solution in hand, one that requires only the client's approval to get launched.
- **Timing:** Do this as soon as possible after the mistake. You want to make sure the client hears about this from you, not someone else.
- **Behavior:** Having this conversation over the telephone could show a sense of urgency, and can also insulate you somewhat. Be prepared to absorb some anger. However, don't let unjustified threats go by—they're uncalled for unless your mistake was malicious or your conduct was unethical.

57. Apologizing to a Client for Your Own Mistake

Icebreaker: I've made a miscalculation that has created a problem for you. I have what I believe is a solution, but first I need to apologize to you. When I was scheduling your project, I failed to take into account that there were two religious holidays that fell during the time I'd set aside for printing. We're not going to be able to meet the schedule I laid out for you.

Accepting: *I'm not happy about this, but I admire your candor. I want you to know I expect special help from you. Now what's your plan?*

Angry: *I can't believe you could have been so stupid and negligent. What were you thinking? Weren't you paying attention? What's wrong with you?*

Outright apology: My relationship with you is very important to me. I feel horrible about what has happened. All I can do is apologize. I don't expect you to just pass this off, but I'd like a chance to earn your confidence back.

Offers another chance: *All right. How do you plan on working this out?*

Offer plan: Thanks for your continued confidence in me. I won't let you down. I suggest we start by contacting another, larger printer I've lined up to find out if he can get the job done in time.

Still angry: *I can't afford to give you another chance. Not after the screwup you just made.*

Ask what can be done: Our relationship is important to me. Since an apology won't suffice, what can I do that would make up for this mistake? If I can do it, I will.

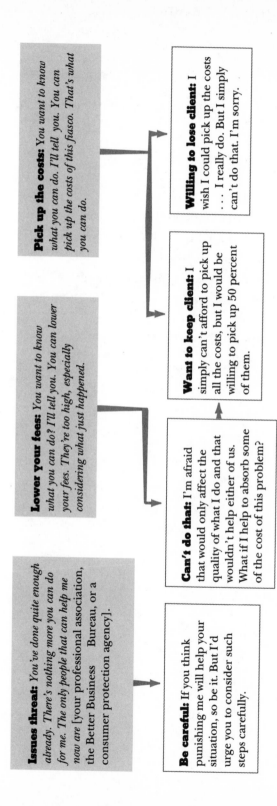

Issues threat: *You've done quite enough already. There's nothing more you can do for me. The only people that can help me now are* [your professional association, the Better Business   Bureau, or a consumer protection agency].

Lower your fees: *You want to know what you can do? I'll tell you. You can lower your fees. They're too high, especially considering what just happened.*

Pick up the costs: *You want to know what you can do. I'll tell you. You can pick up the costs of this fiasco. That's what you can do.*

Be careful: If you think punishing me will help your situation, so be it. But I'd urge you to consider such steps carefully.

Can't do that: I'm afraid that would only affect the quality of what I do and that wouldn't help either of us. What if I help to absorb some of the cost of this problem?

Want to keep client: I simply can't afford to pick up all the costs, but I would be willing to pick up 50 percent of them.

Willing to lose client: I wish I could pick up the costs . . . I really do. But I simply can't do that. I'm sorry.

ADAPTATIONS

This script can be modified to:

- Explain a material disappointment or injury, created unintentionally by you, to a family member or friend

KEY POINTS

- Be direct, frank, and contrite. Offer an explanation but not an excuse.
- If the client accepts your apology, immediately describe your plan.
- If the client gets angry, offer an outright, humble, and candid apology.
- If the client remains angry, ask what else you can do.
- If the client issues an unjustified threat, urge her to be cautious.
- If the client asks you to lower your fees, suggest absorbing some costs instead.
- If the client asks you to pick up the costs, say you'll absorb a share of them.

CHAPTER SEVEN

Lifescripts for Lenders and Investors

Being Interviewed by an Institutional Investor

STRATEGY

Just as with job interviews, getting interviewed by an institutional investor means that you're more than halfway to getting what you want—in this case, money. Since they've already seen your business plan and supporting documentation, and have agreed to meet with you, they're interested. They think your idea is a good one. They've tested the validity of your numbers. They've found your proposal meets their criteria. What they haven't done is evaluate the quality of management—that's you. This meeting is all about you overcoming any hesitations they may have about your ability to manage a growing company. Everything about you, from your garb and manners to the words you choose and the things you say, is under a microscope. Pass this audition and you'll get your money. Beyond that, the secret to responding correctly to their questions is understanding what it is they're looking for—and giving it to them.

TACTICS

- **Attitude:** You can be secure that your plan or application has passed inspection—otherwise you wouldn't have the interview. Now it's just you they're concerned with. Be confident, enthusiastic, eager, and alert.
- **Preparation:** You must know everything there is to know about your business plan, including the life stories of your proposed staff and your ideas for expansion. Learn as much as you can about the investors. Prepare a list of questions of your own to ask them.
- **Timing:** The meeting should be scheduled at their convenience.
- **Behavior:** Dress and act as you would if on a job interview for your dream position with your ideal company. Expect more than one person to be in the room, and respond to each one as if he is the most important person in the world. Never interrupt.

58. Being Interviewed by an Institutional Investor

Invite inquiries: I'm really very pleased to discuss my proposal with you. I think investors like you offer my plan its best chance for success. From what I've heard about your company, you could contribute tremendously to my success by providing experience and wisdom. I'd be happy to answer any questions you might have.

Succession?: *Tell us about your support people.*

Not one-man operation: I picked them not only because I've had a great deal of experience with them, but because each is knowledgeable with more than one discipline. I've never had to worry when I've been away on a sales conference.

Open to advice?: *You have a strong marketing background, but how will you make up for your lack of experience in finance?*

Validity?: *How did you arrive at such optimistic numbers?*

Conservative numbers: I spent an enormous amount of time in validating my sources of revenue, and I tried to be very conservative. I too was pleased with the results.

Ready for competition?: *How do you expect to compete against the big guys when they see your success and copy your product [or] service?*

Authorship?: *We think your plan is very interesting. Who helped you write it?*

My plan: The plan is essentially mine. Of course I had my lawyer and accountant look at it as well.

Support at home?: *To what extent will your family get involved in the business?*

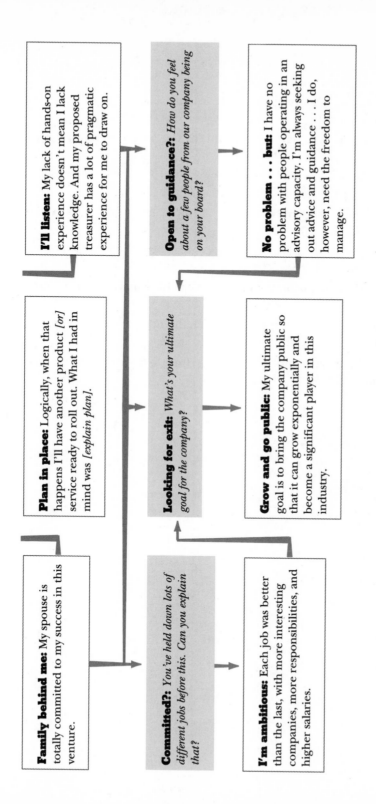

Family behind me: My spouse is totally committed to my success in this venture.

Plan in place: Logically, when that happens I'll have another product [or] service ready to roll out. What I had in mind was [explain plan].

I'll listen: My lack of hands-on experience doesn't mean I lack knowledge. And my proposed treasurer has a lot of pragmatic experience for me to draw on.

Committed?: *You've held down lots of different jobs before this. Can you explain that?*

Looking for exit: *What's your ultimate goal for the company?*

Open to guidance?: *How do you feel about a few people from our company being on your board?*

I'm ambitious: Each job was better than the last, with more interesting companies, more responsibilities, and higher salaries.

Grow and go public: My ultimate goal is to bring the company public so that it can grow exponentially and become a significant player in this industry.

No problem . . . but: I have no problem with people operating in an advisory capacity. I'm always seeking out advice and guidance . . . I do, however, need the freedom to manage.

KEY POINTS

- Be confident, eager, and enthusiastic.
- Questions about authorship are an effort to determine whether you're truly the person behind the idea.
- Questions about your staff are attempts to find out if the business will remain afloat if you die or leave.
- Questions about your numbers are designed to see if you've been conservative in your projection.
- Questions about your family are probes to see whether they support your efforts.
- Questions about your lack of experience in an area are intended to test your openness to advice.
- Questions about your job-hopping are tests of your commitment and determination.
- Questions about your response to future competition are probes for long-range planning.
- Questions about your ultimate goals are efforts to find out if they'll have a profitable exit.

Asking an Institutional Investor for More Money

59

STRATEGY

Institutional investors are aware of the potential that they'll have to sink more money into a business before they turn a profit. They may not like it, but they have enough experience in business to realize that there are occasionally unpredictable circumstances that throw even the best plans out of alignment. The key to this dialogue is in the timing. The sooner you approach the investor, the better your chance of getting a loan. That's because spotting the trouble well ahead of time actually indicates good management. Of course, the problem has to have been caused by something beyond your control. Show up at an investor's office on Friday for money to meet Monday's payroll and, while you might be bailed out, the assistance is likely to be short-term only.

TACTICS

- **Attitude:** Be concerned, but confident in the long-term health of the business.

- **Preparation:** Be prepared to explain why the situation was a total surprise, and to offer one or two optional plans.

- **Timing:** Do this as soon as you realize there's the potential for problems. The more lead time you give, the more likely the investor will retain a high opinion of you and your abilities.

- **Behavior:** Hold this meeting in person, at the investor's office. Demonstrate that you've exhausted all your other options before coming back. Ignore probes for other problems and press your case. Any reluctance should be met by even more confidence on your part.

59. Asking an Institutional Investor for More Money

Icebreaker: The reason I'm here is that I need your help in overcoming an obstacle that may arise for the company in three to six months: a shortfall in our cash position.

↓

Probe for trouble: *Does this mean that one of the assumptions in your cash flow budget was overly optimistic?*

↓

Explain situation: What has happened is that there has been labor unrest with one of our suppliers. They won't be able to deliver raw materials for a period of months and we will have to stop production.

→

You're responsible: *What do you plan to do about that?*

→

Need your help: I was hoping that I could overcome this problem without coming to you for help, but our bankers have taken the position that we don't have sufficient capital to warrant additional funding.

↑

Accepts some responsibility: *So what do you want us to do about that?*

→

Make proposal: You could arrange to have one of your banks provide us with a loan, in which case I would be willing to give you options to buy additional equity in the company for a period of time. Or, you could increase your equity position in the company at terms you find attractive.

Needs reassurance: *How do we know this won't happen again?*

Grudging acceptance: *You've pushed our backs to the wall. We really have no choice.*

Unpredictable situation: What happened was totally unpredictable. I've been watching this company for years and it has had no history of labor unrest.

Reiterate confidence: This isn't a sign of trouble for the business. I'm prepared to take an equity loan on my home and make whatever loans I can to the company because I feel this business is an even better idea now than when I drafted the plan.

ADAPTATIONS

This script can be modified to:

- Get investors' consent to bring in new equity financing
- Prepare investors for the sale of the company

KEY POINTS

- Be concerned, yet still confident.
- Ignore probes for weaknesses in your operations and planning.
- Present at least two options, both of which have clear advantages, to the investor.
- Answer fears of future problems with explanations of why the problem was unforseeable.
- Respond to reluctance or hesitation with strong signs of your own confidence and commitment to the future of the business.

Approaching a "Friendly" Investor

60.

STRATEGY

Entrepreneurs can seldom get start-up funds from a bank. Instead, they must turn to family and friends—as well as their own resources—for the money to turn their dream into reality. This is one script where the preparation is more important than the actual dialogue. Your targets must be selected carefully. The one objection you can't overcome is their lack of funds, so make sure they've got the money to possibly help you. You must also have enough solid information for them to make an investment decision. Your business plan— prepared with the help of a CPA—not only should show them when they'll recover their investments, but should also project into a time when they'll be receiving a yield for their money and ultimately into an exit. Your plan should also be firmly grounded with market projections that show its viability. Even though they're friendly investors, these folk shouldn't feel as though they're getting any less for their money, or taking any greater risks, than they would with any other comparable investment. Your relationship with them should be the reason they choose your business rather than another equivalent one to invest in, not a reason to take a risk they wouldn't otherwise take.

TACTICS

- **Attitude:** Be positive and confident. Any doubts you have will translate into reasons for them to turn you down.

- **Preparation:** Not only should you have a thoroughly documented, professionally prepared business plan for them or their advisors to study, but you should also have selected them carefully. You can't overcome their actual lack of funds.

- **Timing:** Approach friendly investors only after you've got all your plans and projections in place. Going to them too early will mark you as an amateur and your business as just a pipe dream. Schedule the meeting for nonbusiness hours to accentuate your personal relationship.

- **Behavior:** Try to hold this meeting at their homes. Suggest that they can have their spouses present as well. At the same time, keep your conversation businesslike. Both courses will accentuate the personal links. The timing and location should suffice for setting the context. Combine your

60. Approaching a "Friendly" Investor

Icebreaker: I've come to you for a combination of advice and help. I have some really good news. I've decided to leave my job and go into business. I've been waiting for the right moment, researching, and studying, and the time has come.

Subtle negative: *I don't discuss business with family and friends. Why don't you call my office instead.*

Outright negative: *I'm not the one to help you.*

Warning: *Take it from me. Put your money in the bank and hold on to your job. Being in business for yourself is nothing but misery.*

Happy and open: *That's great. I'm happy for you. What can I do to help?*

I need you: I'm seeing you because I need advice. I'd like a hearing. Then I'll give your office a call.

You are: I think you are. Of all the people I know you're the most creative and savvy about business.

You see: What you've just said is why I'm speaking with you. You have a lot of insight about the ways of business.

Thanks: Thanks so much for being so receptive and willing to listen.

Pitch: Over the years I've developed what I've been told is an excellent business plan for *[your product/service]*. I'm prepared to start raising money to supplement my own. What I need is your stamp of approval and your financial help. Let me tell you the details. *[Present plan.]*

Speak to others: *Sounds interesting. But as I said, you need to speak with my office about these things.*

Age fear: *Sounds interesting, but should someone my age put so much in something this risky?*

Big gamble: *Sounds interesting, but these small start-ups are really just crap shoots.*

Overly invested: *Sounds interesting, but I'm overly invested right now.*

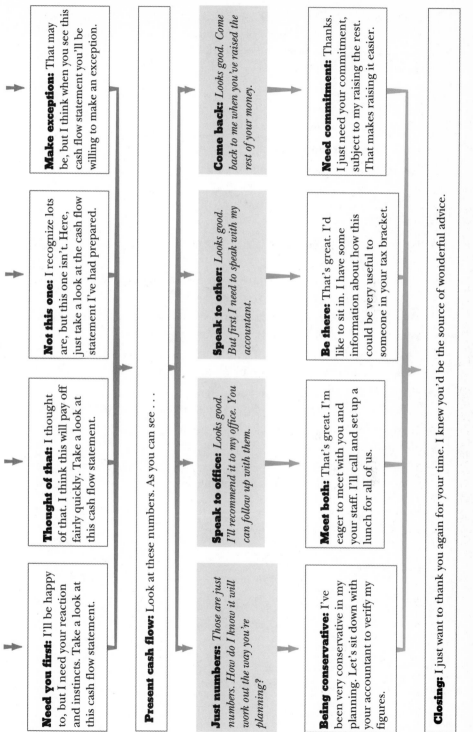

Need you first: I'll be happy to, but I need your reaction and instincts. Take a look at this cash flow statement.

Thought of that: I thought of that. I think this will pay off fairly quickly. Take a look at this cash flow statement.

Not this one: I recognize lots are, but this one isn't. Here, just take a look at the cash flow statement I've had prepared.

Make exception: That may be, but I think when you see this cash flow statement you'll be willing to make an exception.

Present cash flow: Look at these numbers. As you can see . . .

Just numbers: *Those are just numbers. How do I know it will work out the way you're planning?*

Speak to office: *Looks good. I'll recommend it to my office. You can follow up with them.*

Speak to other: *Looks good. But first I need to speak with my accountant.*

Come back: *Looks good. Come back to me when you've raised the rest of your money.*

Being conservative: I've been very conservative in my planning. Let's sit down with your accountant to verify my figures.

Meet both: That's great. I'm eager to meet with you and your staff. I'll call and set up a lunch for all of us.

Be there: That's great. I'd like to sit in. I have some information about how this could be very useful to someone in your tax bracket.

Need commitment: Thanks. I just need your commitment, subject to my raising the rest. That makes raising it easier.

Closing: I just want to thank you again for your time. I knew you'd be the source of wonderful advice.

search for cash with a quest for advice from a potential mentor. That makes the discussion less confrontational. It's a thin disguise, but one that makes both parties more comfortable.

ADAPTATIONS

This script can be modified to:

- Ask relatives for money to pay for a wedding
- Ask relatives for money to pay for college tuition

KEY POINTS

- Be confident, well-prepared, and businesslike. Let your personal relationship speak for itself.
- Whatever the initial response to your statement about going into business, move directly into your pitch.
- Your response to secondary objections should lead directly into presenting your projections of their potential return on the investment.
- Qualms about the accuracy of your numbers should be met by a request to meet with your friend or relative's advisor.
- Requests that you speak with your friend or relative's advisor should be met with enthusiasm and a request to have him attend the meeting.
- If your friend or relative begs off, saying he'll speak with his advisor, ask to come along.
- If he doesn't want to be the first investor, ask him to make a verbal commitment subject to others investing too.

Asking a "Friendly" Investor for More

61

STRATEGY

Almost every small business experiences a cash flow emergency in its early years. In many instances, it has nothing to do with a management problem or forecasting miscalculation, but stems from situations beyond the business's control. The best response to such unforeseen problems is to turn to your original investors for help. Since they are now partners in the business, they're involved whether they like it or not. The best strategy is to approach them for a loan, rather than for an increased investment. That way you maintain the same degree of control over the business. The key is to demonstrate that the problem had nothing to do with either you or the conduct of the business.

TACTICS

- **Attitude:** Be direct and businesslike. Refer to your relationship to the investor only when such a reference makes sense. Flattery isn't mandatory, but it wouldn't hurt.

- **Preparation:** Draft a thorough explanation of what caused the current problem, and have a plan ready in response. Documentation and a written loan proposal should be assembled prior to this meeting.

- **Timing:** Do this as soon as you realize you'll need additional cash.

- **Behavior:** Hold this meeting in person, either at the investor's place of business or home. Maintain and project your optimism and enthusiasm for the long-term success of the business. Show gratitude for past help, but demonstrate that future participation in the business will require additional help.

61. Asking a "Friendly" Investor for More

Icebreaker: I'm seeing all the partners. I'm going to have to modify the timetable for profits and add another six months to break even.

Sophisticated no: *That means you need more money and you're talking to the wrong guy.*

Sophisticated maybe: *I thought your plan was a bit optimistic. What do you plan to do about this?*

Unsophisticated: *I don't understand. You said the business was doing well. What happened?*

Explanation: This has nothing to do with the viability of the business or the quality of management. One of the other partners was supposed to provide funds and hasn't. *[or]* Acme, one of our biggest customers, has just declared bankruptcy. There was no way we could have anticipated or prevented this from happening. It was outside our control.

There's no more: *You know, I went into this because of our relationship. I was willing to put in $5,000 and take a shot with you. But that's it. I'm not going to put in any more money. [or] I can't afford to put in any more money.*

I'd have done better: *You know, if I had put your numbers together I would have made sure there was enough of a contingency fund for just this kind of situation.*

Deflect criticism: Perhaps, but if I put too much into the budget contingencies I could never have raised enough money from other, less sophisticated investors. In any case, I think I have a solution.

Push for loan: I'm not asking you to invest any more money. I'm asking you to make a short-term priority loan to the company of $3,000, which it will pay back at the prime rate within 12 months. That way you'll be able to protect your investment and receive a fair yield.

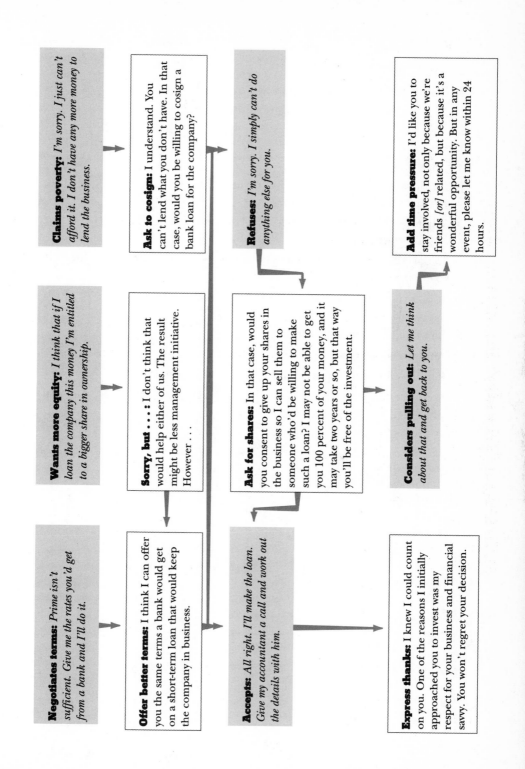

Claims poverty: *I'm sorry. I just can't afford it. I don't have any more money to lend the business.*

Ask to cosign: I understand. You can't lend what you don't have. In that case, would you be willing to cosign a bank loan for the company?

Refuses: *I'm sorry. I simply can't do anything else for you.*

Add time pressure: I'd like you to stay involved, not only because we're friends *[or]* related, but because it's a wonderful opportunity. But in any event, please let me know within 24 hours.

Wants more equity: *I think that if I loan the company this money I'm entitled to a bigger share in ownership.*

Sorry, but . . . : I don't think that would help either of us. The result might be less management initiative. However . . .

Ask for shares: In that case, would you consent to give up your shares in the business so I can sell them to someone who'd be willing to make such a loan? I may not be able to get you 100 percent of your money, and it may take two years or so, but that way you'll be free of the investment.

Considers pulling out: *Let me think about that and get back to you.*

Negotiates terms: *Prime isn't sufficient. Give me the rates you'd get from a bank and I'll do it.*

Offer better terms: I think I can offer you the same terms a bank would get on a short-term loan that would keep the company in business.

Accepts: *All right. I'll make the loan. Give my accountant a call and work out the details with him.*

Express thanks: I knew I could count on you. One of the reasons I initially approached you to invest was my respect for your business and financial savvy. You won't regret your decision.

ADAPTATIONS

This script can be modified to:

- Return to contributors for additional money
- Approach subcontractors to reduce their bills

KEY POINTS

- Be optimistic, yet realistic. Keep things on a businesslike level. Let personal relations be a subtext.
- Whatever the initial response, explain that the current problem was beyond your control.
- Initial criticism should be deflected and the dialogue steered toward your loan proposal.
- Initial rejections should be countered by a description of your loan proposal.
- Be willing to negotiate terms.
- Answer claims of poverty with a request to be a cosigner of a bank loan.
- Requests for more equity should be deflected into improved loan terms.
- Continued refusal should be met by a request to give up shares by a fixed deadline.

Asking an Institutional Lender for More

62.

STRATEGY

It's surprisingly simple to get an institutional lender to increase the amount of its loan to you, as long as you know which buttons to press, and who to press them on. The key here is to approach the loan officer who sponsored your original loan. Part of his job was to make sure the bank was loaning you enough money to generate the kind of revenue required to pay off the loan. He will be anxious to keep you from defaulting and making him look bad. He's concerned, not with your business's long-term health, but with your ability to repay the money you already owe his institution. If you can impress on him that you need the additional funds in order to make the payments, you're likely to turn him into a strong ally. And if you can provide him with ammunition to make your (and his) case, it's even better. Hold some information back early in the conversation so you force the banker to ask obvious questions. That will help you steer the conversation where you want it to go.

TACTICS

- **Attitude:** Be direct and clear. You need help in order to pay off his loan to you in accordance with its terms, not in order to keep your company afloat.

- **Preparation:** Draw up a new loan proposal that offers the bank as much comfort as possible. Include opinions from lawyers and accountants if appropriate.

- **Timing:** Do this as soon as you know you'll have a problem. Bankers hate surprises.

- **Behavior:** Subtly make it clear you know the banker is in this mess with you. Use words like "we" and "us" that reinforce the idea. Stress that there's nowhere else for you to go and that without the added funds, you won't be able to pay off your loan as promised.

62. Asking an Institutional Lender for More

Icebreaker: I need to speak to you about a problem we have. The company has had some incredibly bad fortune, but I think that together we can solve the problem.

Asks for info: *What's the problem? What's gone wrong?*

Offer explanation: We've had a train car load of onions go rotten on the siding because the refrigeration in the car failed. The insurance company is refusing to pay, and as a result we're going to have a shortfall in our cash. We're going to be litigating against the insurance company, but that will take some time. We need $100,000 to sustain ourselves while that's going on.

Asks for risks: *What's the alternative? What will happen if you don't get the $100,000?*

Grave . . . but I'll help: I don't want to even look at that possibility since it probably means a Chapter 11. I've prepared a memo for your lending committee with an opinion from my lawyer. The numbers I've drawn up show how the request fits the bank's lending criteria. I think with this information you'll be able to cover all your bases with the loan committee and make an advance to protect your investment. In addition, if you'd like me to come with you to speak to the committee I'd be happy to.

Offers thanks: *Thanks for preparing the memo. That will save me a lot of time and work. I'll let you know when the next meeting of the loan committee will be. Maybe I'll ask you to be there.*

ADAPTATIONS

This script can be modified to:

- Obtain the return of collateral for use with an alternate lender
- Obtain additional time or inventory from a supplier/creditor

KEY POINTS

- Be direct, honest, and willing to do all you can to help.
- Make it clear, subtly if possible, that you know the banker is at risk too.
- Leave information out of your early statements, forcing the anxious banker to ask obvious questions. This will let you control the direction of the conversation.
- Try to demonstrate that you (and the banker) weren't responsible for the present situation.

Asking an Institutional Lender to Recast Terms

63.

STRATEGY

Asking an institional lender to recast the terms of an existing loan can be an uphill battle. Even though the last thing the lender wants is for you to default, he will try to do everything possible to get you to go to another lender to fulfill your obligations to him. Recasting your original loan will require the same kind of approval required for your initial loan. And this time you've acknowledged that your ability to pay back the loan is no longer the same. You need to demonstrate that this inability is due to some factor totally beyond your control, and that you still have the willingness to pay it back.

TACTICS

- **Attitude:** Be concerned, but also confident in the inherent strength of your business and secure in the knowledge that the last thing the lender wants is for you to default.

- **Preparation:** You must have comprehensive documentation of the problem, as well as the same kind of thorough proposal you used to secure the loan initially . . . but this time it should demonstrate your ability to pay back the recast loan.

- **Timing:** Do this as soon as you realize you'll have problems. The worst thing you can do is surprise a bank by not making a payment. Take the loan officer into your confidence early, and the institution is more likely to become an ally than an adversary.

- **Behavior:** This is a business meeting. Treat it as you did your initial loan meeting. But this time, don't hesitate to respond somewhat aggressively to any bullying from the loan officer. You're still a supplicant, but you've got more leverage now that you owe the bank money.

63. Asking an Institutional Lender to Recast Terms

Icebreaker: I'm finding it increasingly difficult to keep current in my loan because of a circumstance that has affected my stream of income. Shortly, I'll find it impossible. I think I have a solution, however. I came to you as soon as I knew.

Concerned: *I'm sorry to hear that. What happened?*

Reflexively negative: *You're going to have to go elsewhere for help. You signed an agreement with us and you must fulfill your obligations.*

Offer explanation: My income from my largest customer has been dramatically lowered and will remain so for the foreseeable future. They've had problems of their own and weren't able to help themselves. So, in order to pay this loan back I'll need to extend the term to six years rather than the three we had planned.

Subtly aggressive: I came here to try to avoid a default. That wouldn't be good for me and my credit, and you wouldn't want a defaulted loan on your books. I'd like to keep our relationship. The last thing I want to do is to have to plead my case to your boss. I think you and I can work this out together.

Your fault?: *That's all very well, but the bank is going to wonder why you couldn't have anticipated this happening and protected yourself.*

Willing to listen: *I'm not sure about that, but what did you have in mind?*

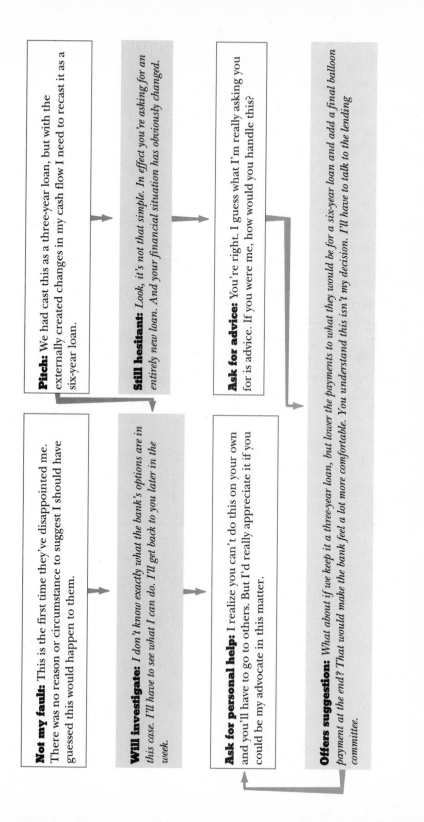

Not my fault: This is the first time they've disappointed me. There was no reason or circumstance to suggest I should have guessed this would happen to them.

Pitch: We had cast this as a three-year loan, but with the externally created changes in my cash flow I need to recast it as a six-year loan.

Will investigate: *I don't know exactly what the bank's options are in this case. I'll have to see what I can do. I'll get back to you later in the week.*

Still hesitant: *Look, it's not that simple. In effect you're asking for an entirely new loan. And your financial situation has obviously changed.*

Ask for personal help: I realize you can't do this on your own and you'll have to go to others. But I'd really appreciate it if you could be my advocate in this matter.

Ask for advice: You're right. I guess what I'm really asking you for is advice. If you were me, how would you handle this?

Offers suggestion: *What about if we keep it a three-year loan, but lower the payments to what they would be for a six-year loan and add a final balloon payment at the end? That would make the bank feel a lot more comfortable. You understand this isn't my decision. I'll have to talk to the lending committee.*

ADAPTATIONS

This script can be modified to:

- Change a pledge of time or effort to an institution
- Change the terms of an employment contract
- Change the terms of an equipment or auto lease

KEY POINTS

- Be businesslike, secure in your leverage, and confident in your business.
- If the banker shows concern, offer an explanation of your problem.
- If the banker is reflexively negative, feel free to show you know you have some leverage.
- If the banker probes to see if you're at fault, demonstrate the problem was unforseeable and unavoidable.
- If the banker remains hesitant about your proposal, treat it as an offer to negotiate your proposal.
- Whether the banker offers an alternative plan or asks for time to prepare a response, ask him to serve as your advocate.

Approaching a "Friendly" Lender

64.

STRATEGY

If you're going to borrow money from friends or relatives for your business, it's best to make sure it's for the right reasons. That means money to expand or to buy new equipment. Borrowing from "friendly" lenders should be in order to enhance the business, not to get out of trouble. And such loans shouldn't be for start-up money either—any such funds should be equity investments. The reasons for going to family and friends are that this may be less expensive than borrowing from an institutional source, the paperwork can be much less, and the terms can be much more flexible. For the friendly lender, such loans have benefits over other investments, including the possibility of tax advantages and equity options. It's best to approach someone who you know has liquid funds. Bring this person, or his advisor, a proposal custom-designed for his needs. Often, a private individual with the money to lend a family member's business will have a financial advisor. Therefore, your goal in this dialogue might be to get the prospective lender's approval for you to speak with his advisor, and perhaps put in a good word for you.

TACTICS

- **Attitude:** You're not looking for help, you're offering a proposal that's beneficial to both parties.
- **Preparation:** Be certain the individual has funds available. Have a potential deal in mind that has been customized for this individual's needs. If possible, have a third party, preferably another family member, serve as the source of the idea.
- **Timing:** Hold this meeting at a time convenient to the other party.
- **Behavior:** Break the ice with a telephone call first. Then meet the other party at his home to reinforce the personal ties you have. Be serious, but feel free to relate as you normally would. You aren't asking for help, you're proposing a mutually beneficial arrangement. However, dress as you would for a business meeting.

64. Approaching a "Friendly" Lender

Telephone set-up

Icebreaker 1: Hello, Uncle Sam. This is Sheryl. I'm calling for a business reason today. I wanted to sit down with you and talk about a great opportunity I have. Uncle Henry suggested I speak with you. It would take too long to go over it on the telephone, so can I stop by to see you next Monday afternoon?

Face-to-face meeting

Icebreaker 2: Uncle Sam, for years I've been trying to figure out ways for the business to grow bigger. You know we're paying for Junior's tuition at Yale and little Millie's piano lessons. What I've done is taken some steps to make the company bigger so we can make more money to pay for our growing needs. I was going to go to my bank to get a loan for this expansion program. But when I told Uncle Henry about what I was doing he said it could be a wonderful financial opportunity for the family. I'd like to discuss that possibility with you.

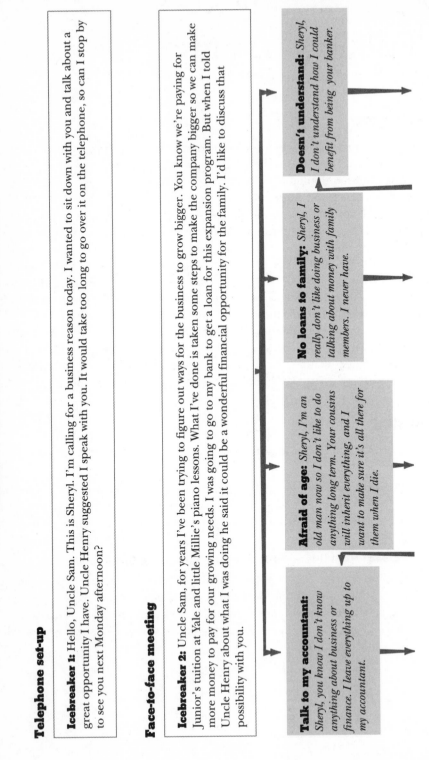

Talk to my accountant: *Sheryl, you know I don't know anything about business or finance. I leave everything up to my accountant.*

Afraid of age: *Sheryl, I'm an old man now so I don't like to do anything long term. Your cousins will inherit everything, and I want to make sure it's all there for them when I die.*

No loans to family: *Sheryl, I really don't like doing business or talking about money with family members. I never have.*

Doesn't understand: *Sheryl, I don't understand how I could benefit from being your banker.*

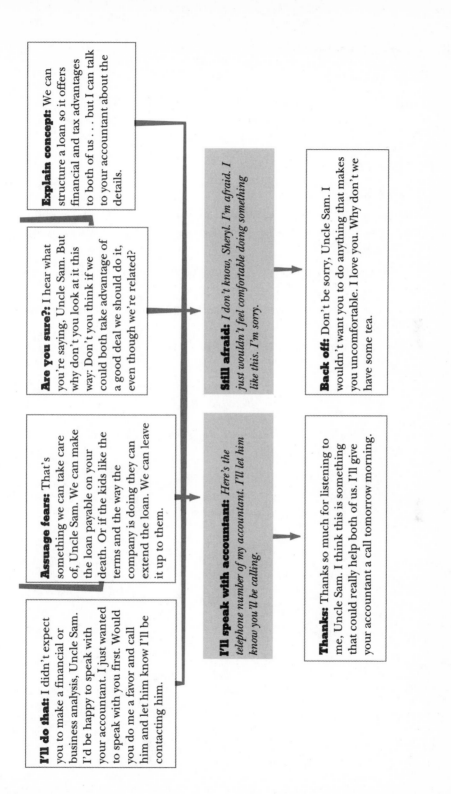

Explain concept: We can structure a loan so it offers financial and tax advantages to both of us . . . but I can talk to your accountant about the details.

Are you sure?: I hear what you're saying, Uncle Sam. But why don't you look at it this way: Don't you think if we could both take advantage of a good deal we should do it, even though we're related?

Still afraid: *I don't know, Sheryl. I'm afraid. I just wouldn't feel comfortable doing something like this. I'm sorry.*

Back off: Don't be sorry, Uncle Sam. I wouldn't want you to do anything that makes you uncomfortable. I love you. Why don't we have some tea.

Assuage fears: That's something we can take care of, Uncle Sam. We can make the loan payable on your death. Or if the kids like the terms and the way the company is doing they can extend the loan. We can leave it up to them.

I'll do that: I didn't expect you to make a financial or business analysis, Uncle Sam. I'd be happy to speak with your accountant. I just wanted to speak with you first. Would you do me a favor and call him and let him know I'll be contacting him.

I'll speak with accountant: *Here's the telephone number of my accountant. I'll let him know you'll be calling.*

Thanks: Thanks so much for listening to me, Uncle Sam. I think this is something that could really help both of us. I'll give your accountant a call tomorrow morning.

ADAPTATIONS

This script can be modified to:

- Borrow a substantial sum of money from a family member for a major personal investment, such as buying a home

KEY POINTS

- Be sober, but personable.
- If the potential lender doesn't understand your idea, explain it simply.
- If the potential lender is fearful of age or estate factors, say those can be accommodated.
- If the potential lender is leery of doing business with family members, say it can be mutually beneficial.
- If the potential lender suggests you speak with an advisor, agree, but ask for an introduction.
- If the potential lender remains hesitant, back off and shift to an entirely personal visit.

Asking a "Friendly" Lender to Recast Terms

65

STRATEGY

Sometimes unforeseen events force entrepreneurs to alter their loan repayment schedules so as to stay afloat. When the lender is a family member or friend, the request to recast terms is even more difficult than when the lender is an institution. That's because there's an added element of personal responsibility to the exchange that opens the borrower up to guilt feelings. The secret to this dialogue is realizing that your friendly creditors are, in this situation, no different than your institutional creditors. If you don't have the money to pay them back as planned, they'll simply have to accept that and deal with it. Their only recourse is to sue you, and that will result in their not getting their full loan back, since it's likely to bankrupt the business. Still, you can't be so abrupt or direct with friends. Instead, let them vent, but keep discreetly steering them back to the fact that they've no option. Call every bluff, and deal directly with every threat. Eventually they'll have to back down. Of course, don't count on getting another loan from them in the future.

TACTICS

- **Attitude:** Be compassionate and caring, but also realize that you have all the leverage and there's really nothing they can rationally do, other than accept the situation.

- **Preparation:** Have thorough documentation of the unforeseen and unavoidable occurrence, its impact on your finances, and your recast pay back plan.

- **Timing:** Do this as soon as you know you'll have a problem meeting your payments, but not before you've had time to draft a new plan.

- **Behavior:** Even though you know you have all the leverage in this situation, don't be haughty. Address all their fears, anger, and worries to the extent possible. Offer to do all you can to help, but make it clear there's no way you can meet the previously agreed schedule and that you've exhausted all other options.

65. Asking a "Friendly" Lender to Recast Terms

Icebreaker: I have a serious problem I need to tell you about. I won't be able to repay the loan you made to me as quickly as I wanted to. My major customer has just gone bankrupt.

Blames third party: *Listen, I borrowed this money to lend it to you. It has to be paid back . . . as promised.*

Needs money: *What happened? I was counting on this money. Junior's tuition bills are coming up.*

Issues threat: *Hey, I want the money as you promised. If I don't get it I'll sue you for it.*

Blames spouse: *My wife told me I shouldn't lend money to family [or] friends. She's never going to let me change the deal.*

Show dismay: If I had known you were borrowing the money, I'd never have accepted it. I wouldn't have come to you unless I thought you had the money. I didn't know I was dealing with a third party.

Didn't know: I had no idea you were counting on this money for Junior's tuition. What do you want me to do? I simply don't have it.

Suing won't help: I was hoping you wouldn't respond that way. If you sue and get a judgment, it will just put me out of business because I don't have the money. It won't help either of us. Please reconsider.

Reason with spouse: If you explain to her that this has nothing to do with the health of the business or the quality of management, and that it's temporary, surely she'll understand.

Don't get angry: *Look, I just wanted to help you out. Don't get mad at me.*

Seeks reassurance: *You can't pay if you don't have it, but how do I know it won't happen again?*

That won't help: *No. That won't make any difference. She'll want the money back just as we'd agreed.*

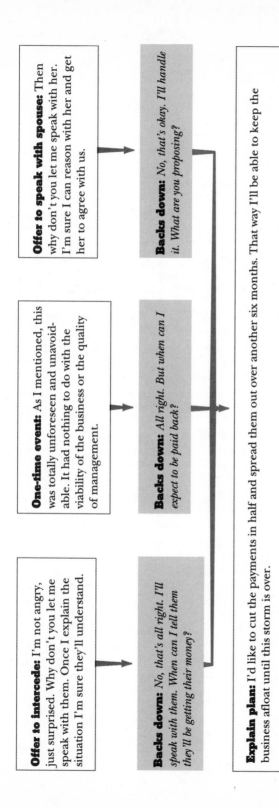

Offer to intercede: I'm not angry, just surprised. Why don't you let me speak with them. Once I explain the situation I'm sure they'll understand.

Backs down: No, that's all right. I'll speak with them. When can I tell them they'll be getting their money?

One-time event: As I mentioned, this was totally unforeseen and unavoidable. It had nothing to do with the viability of the business or the quality of management.

Backs down: All right. But when can I expect to be paid back?

Offer to speak with spouse: Then why don't you let me speak with her. I'm sure I can reason with her and get her to agree with us.

Backs down: No, that's okay. I'll handle it. What are you proposing?

Explain plan: I'd like to cut the payments in half and spread them out over another six months. That way I'll be able to keep the business afloat until this storm is over.

ADAPTATIONS

This script can be modified to:

- Withdraw from a commitment to help a family member or friend

KEY POINTS

- Be understanding, compassionate, and concerned on the outside, but confident and secure inwardly.
- If the creditor says there's a third party involved, show your dismay, and then offer to intercede.
- If the creditor issues a threat, explain that such actions will help no one.
- If the creditor stresses his need for the money, show understanding and concern, but reiterate there's nothing you can do about the situation.
- If the creditor blames his spouse, suggest reasoning with the spouse, and then offer to intercede.
- Launch into your plan only after the creditor has accepted, he has no choice but to accept a change in plans.

Approaching the Representative of a "Friendly" Lender

STRATEGY

Most individuals who have sufficient funds to be potential lenders to other family members' businesses will have financial advisors. Part of the reason is that they don't want to have to make decisions on the very type of proposal you're bringing them. Hopefully you'll have persuaded your relative to put in a good word for you with the advisor prior to your meeting. You can assume this meeting will be short, since the advisor will prefer working from a written proposal, rather than your oral presentation. The goal of this meeting, therefore, is to demonstrate to the advisor that you are just as concerned with your relative's welfare as the advisor. Your proposal is one that, you believe, will benefit your relative as well as your business. A brief explanation of your idea is all you'll be able to hope for, so make sure to hit on its benefits to your relation. If you're impressed by the advisor, it wouldn't hurt to express your willingness for the advisor himself to get more deeply involved. It won't be construed as a bribe if you frame it as being in your relative's best interests.

TACTICS

- **Attitude:** Be businesslike and concise . . . except when you discuss your concern for your relative.
- **Preparation:** Your written proposal should be just as comprehensive and exhaustive as one that you would present to a banker or venture capitalist.
- **Timing:** Hold this meeting at the advisor's convenience.
- **Behavior:** Act and dress as you would if you were meeting a banker. For the advisor, this is entirely a business meeting. Don't have this meeting at your home, even if it's suggested.

66. Approaching the Representative of a "Friendly" Lender

Icebreaker: Thanks for seeing me. Aunt Sadie thinks the world of you. She not only regards you as a good professional, but as her financial mentor. I was delighted when she suggested that I speak with you about the proposal I made to her.

Establishes role as protector: *Your aunt is a lovely woman. Let me make it clear that I represent your aunt. My responsibility is that she should live out the rest of her days happy and without any worries about her money or where it's invested.*

Establish you care and pitch: I would expect no less from you. It just so happens that I love her. When I came to her with my proposal it was with the idea that it could benefit her, as well as me. I'm as concerned about her as you are. I believe my proposal is bankable. But because of the nature of my company, I think a banker would charge me as much as he could get. I also believe this is the kind of deal where, if the interest on the loan was modest, I could afford to give the lender a participation in profits or an equity position in the company. While a banker can't do something like that, it could be an ideal safe harbor for a person like my aunt.

Open to idea: *Let me take a look at your proposal and get back to you.*

Hesitant about idea: *Your aunt is a conservative investor. She is not in the venture capital business.*

Tries to close meeting: *I'll get back to you as soon as I've had a chance to go over your proposal.*

Optional

Not risky: This loan would not be a venture loan. It wouldn't be risky at all. I just need the loan to be inexpensive, and I'm willing to trade a participation in profits or equity for that lower cost. I thought this would be ideal for my aunt. She gets her interest, and her money back, and if the company is successful she gets a bonus.

Added bonus: You've been very fair and caring during this meeting. Whether we do a deal or not, I'll let my aunt know how impressed I am with you and your concern for her welfare. If you do decide my aunt can get involved, I'd be happy to work out some way for you to continue to watch over her interests, either by representing the firm or with a seat on the board.

ADAPTATIONS

This script can be modified to:

- Approach any professional who represents someone near and dear to you

KEY POINTS

- Be businesslike and direct.
- Establish that you care about your relative.
- Demonstrate why your offer is ideal for your relative.
- If you're impressed with the professional, suggest further involvement.

CHAPTER EIGHT

Lifescripts for Vendors

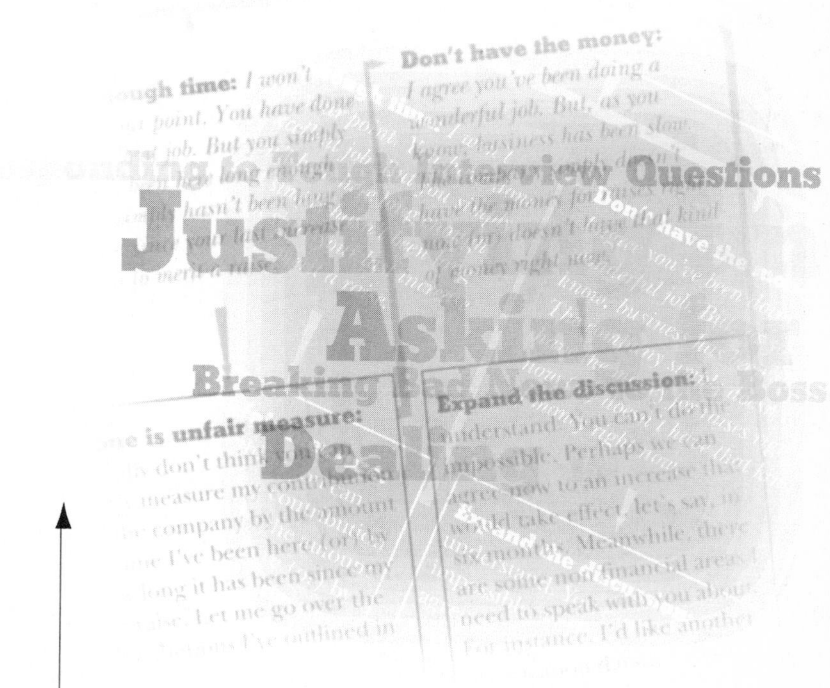

Asking a Vendor
to Reduce a Price

67

STRATEGY

The secret to getting a price reduction from a vendor is to have an external reason for the request. It can't simply be that you want a higher profit at her expense. The external reason can be anything from a difficult client to an outside auditor or an unfair competitor. Obviously, the more important you are to this supplier, the more likely you are to get a reduction. Similarly, it will be easier if this is a one-time reduction. You can make longer-term reductions more palatable by making them temporary, agreeing to have another discussion at a specific point in the future. Make sure you're speaking with someone who has the power to make such a decision. Also, make sure this request is truly essential for your bottom line. This isn't something you can do regularly when your cash flow gets tight.

TACTICS

- **Attitude:** You're not asking the vendor to take a loss, simply to lower her profits temporarily in order to keep your business.
- **Preparation:** The more you know about the vendor's profit margins the better, so do some research. If you find out she has given price concessions to others, your case is strengthened. Also, make sure you have targeted someone with the power to make this decision.
- **Timing:** The best time to do this is either just after you have paid your most recent bill, or just after placing a large order at your regular price. The idea is that there will be fresh evidence of your importance to the vendor.
- **Behavior:** It's okay to have this conversation on the telephone. Don't start out with a threat to shift your business. Instead, present it as a favor from one business person to another. If that doesn't work, ratchet up the pressure incrementally until you finally say directly that you'll have to shift your business unless the vendor agrees. Agree to any vague request for a quid pro quo. It's more of a face-saving gesture than a real request.

67. Asking a Vendor to Reduce a Price

Icebreaker: I consider you to be much more than a vendor *[or]* supplier. That's why I know I can take you into my confidence.

Ongoing reduction: My bank has been reviewing my lines of credit and my margins. They've told me I have to improve my profitability if I want to keep my credit. To do that, and stay in business, I'm going to need your help.

One-shot reduction: I'm doing a project for Acme Cable. They're very tough, as you may have heard. I'm working on a very tight margin on this one and I need your help. I need you to reduce your profit on this one and charge me *[desired price]*.

Agrees: *You're really killing me, but I don't want to be the one who puts you under. This can't go on forever. In three months we've got to return to normal.*

Can't do it: *I've always given you my preferred price. To do any more will only hurt me. I don't think I can help you.*

Temporary situation: Look, I really want to keep on working with you. I value our relationship, but I need your help. Once the bank is off my back we can have another conversation.

Won't do it: *When I deal with you it's always straight. I've always given you my best price.*

Agrees: *I hate to do it, but if this job is that important to you I'll do it. But it's just this once, and you owe me one.*

Extraordinary situation: I've never questioned that. But right now I'm involved in an extraordinary situation. I want to stay with you, but I'm going to need your help.

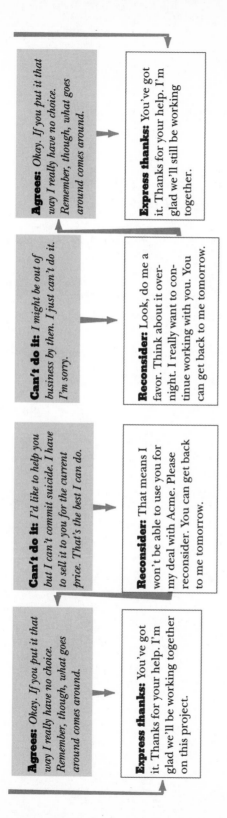

Agrees: *Okay. If you put it that way I really have no choice. Remember, though, what goes around comes around.*

Express thanks: You've got it. Thanks for your help. I'm glad we'll still be working together.

Can't do it: *I might be out of business by then. I just can't do it. I'm sorry.*

Reconsider: Look, do me a favor. Think about it overnight. I really want to continue working with you. You can get back to me tomorrow.

Can't do it: *I'd like to help you but I can't commit suicide. I have to sell it to you for the current price. That's the best I can do.*

Reconsider: That means I won't be able to use you for my deal with Acme. Please reconsider. You can get back to me tomorrow.

Agrees: *Okay. If you put it that way I really have no choice. Remember, though, what goes around comes around.*

Express thanks: You've got it. Thanks for your help. I'm glad we'll be working together on this project.

ADAPTATIONS

This script can be modified to:

- Make an unusually large purchase from an often-used retailer

KEY POINTS

- Be direct and unambiguous. If possible, make a specific request.
- Make it clear whether this will be a one-time reduction or an ongoing reduction.
- If the vendor agrees right away, however grudgingly, immediately express your thanks.
- If the vendor balks, stress that the situation is either extraordinary or temporary, and that you want to continue to use her services.
- If the vendor continues to balk, ask her to reconsider and make it clear that otherwise you'll have to take your business elsewhere.
- If the vendor asks for a vague quid pro quo, agree immediately.

Complaining to a Vendor About Service

68.

STRATEGY

It's not uncommon for vendors, particularly consultants who come into your office, to run way behind schedule or to have problems getting things right. Whatever the reason for the unsatisfactory service, it's essential you get the results you're paying for as quickly as possible. You don't need the consultant to become a permanent staff member or to get paid for making mistakes. The secret to getting better service is to have a concise discussion that first, says you have a problem with the service, and second, probes for a reason. Your goal in this dialogue is to get better service, so be prepared to call any bluffs the vendor makes about your staff, to absorb any criticisms she offers, and even to eat a little crow if need be.

TACTICS

- **Attitude:** Be direct and clear. The service is unsatisfactory. You want to know why.
- **Preparation:** Go back to the original plans or proposal the vendor is working from and see if there's been a deviation. Interview anyone assigned to interface with the consultant to find out if there's a problem in-house. Finally, prepare a memo that reiterates your goals and needs.
- **Timing:** Call the vendor to set up a meeting, at your convenience.
- **Behavior:** Hold this meeting in your office. Make sure it's entirely private and confidential. Speak quietly. Make it clear you care about one thing only—getting the job done. Force the vendor to give a reason for the problem, address the reason directly, and tell the vendor to get on with the job.

68. Complaining to a Vendor About Service

Telephone teaser

Icebreaker 1: We need to have a meeting about the computer system in the office. I'd like you to come in Tuesday afternoon.

Face-to-face dialogue

Icebreaker 2: I'm very concerned about the length of time it's taking to get the system operational. I need to get it up and running. If there's been a problem with one of my people, tell me right now. If you're having a problem then I need you to do something about it, even if it means going out and hiring your own consultant.

Blames your staff: *I know it's taking longer than anticipated. But June keeps giving me conflicting directions. I don't think that she's fully familiar with your requirements, or if she has enough time to put into this.*

Acquiesces: *I had no idea that you were having more than the average problems. I'll redouble my efforts and if I need any help I'll bring it in.*

Blames you: *Listen. Rome wasn't built in a day. This is a complicated system. You've barely been involved in the process and you have no idea of the problems I've had on this job.*

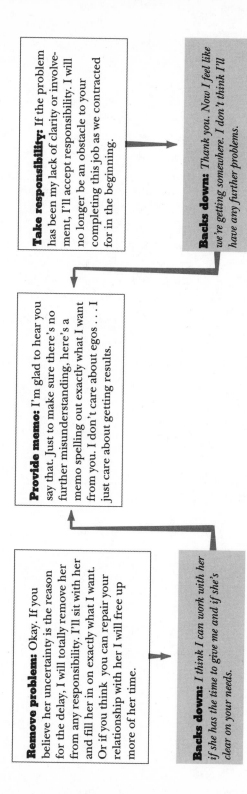

Take responsibility: If the problem has been my lack of clarity or involvement, I'll accept responsibility. I will no longer be an obstacle to your completing this job as we contracted for in the beginning.

Backs down: *Thank you. Now I feel like we're getting somewhere. I don't think I'll have any further problems.*

Provide memo: I'm glad to hear you say that. Just to make sure there's no further misunderstanding, here's a memo spelling out exactly what I want from you. I don't care about egos . . . I just care about getting results.

Remove problem: Okay. If you believe her uncertainty is the reason for the delay, I will totally remove her from any responsibility. I'll sit with her and fill her in on exactly what I want. Or if you think you can repair your relationship with her I will free up more of her time.

Backs down: *I think I can work with her if she has the time to give me and if she's clear on your needs.*

ADAPTATIONS

This script can be modified to:

- Complain to a service provider working with your child
- Complain to a service provider working with your parent

KEY POINTS

- Be direct and very concise. The meeting should have no digressions—just as the vendor should have no digressions from getting the job done.
- If the vendor blames one of your staff, say you'll either remove the person or take the authority yourself, and insist on getting the job done now.
- If the vendor blames you, accept responsibility, say you won't be a problem anymore, and insist that the job get done now.
- If the vendor backs off or acquiesces, thank her, and offer a memo reiterating your goals and needs.

Getting a Vendor to Come in with a Very Low Bid

69.

STRATEGY

This is probably the shortest script in this book. Yet it's one of the most important for business people. Very often, faced with having to bid on a very competitive, potentially lucrative project, business people are limited by the profitability of their own subcontractors. One way of landing that big project is to put the pressure on your own vendors to, in effect, become partners with you in the project. The only way this is going to work, however, is if you can hold out the opportunity of a big, profitable payoff down the road. Farsighted vendors with the ability to take a chance will be willing to do some initial work at their cost, or even at a loss, if it results in a long-term profitable relationship. The secret here is to ask for bids on both parts of the project so the vendor can see that you're not just pushing for a low price. By the way, keeping the name of your own client under wraps could help.

TACTICS

- **Attitude:** Be completely honest and clear about what you need. Don't feel guilty: She's helping you in a marketing effort that will be of long-term benefit to her as well.

- **Preparation:** If this is a new relationship, make sure the vendor comes highly recommended and is established enough to be able to "invest" with you in a major project. Find out who the decision maker is and speak with her directly.

- **Timing:** This dialogue can be held at your own convenience.

- **Behavior:** Have the conversation over the telephone. Be upfront about exactly what you need. Let the vendor make her usual statements about how good she is at what she does. Close by reiterating exactly what you expect from her.

69. Getting a Vendor to Come in with a Very Low Bid

Icebreaker and pitch: This is Mr. Jones of the Jones Agency. You were recommended to me by Sharon Chartling of Acme & Zenith. I'd like you to bid on a printing order. However, before I send you the specs there are a few things you should know about the job. The initial press run on this job is only 5,000 because our client is testing the market. If the test is successful the press run will be 500,000 . . . monthly. I need a bid on both the test and the full runs. Our client is a large multinational that measures risk very carefully. They want to limit their investment in this testing period to the bare minimum. We're willing to run with them and invest in the concept. We need our subcontractors to make the same kind of investment.

We're competitive: *As I'm sure you heard from Sharon, we're as competitive as anyone in the business . . . and we provide better, more reliable service than any of our competitors. I'm sure you'll be happy with our bid and our work.*

Reiterate: That's why we're calling you to put in a bid. I just need to stress that your bid on the initial run cannot have profit built into it. As for your bid on the rest of the run we just need it to be competitive. I'll send the specs along. If you have any questions, call me. I look forward to seeing your bid.

ADAPTATIONS

This script can be modified to:

- Ask for any kind of help from a vendor with whom you have had a good relationship

KEY POINTS

- Be very clear about what you need.
- Consider keeping the name of your client from the subcontractor.
- Offer a long-term, sizable, profitable relationship in exchange for a bare-bones initial bid.
- Suggest the subcontractor submit simultaneous bids for both elements: the loss leader and the profit maker.
- Close by reiterating your needs.

Asking a Vendor to Accelerate Work

70.

STRATEGY

Every service you buy from a vendor has four elements to it: speed, quality, scope, and cost. If you're going to request speedier service, you have got to accept that at least one of the other elements must change. In general, it's a mistake to accept a reduction in quality. Therefore you must be willing either to narrow the scope of the assignment or to increase the amount of money you're paying for it. Be aware that the more advance warning you can give, the less you'll have to reduce the scope or increase the price. Your best leverage in this dialogue is the potential you have to offer additional work, so save that as reward for agreement. Similarly, your biggest stick is taking the assignment away from the vendor, so save that as your final pitch. Avoid getting into detail about why the work has to be accelerated. The more details you offer, the more opportunity the vendor has to look for another solution. You've already made that analysis, so there's no point in getting the vendor involved.

TACTICS

- **Attitude:** Be clear and concise. Do not apologize—that just lays the groundwork for a price increase. As long as you're willing to increase your payment or reduce the scope of the project, you're not asking for anything unreasonable.

- **Preparation:** Exhaust all your other options before going to your vendor. Then, go over the details of the project carefully, looking for ways the scope can be reduced. If you don't find any, be prepared to increase the fee.

- **Timing:** Do this as far in advance of the deadline as possible. The more advance warning you give, the less you'll have to pay as a bonus, the less you'll have to reduce the scope of the project, and the more willing the vendor will be to make changes.

- **Behavior:** You can have this conversation over the telephone. Be single-minded. There should be no hint of the new deadline being negotiable. Deflect initial objections and launch right into your suggestion. Mitigate fears by hinting at additional work or make the threat to take the project elsewhere.

70. Asking a Vendor to Accelerate Work

Icebreaker: I need to speak with you about the project you're working on for me. We're facing a different situation now and I need you to adjust the schedule. I need it to be completed by the 15th . . . and it's urgent.

Can't be changed: *I'm sorry but my schedule is very tight this time of year and I simply can't get it done by then.*

Sympathetic response: *What happened? What's the matter?*

Sees dollar signs: *Anything is possible. You know that. But it's going to cost. You're talking about lots of overtime.*

You're resourceful: I appreciate your problem. But one of the reasons I hired you was your resourcefulness. I think we can work this out.

Vague but firm: Unanticipated outside factors have come up forcing us to move the date up, and there's no option. But I think we can work this out.

You're professional: I knew you'd be able to deal with this. I didn't hire you solely on price, but on your professionalism too. I think we can work this out.

Suggest reduced scope: I don't think we need to include all original art. Canned images would be sufficient. That should cut down on the amount of time and minimize the impact on your schedule.

Suggest increased budget: I would have no objection to picking up the cost of your bringing in a part-timer who, under your supervision, could help complete the job on time.

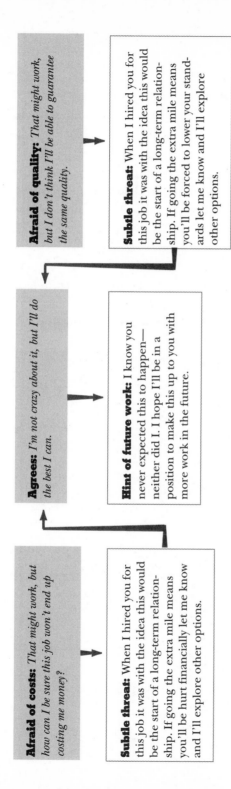

Afraid of quality: *That might work, but I don't think I'll be able to guarantee the same quality.*

Subtle threat: When I hired you for this job it was with the idea this would be the start of a long-term relationship. If going the extra mile means you'll be forced to lower your standards let me know and I'll explore other options.

Agrees: *I'm not crazy about it, but I'll do the best I can.*

Hint of future work: I know you never expected this to happen—neither did I. I hope I'll be in a position to make this up to you with more work in the future.

Afraid of costs: *That might work, but how can I be sure this job won't end up costing me money?*

Subtle threat: When I hired you for this job it was with the idea this would be the start of a long-term relationship. If going the extra mile means you'll be hurt financially let me know and I'll explore other options.

ADAPTATIONS

This script can be modified to:

- Accelerate the work of professionals
- Broaden the scope of an assignment without significant additional costs

KEY POINTS

- Be single-minded about the new deadline, but flexible on scope and cost.
- If the vendor reflexively says it can't be done, praise her resourcefulness and launch into your suggestion.
- If the vendor reflexively sees dollar signs, show that you're open to negotiation.
- If the vendor probes for details, offer vague answers and launch into your suggestion.
- If the vendor is fearful of costs or quality, subtly threaten to take the project elsewhere.
- If the vendor agrees, offer the vague hope of future projects.

CHAPTER NINE

Lifescripts
for Partners

Asking a Partner to Do More Work

STRATEGY

Sometimes, when a business has been established and become stable, a partner can grow complacent. It's only human nature. After the stressful early stages your partner may need a rest. Or, he may grow bored with the status quo. Whatever the reason, it's essential that all the active partners in a business remain energized. If a business isn't growing, it's dying. To reenergize your partner, you'll have to make it clear that you both need to bring your energy levels back up to where they were when you started the business. The dialogue is softened by making it a shared problem, but the situation can't be ignored. It must be presented as a matter vital to the continued survival of the business. You must make it clear to your partner that failing to get reenergized means giving up on the business. Be prepared that he may truly be burned out, and no longer interested in the company. In that case, this dialogue will precipitate a discussion of how to dissolve the partnership.

TACTICS

- **Attitude:** Accept that although this dialogue is necessary for the continued survival of the business, it might trigger the dissolution of the partnership.
- **Preparation:** Develop a plan of action, with a set of new goals, that can serve as the means to reenergize your partner.
- **Timing:** Do this on a slow day at the office, preferably at a period in the day when you have some uninterrupted time.
- **Behavior:** Don't give your partner advance warning of this dialogue. Go to his office to have the conversation, and try to keep him from leaving in order to escape the conversation. You can do that by either remaining standing between your partner and the door to the office, or by closing the door behind you and subtly shifting a chair so that you're between your partner and the door.

71. Asking a Partner to Do More Work

Icebreaker and pitch: I've come up with an idea that I think is going to please you a lot. We both know there's no such thing as standing still in business. If you're not moving ahead you're falling behind. While the business has done well, it has become stagnant. *[Offer some evidence.]* Both of us have been relying on each other to cover the basics too much. It has minimized our energy and diluted our efforts. Maybe we should turn the clock back to how it was when we started off. We can divide up the tasks and each take half.

Reads between lines: *Are you saying that I'm not pulling my weight in this business?*

Open to change: *Hey, I'm always in favor of doing better. If you think this will improve the business, let's do it.*

Burned out: *Listen. I think I'm doing the best I can. We've worked hard and had a good run. Now I think we've earned a rest.*

Shared problem: No. I think we both have a problem. We've been in this together from day one and we're still in this together. I think I've figured out a solution for us.

Regain spark: Remember when we first started out, we'd meet together early in the morning, divide up all the work, and race to see who would be the first to get done? We need to apply that same energy again. Why don't we meet for breakfast tomorrow at the same diner where we used to meet. The business is in a different place now, but it needs our energy again.

That means end: I like the idea of a rest too. But for us both to rest we'd have to sell the business. If we rest while still in business the business will die.

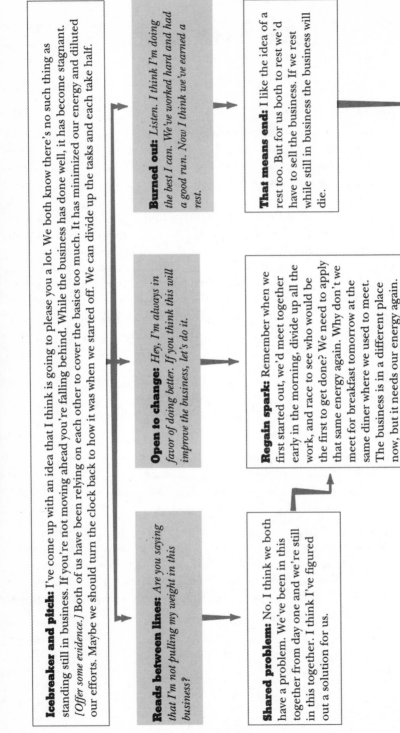

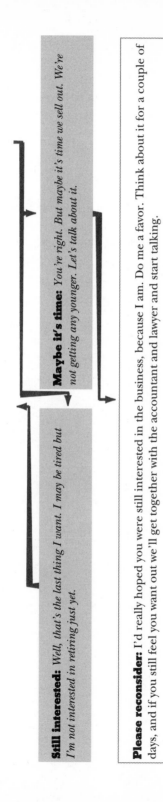

Still interested: *Well, that's the last thing I want. I may be tired but I'm not interested in retiring just yet.*

Maybe it's time: *You're right. But maybe it's time we sell out. We're not getting any younger. Let's talk about it.*

Please reconsider: I'd really hoped you were still interested in the business, because I am. Do me a favor. Think about it for a couple of days, and if you still feel you want out we'll get together with the accountant and lawyer and start talking.

ADAPTATIONS

This script can be modified to:

- Invigorate an employee or peer whose efforts have become lethargic

KEY POINTS

- Be friendly, compassionate, and caring, yet determined to do what's best for the business.
- Present this as a shared problem vital to the continued health of the company.
- If your partner gets defensive, reiterate that it's a shared problem.
- If your partner admits to burnout, point out that that means the demise of the company.
- If your partner doesn't object to ending the partnership, ask for reconsideration.
- If your partner appears willing to regain the spark, present your plan of action.

Getting a Partner to Improve Behavior

72

STRATEGY

If your partner's behavior is somehow inappropriate—whether with customers, employees, or vendors—it's vital you do something about it. Businesses are built on personal relationships. If a partner's behavior or personality is problematic, the business will have trouble surviving. Your goal here is to keep your partner's behavior from causing problems for the business. The best way to deal with this at first is to say that the company (not your partner) has a problem and to ask what it could be, in a way that's likely to prompt the problem behavior. Then identify the behavior as the problem. Rather than suggesting a change in behavior, propose keeping your partner from situations where his behavior is a problem. Expect some resistance, but if you stand firm, your partner will either accept the idea or offer to change the behavior. Either way you'll have achieved your objective.

TACTICS

- **Attitude:** Realize that while this may be awkward, you have no choice if you want the business to survive.
- **Preparation:** It will be helpful if you have some specific examples ready in case you meet with denial. In addition, have a plan that will allow the company to overcome the problem without your partner having to change.
- **Timing:** Do this as soon as possible after an incident where your partner's behavior was a problem.
- **Behavior:** Hold this meeting in your partner's office. It's not your role to explore the causes of the problem. Your job is to make it clear that the behavior is affecting the company and you cannot allow that to continue. Try to keep him from leaving in order to escape the conversation. You can do that by either remaining standing between your partner and the door to the office, or by closing the door behind you and subtly shifting a chair so that you are between your partner and the door.

72. Getting a Partner to Improve Behavior

Icebreaker: Joe, I'm very worried about the business. The last three or four meetings we've had with clients have failed miserably. You've gotten angry at them, not without cause, but we've been striking out. Frankly, I'm worried about our future. Are we doing something wrong? Is there anything you think I should be doing different? Is there something bothering you?

Demonstrates problem: *It's not us, it's them. Those sons of bitches were trying to screw us. We're better off without them.*

That's the problem: You know, what you just said could be the problem. We're in a service business. Whether they're sons of bitches or not we've got to deal with them. I don't like it either, but to keep the business afloat we may just have to swallow some of our pride. If that's tough for you to do, maybe I should go on the sales calls on my own.

Gets defensive: *I'm surprised to hear you say that. I care about this business just as much as you do.*

Gets suspicious: *What are you getting at? What are trying to tell me? Are you saying something about our partnership?*

Agree: I know you do. That's the point. We've got to make sure we don't lose any more customers or else the business is in trouble. I think maybe I should go on these sales calls on my own for a while.

Reiterate: All I'm saying is that we can't go on like this. We're losing a lot of business. I don't want to ask you to change. That's not right and it wouldn't work. So I think I should go on these sales calls on my own for a while.

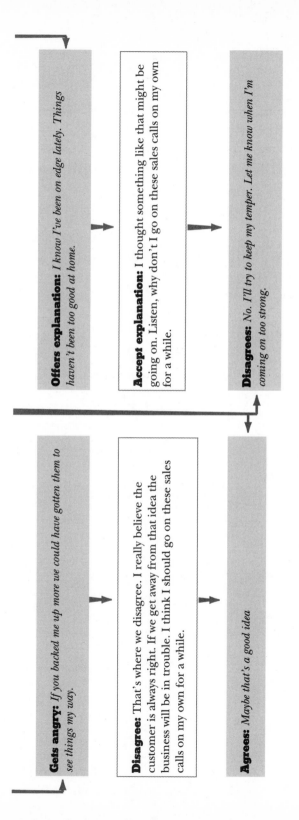

Gets angry: *If you backed me up more we could have gotten them to see things my way.*

Disagree: That's where we disagree. I really believe the customer is always right. If we get away from that idea the business will be in trouble. I think I should go on these sales calls on my own for a while.

Agrees: *Maybe that's a good idea*

Offers explanation: *I know I've been on edge lately. Things haven't been too good at home.*

Accept explanation: I thought something like that might be going on. Listen, why don't I go on these sales calls on my own for a while.

Disagrees: *No. I'll try to keep my temper. Let me know when I'm coming on too strong.*

ADAPTATIONS

This script can be modified to:

- Chastise an assistant or confidential secretary who has been with you for a long time
- Correct the behavior of a volunteer
- Chastise a member of your family whose behavior has been detrimental to your home-based business

KEY POINTS

- Make it clear that this is a problem for the business, not a personal problem for your partner.
- Suggest a way to avoid the problem rather than a change in your partner's behavior.
- If he gets angry, absorb the anger and reiterate your plan.
- If he gets suspicious, allay fears but reiterate your plan.
- If he gets defensive, agree with the defense but reiterate your plan.
- If he offers an explanation, accept it but reiterate your plan.

Asking a Partner to Contribute More Money

73

STRATEGY

There are times in the history of a business when the owners have no choice but to pour more of their own money into the company's coffers. Whether your partner is a silent or active one, the script for requesting more money from him is the same. Make sure your request is for a specific amount for a specific reason, for a finite period of time, and that there are no other possibilities. If the reason is an emergency beyond management's control, the request will be easier. Know the answers to every potential question. The less abstract and open-ended your request, the better it will be received. Finally, realize that your partner has little choice but to go along with the request if he wants to maintain the partnership and the business.

TACTICS

- **Attitude:** Realize that your partner really has little choice but to agree, but that you may have to let him vent; and subtly point out the lack of options.

- **Preparation:** Have all the facts at the tip of your tongue. Know what caused the problem, why there are no other options, exactly how much is needed, for how long, and how it could be raised.

- **Timing:** Have this dialogue as soon as you know there's a problem. Do it during business hours, if possible.

- **Behavior:** Hold this meeting at the business, even if yours is a silent partner. That makes you less of a supplicant and the problem less abstract. Be prepared for anger, denial, or attempts to avoid responsibility. Absorb or deflect such responses by stressing that there's no choice for either of you but to put more of your own money into the company.

73. Asking a Partner to Contribute More Money

Icebreaker and pitch: I've got something important to discuss with you. I just found out that Beacon Inc., our top customer, has declared bankruptcy. I've called the bank and our suppliers to do everything possible to slow down the cash flow out, but unless we do something quick we're not going to have enough money to pay the bills. We each need to come up with another $15,000 in cash to keep the business afloat.

Blames third party: My wife won't let me put any more money into the business.

He's not a partner: She's not a partner in this business . . . you are. You'll have to deal with her. Do you want me to have a talk with her?

Backs down: No, that won't be necessary. I'll speak with her.

It's your problem: Hey, you're the financial guy. I'm taking care of sales and marketing. This is your job.

It's our problem: I'm shocked to hear you say that. We're partners. We're in this together. Are you suggesting we reconsider our relationship?

Backs down: Don't get me wrong. I'm not blaming you. It's just that this is a pretty big shock. Besides . . .

Pleads poverty: What are we going to do? I don't have that kind of money.

Go to others: Neither do I. You're going to have to do what I'm doing, go to third parties and ask for loans. I don't want to have to sell this business because of a temporary problem that's not our fault.

Claims no options: I agree, but I don't have anyone I can go to for that kind of money.

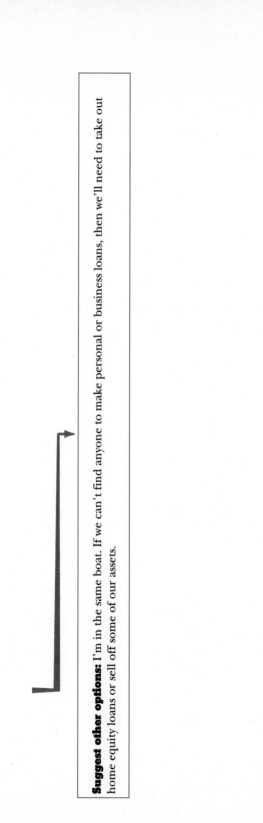

Suggest other options: I'm in the same boat. If we can't find anyone to make personal or business loans, then we'll need to take out home equity loans or sell off some of our assets.

ADAPTATIONS

This script can be modified to:

- Ask friends or relatives to increase their stake in any joint venture

KEY POINTS

- Be direct and determined, but allow your partner to vent.
- If your partner pleads poverty, suggest going to others for the money.
- If your partner tries to avoid responsibility, ask if he wants to end your relationship.
- If your partner blames a third party, offer to intervene.
- If your partner says he has no options, suggest ways of raising the money.

Complaining to a Partner about One of His Family Members

74

STRATEGY

Most people have blind spots about their family, particularly their children. A business person who ordinarily wouldn't tolerate the least bit of rudeness to clients or customers may turn a blind eye to even worse behavior if it's from a member of his own family. But since the continued success of the business may be at stake, it's essential for a partner to bring this up. First, do not approach the family member/employee on your own. That's sure to spark trouble, regardless of how you handle the dialogue. Instead, awkward as it may be, bring the matter to your partner's attention. Generally, all you'll need to do is let him vent, then describe what's clearly a business problem, and offer to take care of it yourself if he doesn't want to. Rather than letting you reprimand the relative, your partner will accept the responsibility.

TACTICS

- **Attitude:** Accept that this will be awkward for both of you, but realize that it must be taken care of.
- **Preparation:** Make some notes about specific examples of the problem behavior.
- **Timing:** Do this as soon as possible after an incident.
- **Behavior:** Come right out and acknowledge the awkwardness of the situation, but press ahead. Absorb anger, deflect criticism, and agree with any rationalizations, but insist that the matter is important and must be addressed. Finally, offer to do it yourself. That should force a response.

74. Complaining to a Partner about One of His Family Members

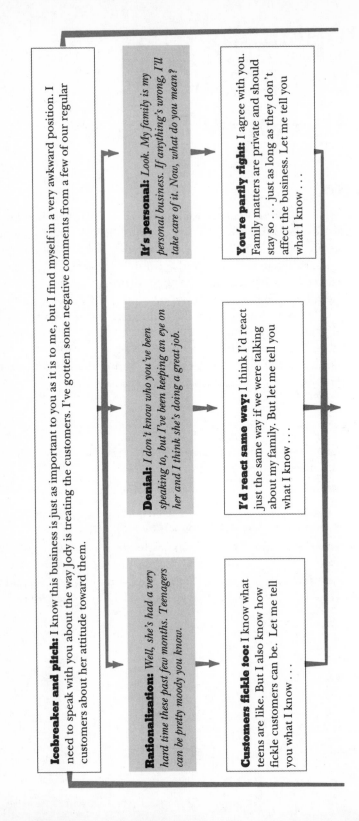

Icebreaker and pitch: I know this business is just as important to you as it is to me, but I find myself in a very awkward position. I need to speak with you about the way Jody is treating the customers. I've gotten some negative comments from a few of our regular customers about her attitude toward them.

Denial: I don't know who you've been speaking to, but I've been keeping an eye on her and I think she's doing a great job.

It's personal: Look. My family is my personal business. If anything's wrong, I'll take care of it. Now, what do you mean?

Rationalization: Well, she's had a very hard time these past few months. Teenagers can be pretty moody you know.

I'd react same way: I think I'd react just the same way if we were talking about my family. But let me tell you what I know . . .

You're partly right: I agree with you. Family matters are private and should stay so . . . just as long as they don't affect the business. Let me tell you what I know . . .

Customers fickle too: I know what teens are like. But I also know how fickle customers can be. Let me tell you what I know . . .

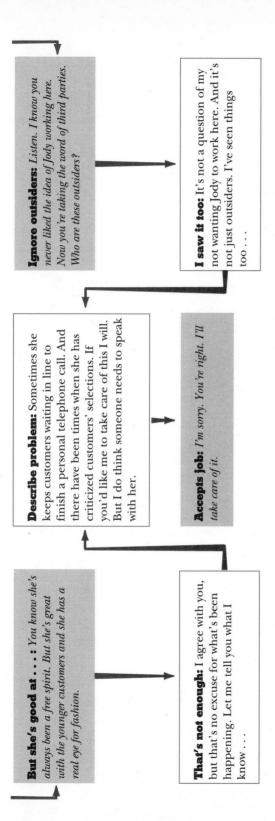

Ignore outsiders: *Listen. I know you never liked the idea of Jody working here. Now you're taking the word of third parties. Who are these outsiders?*

I saw it too: It's not a question of my not wanting Jody to work here. And it's not just outsiders. I've seen things too . . .

Describe problem: Sometimes she keeps customers waiting in line to finish a personal telephone call. And there have been times when she has criticized customers' selections. If you'd like me to take care of this I will. But I do think someone needs to speak with her.

Accepts job: *I'm sorry. You're right. I'll take care of it.*

But she's good at . . . : *You know she's always been a free spirit. But she's great with the younger customers and she has a real eye for fashion.*

That's not enough: I agree with you, but that's no excuse for what's been happening. Let me tell you what I know . . .

ADAPTATIONS

This script can be modified to:

- Speak to a neighbor about the conduct of his child or pet

KEY POINTS

- Acknowledge that the situation is awkward, but stress that it's the business that counts.
- If your partner rationalizes, show you understand, but offer examples.
- If your partner denies there's a problem, say you'd react the same way, then offer examples.
- If your partner says it's a personal matter, say it's a business matter too, and offer examples.
- If your partner blames either you or others, absorb the anger and offer examples.
- If your partner says there are positive elements too, agree, but say they don't outweigh your examples.
- Finally, force the issue by asking if your partner would like you to take care of it.

CHAPTER TEN

Lifescripts for Sales

Renegotiating a Price with a Client or Customer

75.

STRATEGY

At times your original estimate of what an assignment will cost turns out to have been mistaken. If you will end up with less of a profit than you hoped or you will break even, it's best to simply accept the situation as is, and learn from it. However, if you will end up losing money, it's worth trying to renegotiate your fee. The secret to doing this successfully is demonstrating that the project is more complex than you'd originally thought, and that in order for you to do the quality of work you'd promised, you'll need to increase your fee. By admitting you have made a mistake but linking the quality of the job to the increased fee, you may be able to get by with only a minimal amount of anger or annoyance from the client. However, be aware that you're putting your long-term relationship with the client or customer at risk.

TACTICS

- **Attitude:** Realize that you're going to have to admit an error of judgment and that you'll be placing your long-term relationship at risk.
- **Preparation:** Have an explanation for your miscalculation and a plan for moving forward ready before the conversation. In addition, have an answer ready if the client tries to negotiate the amount of the increase.
- **Timing:** Do this as soon as you realize your original estimate was wrong.
- **Behavior:** You can have this conversation over the telephone. Absorb any anger or resentment, but impress that the quality of service is contingent on an increase in the fee. Indicate that you're only looking to break even. Don't press for a final answer in this conversation.

75. Renegotiating a Price with a Client or Customer

Icebreaker and pitch: Paula, this is Jack. You're not only one of my most important clients, you've also become a close friend. That's why I have to share with you a problem I have with the estate plan you asked me to prepare for you. In order for me to do an effective job I've got to bring in a tax expert. Of course, I'm not going to mark up his cost, but it will increase the price another $5,000.

Forget it: *I can't afford that. Maybe we should just forget about it and continue another time when I have the money.*

How did this happen: *I don't understand how this could happen. A month ago you said the price would be $10,000. Nothing has changed. Why has the price gone up?*

Eat it: *You can't make that my responsibility. I relied on your price to get my husband to agree to this project. You're a business man. When I make a mistake I have to eat it. This is your problem, not mine.*

You said you could do it: *I thought you were an expert in this field. That's what you told me. If you had told me I needed an expert, I would have gone to one in the first place.*

I've already done work: That would be extremely difficult for me. I've already invested over 100 hours of my own time in this project.

Not extraordinary: I understand your confusion. What happened isn't that extraordinary. We've just discovered that you're a wealthier woman than you thought. That means we need to bring in another specialist.

Quality at risk: Look, the whole issue here is that I want to do the best job possible for you. I can, if you wish, stick to the original price. But I have to warn you that we're taking a risk. The decision is yours.

I can but . . . : I am an expert. My reputation is important to me and so is the quality of what I do. That's why I'm recommending we get a second opinion. Besides, you couldn't go directly to this kind of expert.

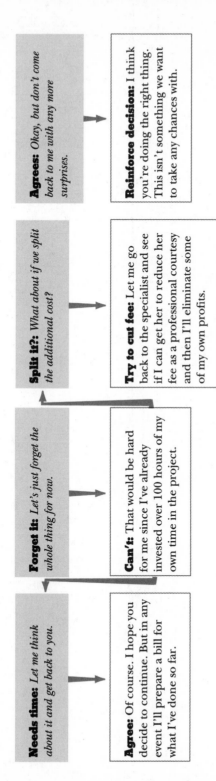

Needs time: *Let me think about it and get back to you.*

Agree: Of course. I hope you decide to continue. But in any event I'll prepare a bill for what I've done so far.

Forget it: *Let's just forget the whole thing for now.*

Can't: That would be hard for me since I've already invested over 100 hours of my own time in the project.

Split it?: *What about if we split the additional cost?*

Try to cut fee: Let me go back to the specialist and see if I can get her to reduce her fee as a professional courtesy and then I'll eliminate some of my own profits.

Agrees: *Okay, but don't come back to me with any more surprises.*

Reinforce decision: I think you're doing the right thing. This isn't something we want to take any chances with.

KEY POINTS

- Stress the importance of the relationship, personally and professionally, as well as the need to provide top quality.
- If the client wants to abandon the project, note that you'll need payment for what you've already done.
- If the client asks you how this could have happened, stress the increased complexity.
- If the client asks you to absorb the cost, suggest that would lead to lower quality.
- If the client questions your professionalism, explain that that's exactly why you've spotted the need for additional work.
- If the client suggests splitting the added cost, respond with a proposal of your own.

Explaining a Delay to a Client or Customer

76.

STRATEGY

Delays are a fact of life in business. But explaining them to an anxious client or customer isn't easy. Whether the delay was caused by your own miscalculation about your capacity or by an objective circumstance doesn't matter at this point. Since delay is now unavoidable, there's nothing to be gained by going into detailed explanations of what went wrong. In any case, the client is probably not interested in the reason. The secret here is to do whatever you can to accommodate the client. If that means cutting into your profits, so be it. To make the delay tolerable, you have to offer something on the promised date. While it may not be all the client wants, at least she won't be empty-handed.

TACTICS

- **Attitude:** Realize you're going to take some heat for this and risk losing the client.
- **Preparation:** Have ready a very brief and vague explanation of the problem, and prepare a plan that will offer the client something on the promised date of delivery.
- **Timing:** Do this as soon as you realize the scheduled delivery is impossible.
- **Behavior:** Have this dialogue over the telephone—you don't want it going on too long. Absorb any anger and accept full and total responsibility, even while noting that the situation was beyond your control. Then offer your partial product or service and explain how this might be sufficient for the time being. Finally, let the client have the last word—it will help her save face since she really has no alternative but to accept the situation.

76. Explaining a Delay to a Client or Customer

Icebreaker and pitch: I'm calling to let you know the brochure will not be ready in time for your sales meeting before the trade show in Las Vegas. We've had a technical problem at the printer. I'll be able to get them to you the morning of the day the trade show opens.

Fearful: *How could you do this to me? You know I've got to have that brochure before the show to prep the sales staff.*

Angry: *You've had more than enough time to get this done. If I can't count on you for this, I can't count on you for anything.*

You're responsible: *How do you plan on dealing with this? What are you going to do?*

Don't worry: There's no reason to panic. The delay was unavoidable and beyond my control. I think I have a solution to your problem.

Anger won't help: Please don't prejudice our relationship over something that was unavoidable and beyond my control. If you calm down I can tell you my solution to this problem.

Take responsibility: The delay is unavoidable and beyond my control, but I take full responsibility for it. I think I have a solution, however.

Offer solution: I can have working drafts of the brochure, without the edited copy, retouched photos, and four-color graphics, for all of your salespeople by the end of the week. That way you'll be able to go over the brochures with them before the trade show.

Takes parting shot: *Well, I've got no choice, have I, so I suppose that will have to do. But you'd better come through this time . . . understand?*

ADAPTATIONS

This script can be modified to:

- Counter any frustrations you expect from a third party who isn't going to receive what they anticipated

KEY POINTS

- Be businesslike, direct, and concise. State explicitly that there will be a delay and that there's no way to avoid it.
- If the client expresses fears, explain that panic isn't necessary and offer your plan.
- If the client holds you responsible, accept responsibility and offer your plan.
- If the client gets angry, absorb the anger and offer your plan.
- Let the client have the last word.

Overcoming Stalls When Selling

77.

STRATEGY

Most salespeople know that to make a sale, you have to ask for a decision. But by asking potential customers directly, you're putting them on the spot. Some will opt to buy. A few, just as directly, will give you a flat-out "no." But most will equivocate or stall, either because they're still unsure, they're afraid to say no, or they need a little bit more convincing. This script differs from most of the others in this book in that, rather than going through a complete dialogue, it concentrates on one part of the conversation, offering a series of responses to particular stalls.

TACTICS

- **Attitude:** It's better to push beyond a stall and either force a direct "no" or get more information so you can close more effectively.
- **Preparation:** In this case, preparation is more a matter of memorizing the responses you feel are most appropriate to your business.
- **Behavior:** Even though the language may seem a bit confrontational, if delivered in a caring, friendly tone, it will simply be taken as a sign of persistence and concern.

77. Overcoming Stalls When Selling

I'd like to add your name to our client list. Shall we move ahead and fill out the order form?

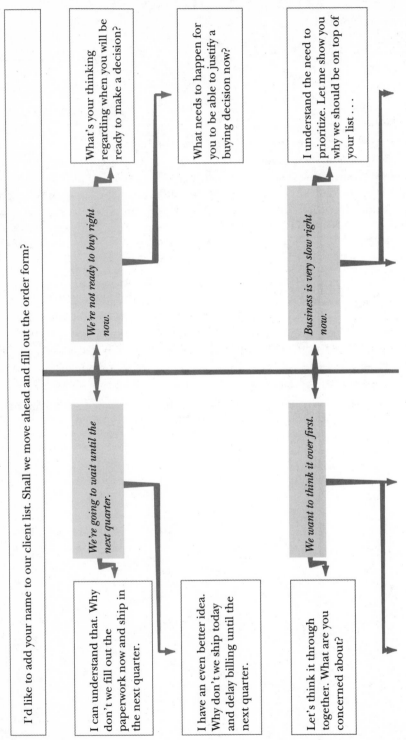

What's your thinking regarding when you will be ready to make a decision?

We're not ready to buy right now.

What needs to happen for you to be able to justify a buying decision now?

I understand the need to prioritize. Let me show you why we should be on top of your list. . . .

Business is very slow right now.

We're going to wait until the next quarter.

I can understand that. Why don't we fill out the paperwork now and ship in the next quarter.

I have an even better idea. Why don't we ship today and delay billing until the next quarter.

We want to think it over first.

Let's think it through together. What are you concerned about?

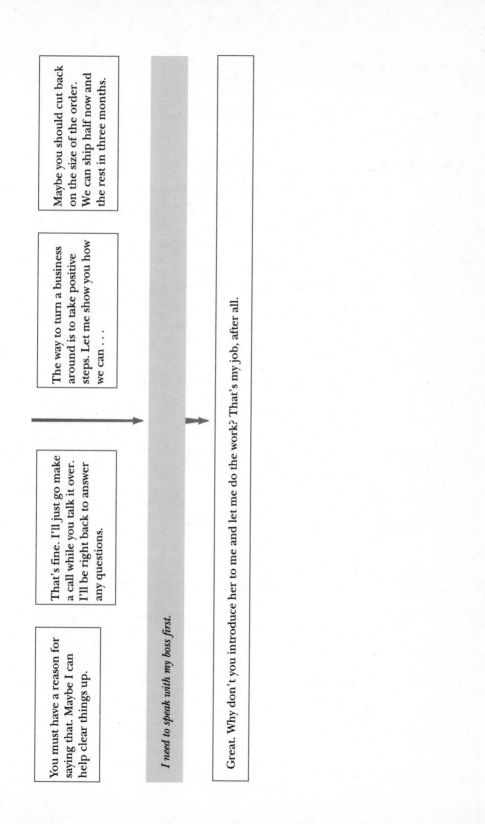

You must have a reason for saying that. Maybe I can help clear things up.

That's fine. I'll just go make a call while you talk it over. I'll be right back to answer any questions.

The way to turn a business around is to take positive steps. Let me show you how we can . . .

Maybe you should cut back on the size of the order. We can ship half now and the rest in three months.

I need to speak with my boss first.

Great. Why don't you introduce her to me and let me do the work? That's my job, after all.

ADAPTATIONS

This script can be modified to:

- Force a client to take an important step that she's delaying

KEY POINTS

- Be caring and friendly, and the response won't sound confrontational.
- If the customer asks for more time, try to find out what the time is needed for.
- If the customer implies she'll buy later, push for a commitment now and either delivery or payment in the future.
- If the customer has to get approval, offer to help.
- If the customer isn't ready to buy, find out what would make her ready.
- If the customer cites poor business, either make the offer more affordable or show how it can boost business.

III

Lifescripts

FOR PERSONAL FINANCE

CHAPTER ELEVEN

Lifescripts for
Consumer Issues

Complaining about a Service Provider's Work

STRATEGY

There's absolutely no reason you should accept anything less than what you've contracted for from a service provider. The first secret to getting satisfaction is not to pay until you're truly satisfied. The only real leverage you have over a service provider is financial. Once you've paid him, there's often little reason for him to come back (unless you could be responsible for repeat business or a formal complaint). The second secret is to reward the service provider's willingness to redo the work with a partial payment. Your goal here is to get the work redone without incurring any further charges.

TACTICS

- **Attitude:** You have every right to get what you contracted for and shouldn't hesitate to complain if you're not satisfied.
- **Preparation:** Make sure you have a clear record of exactly what was agreed to before work began.
- **Timing:** Do this as soon as you realize you have a problem with the work. The longer you wait, the more difficult and expensive it will be to make changes or redo things.
- **Behavior:** It's best to hold this conversation at the work site so the evidence is all around you. It also helps if you speak as early in the day and the work week as possible so the service provider has the rest of the week to make amends. Flatter him for past work, and say that's what puzzles you about this job.

78. Complaining about a Service Provider's Work

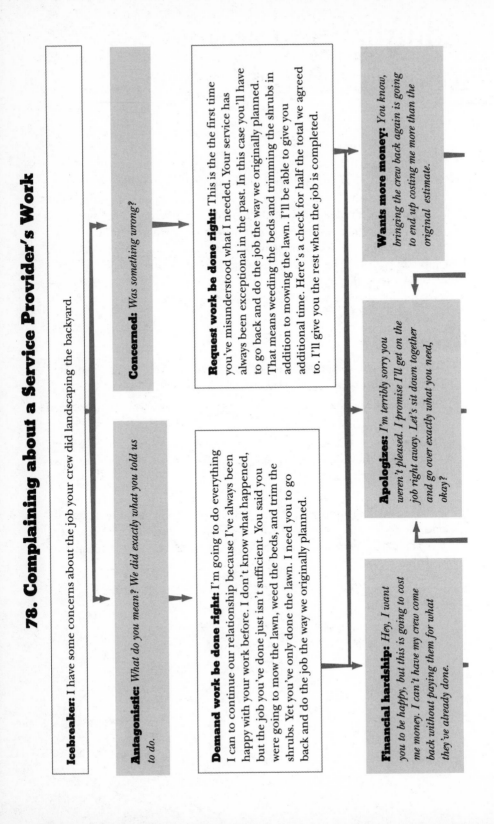

Icebreaker: I have some concerns about the job your crew did landscaping the backyard.

Antagonistic: *What do you mean? We did exactly what you told us to do.*

Concerned: *Was something wrong?*

Demand work be done right: I'm going to do everything I can to continue our relationship because I've always been happy with your work before. I don't know what happened, but the job you've done just isn't sufficient. You said you were going to mow the lawn, weed the beds, and trim the shrubs. Yet you've only done the lawn. I need you to go back and do the job the way we originally planned.

Request work be done right: This is the the first time you've misunderstood what I needed. Your service has always been exceptional in the past. In this case you'll have to go back and do the job the way we originally planned. That means weeding the beds and trimming the shrubs in addition to mowing the lawn. I'll be able to give you additional time. Here's a check for half the total we agreed to. I'll give you the rest when the job is completed.

Financial hardship: *Hey, I want you to be happy, but this is going to cost me money. I can't have my crew come back without paying them for what they've already done.*

Apologizes: *I'm terribly sorry you weren't pleased. I promise I'll get on the job right away. Let's sit down together and go over exactly what you need, okay?*

Wants more money: *You know, bringing the crew back again is going to end up costing me more than the original estimate.*

Won't pay for error: I can understand that, but you can't expect me to pay for an error.

Reaffirm relationship: I think that's an excellent idea. I'd be happy to. Your response has reaffirmed my decision to choose you and your company.

Offer half payment: I understand that. I'll give you a check for half the total now. I'll pay the rest when the job is completed.

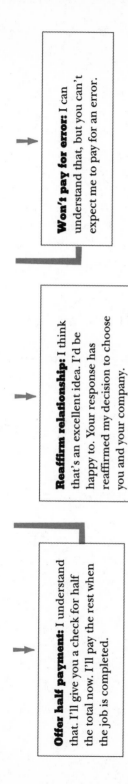

ADAPTATIONS

This script can be modified to:

- Have custom work—clothing, floral arrangements—redone
- Have items reserviced by a repair person
- Have items recleaned by a dry cleaner

KEY POINTS

- Be direct and clear, but not accusatory. Be puzzled rather than annoyed.
- If the service provider is concerned, frame your problem in the form of a request.
- If the service provider is antagonistic, frame your problem in the form of a demand.
- If the service provider asks for more money, refuse to pay for his error.
- If the service provider pleads poverty, offer to pay half the agreed fee now, half when the job is corrected.
- If the service provider apologizes and agrees to correct the problem, reaffirm your relationship with him.

Returning Unwanted Merchandise for a Cash Refund

79

STRATEGY

In today's retail environment, it's rarely a problem to return unwanted merchandise either for a store credit or for another item in exchange. The tough part is getting cash back. First, you must return the item in exactly the same condition as it was purchased, so there's no question that it can be immediately sold again. In addition, you must make it clear that you have no need for an exchange and that a store credit would be useless to you. Finally, you must be willing to humble yourself and say that you need a cash refund, that the money counts for you, and that you're not in a position to accept this kind of financial loss. Realize this isn't an easy task since the policy was probably made clear to you at the time of purchase. You're basically throwing yourself on the retailer's mercy.

TACTICS

- **Attitude:** Realize that you're asking for an exception to the rules and that you have nothing but the retailer's goodwill to draw on.
- **Preparation:** Make sure you have some excellent reasons for not being able to accept either an exchange or a store credit. And be certain the item you're returning is immediately salable.
- **Timing:** Do this as soon after the purchase as possible and during a time of day when the store isn't busy. You want the store manager to have the time to listen to your tale of woe.
- **Behavior:** Don't lose your temper, even if the retailer does. You have no reason to get angry since you're asking for an exception to a clearly defined rule. Instead, rely on determination and appeals for help.

79. Returning Unwanted Merchandise for a Cash Refund

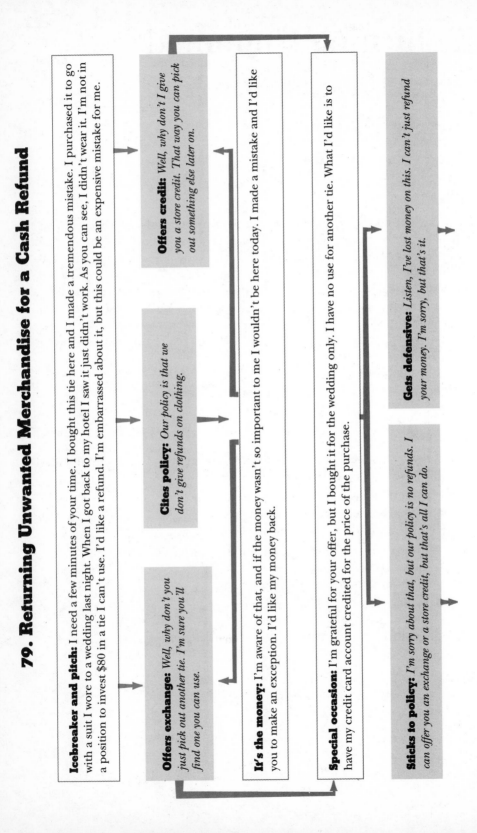

Icebreaker and pitch: I need a few minutes of your time. I bought this tie here and I made a tremendous mistake. I purchased it to go with a suit I wore to a wedding last night. When I got back to my hotel I saw it just didn't work. As you can see, I didn't wear it. I'm not in a position to invest $80 in a tie I can't use. I'd like a refund. I'm embarrassed about it, but this could be an expensive mistake for me.

Offers credit: *Well, why don't I give you a store credit. That way you can pick out something else later on.*

Cites policy: *Our policy is that we don't give refunds on clothing.*

Offers exchange: *Well, why don't you just pick out another tie. I'm sure you'll find one you can use.*

It's the money: I'm aware of that, and if the money wasn't so important to me I wouldn't be here today. I made a mistake and I'd like you to make an exception. I'd like my money back.

Special occasion: I'm grateful for your offer, but I bought it for the wedding only. I have no use for another tie. What I'd like is to have my credit card account credited for the price of the purchase.

Gets defensive: *Listen, I've lost money on this. I can't just refund your money. I'm sorry, but that's it.*

Sticks to policy: *I'm sorry about that, but our policy is no refunds. I can offer you an exchange or a store credit, but that's all I can do.*

Stress financial hardship: Listen, I know $80 doesn't seem like a lot to you, but it cost me a lot of money to take time off work and fly down here for this wedding. Very frankly, I can't afford to lose the $80. Please help me. I need to have my money refunded.

Minimize damage: I realize the damage I did to you in not letting you have this tie available for sale. But it was only for a day *[or]* couple of days. Please help me. I need to have my money refunded.

KEY POINTS

- In your initial pitch, try to make it clear why you need a refund, demonstrate the item's immediate salability, and humbly ask for help.
- If the retailer cites policy, acknowledge he is right but say you need the money and ask for a refund.
- If the retailer offers an exchange or store credit, express your thanks but show why neither would be helpful and again ask for a refund.
- If the retailer sticks to policy, become even more humble, plead poverty, and ask for a refund.
- If the retailer gets defensive, subtly minimize the damage you've done him, and again ask for a refund.

Asking a Craftsperson to Redo Work

80

STRATEGY

Sometimes, despite your best efforts, craftspeople don't do exactly what you asked of them. The issue here isn't who's at fault for the miscommunication, the issue is you're not getting what you contracted for. Your leverage here is, obviously, the money you owe the craftsperson for the work. As long as you haven't paid the bill in full, you'll be able to get the work redone, one way or another. That understood, try to get the craftsperson to do the job as soon as possible. Be willing to compromise a bit on the timing, and you'll be able to deflect efforts to get more money.

TACTICS

- **Attitude:** Don't be angry. Instead, act surprised and disappointed. Anger will only lead to a debate over where the fault lies.
- **Preparation:** If need be, have evidence on hand that the original plan wasn't followed. More importantly, have a new completion date in mind.
- **Timing:** Do this as soon as you realize there's a problem. The earlier you notify the craftsperson, the easier this dialogue will be.
- **Behavior:** Hold this dialogue at the project site. Try to do it when no one else in your family or his crew is around so there's less embarrassment. Since you haven't paid in full, you have no need to get angry. You actually have the power here.

80. Asking a Craftsperson to Redo Work

Icebreaker and pitch: I have a problem with the bookcases you built for me. I was surprised to find they didn't turn out the way I requested. It's unfortunate, but they'll have to be redone. I need them to be...[explain what you want].

It's your fault: *I was careful to do exactly what you wanted. I can't help it if you've changed your mind about your needs now that the job has been finished.*

Now it's clear: Obviously you didn't understand me before. Now that you know what I want, how long will it take for you to fix the problem?

Willing but wants time: *I don't want any trouble and I want you to be happy. As soon as I can I'll come back and redo them.*

Time still important: You're missing the point. The timetable was and still is important to me. You had sufficient time to do it in the first place. If you don't have the time now are you suggesting you'll give back the money I've paid and I call someone else in to redo it?

Willing but wants to share costs: *I'm not sure I agree they didn't turn out right, but if you need it redone in order to be happy I'll supply the labor if you pick up the cost of materials.*

Won't pay extra: It's not a question of me being happy, but of you giving me what I'm entitled to, what we've contracted for, and what I've paid for. I shouldn't have to pay extra for it.

Offers definite time: *Okay. Maybe I can move it up on the schedule. Will three weeks from today be okay?*

Offer closing compromise: I really need this done before my wife's family comes for the holidays. If it can be done in two weeks that would be fine.

KEY POINTS

- Don't get angry. Act surprised and disappointed instead.
- If the craftsperson offers to split the cost with you, remain firm that you expect the job to be done as contracted for at the agreed price.
- If the craftsperson tries to debate blame, deflect the attempt and ask how long it will take to fix the problem.
- If the craftsperson is willing, but asks for more time, insist time is still important to you.
- If the craftsperson offers a date of completion, negotiate a compromise.

Getting a Manufacturer to Honor an Expired Warranty

81.

STRATEGY

Warranties aren't intended as fine print documents for companies to hide behind. They're meant as a pledge that a product will perform as promised for at least that period of time. Therefore, to get a manufacturer to honor a warranty that has expired, you must show that, although the warranty has formally expired based on the date of purchase, your personal use of the product started well after the purchase date. The secret to using this strategy effectively is to find someone in the manufacturer's bureaucracy who can make a reasoned rather than a reflexive judgment. That will require you to go through the same script over and over again until you eventually work your way up the corporate ladder to the right person.

TACTICS

- **Attitude:** Realize that this will be time-consuming and frustrating but can be done if you persevere.
- **Preparation:** Have your story written out before the call. Have a pad and pencil on hand so you can jot down the names and numbers of everyone you've spoken with in case you're disconnected.
- **Timing:** Place your first call early in the day since this process may take a while and you don't want to run up against lunch hour.
- **Behavior:** Always remain calm and friendly. The moment you get angry or obnoxious, you have lost. If you're calm, patient, and determined, you'll get satisfaction.

81. Getting a Manufacturer to Honor an Expired Warranty

Icebreaker: Hello. My name is Dale Smith. I have a problem and I need your help.

Pitch #1: I purchased one of your air conditioners last year at an end of season sale. This year, after running fine for most of the summer, it has broken down. The warranty period has officially expired, but since the product has been used for less time than the warranty covers I believe it should still be honored. I'd like to have it repaired free of charge. I'm sure the intent of your warranty is to cover usage of the product for the stated period of time, not to provide a date that you can hide behind.

Pitch #2: I was given one of your televisions as a wedding gift last year. After returning from my month-long honeymoon I began using the set. It ran fine for two months but has recently broken down. While I'm aware the warranty has officially expired, I'd like you to honor it anyway. After all, even though it was purchased more than three months ago it has only been used for two months. I'd like to have it repaired free of charge. I'm sure the intent of your warranty is to cover usage of the product for the stated period of time, not to provide a date that you can hide behind.

Denies request: *I'm sorry but company policy very clearly states that the warranty period begins on the date of purchase. All I can do is suggest a service shop in your area.*

Express thanks: I understand that your powers are limited in these matters. Thank you for listening to me. I'd appreciate it if you could give me the name of your supervisor and connect me to him or her. I'll be sure to mention how helpful you've been.

Makes connection: *My supervisor's name is Penny Penurious. Her extension is 666. If you hold on I'll connect you.*

KEY POINTS

- Be calm, friendly, and determined.
- State your case clearly and fully.
- Specifically state what you want from the company.
- Each time someone turns you down, thank him for his time, ask to be connected to his superior, and note that you'll report how well you were treated.
- Keep moving up the ladder until you get satisfaction.

Appealing a
Bureaucratic Decision

82

STRATEGY

Bureaucratic decisions, particularly those made by businesses, aren't based on legal grounds. While there are always a series of rules, regulations, policies, and procedures that must be followed, in the final analysis bureaucratic decisions are made on a cost/benefit basis. That's why you can push the up button in a bureaucracy all the way until you reach the executive suite. There is a series of secrets to making these appeals work. First, always be polite and compliment everyone you speak with. Second, insist on your right to present your argument and to appeal decisions up the ladder. Third, always get names and use them and your own so as to personalize the exchange. Lastly, realize your final leverage is pursuing matters legally. Most businesses would prefer to settle, regardless of the facts, than pursue the cost of a legal defense, even in small claims court. However, legal threats will work only when you have exhausted all other avenues of appeal. Only that demonstrates that you have the persistence to actually take the company to court.

TACTICS

- **Attitude:** Realize that this will be time-consuming and frustrating but can be done if you persevere.
- **Preparation:** Have your story written out prior to the call. Have a pad and pencil on hand so you can jot down the names and numbers of everyone you have spoken with in case you're disconnected.
- **Timing:** Place your first call early in the day since this process may take a while and you don't want to run up against lunch hour.
- **Behavior:** Always remain calm and friendly. The moment you get angry or obnoxious, you've lost. If you're calm, patient, and determined, you'll get satisfaction. If you're offered a compromise settlement, negotiate and accept.

82. Appealing a Bureaucratic Decision

Rejection: I'm sorry, Mr. Smith. I understand what you're saying but we're unable to help you. Your claim has still been denied.

Push the up button: I understand, Mrs. Jackson. I want to express my appreciation for all your efforts in processing the claim quickly. I know you've done your best to serve me, but this matter is important to me. I'm going to have to take this to the next level. May I have the name of your supervisor or manager?

Offers name: *My supervisor's name is Ron Wilson and he's at extension 555. If you hold on I'll connect you.*

Appeal #1: Mr. Wilson, my name is John Smith. I'm calling at the suggestion of Mrs. Jackson in your claims department. I'm calling to discuss the rejection of my claim, file number 14850.

Offers chance to argue: *On what basis do you think we should overturn our original decision?*

Present argument: Thank you for the opportunity to present my case. I believe that . . . [present argument].

Rejects argument: *I'm sorry. There's nothing I can do in this matter Mr. Smith.*

Outright no: *I've read your file, Mr. Smith, and Mrs. Jackson was correct in turning you down. There's nothing I can do but sustain his decision.*

Ask for hearing: First, I want to tell you that Mrs. Jackson treated me very well. If what you're saying is that you're rejecting me out of hand, we can both save time by your connecting me directly to your supervisor. But I appreciate the opportunity to explain my position.

Offers compromise: *You do have some points in your favor, Mr. Smith. I think we might be able to pay 50 percent of that claim.*

Push the up button: I appreciate all your efforts, Mr. Wilson, but this matter is important to me. I'd appreciate it if you could give me the name of your superior and connect me with him or her.

Gives name: *Certainly. The vice president of customer service is Richard Rich. His extention is 777.*

Negotiate: I appreciate your efforts. I've gone back to my doctor and he says he's willing to settle with me for 3/4 of the original claim. If you could meet that level I'd be happy to settle.

Agrees: *Done. We'll issue a check today.*

Praise subordinates: Mr. Rich, my name is John Smith. I'm calling you at the suggestion of Mr. Wilson, who I spoke with at the suggestion of Mrs. Jackson. I want to begin by saying that I've been a policy holder for 20 years and I've always been delighted with your service. In addition, both Mrs. Jackson and Mr. Wilson have treated me courteously, even though they've rejected my claim.

What's your argument: *I'm glad to hear that. We pride ourselves on our customer service. That's why I'm interested to hear why you think your claim has been rejected unfairly.*

Present argument: Let me explain . . . *[present argument].*

Rejects argument: *Mr. Smith, I believe both of my people have acted prudently in rejecting your claim. I'm afraid I cannot overrule their decisions.*

Threaten legal action: I simply don't agree, Mr. Rich. That's why I've gone this far with the matter. I wanted to speak with you before handing the matter over to my attorney. I'd appreciate it if you could reconsider overnight before I go to the expense of hiring a lawyer.

The next day

KEY POINTS

- Be calm, friendly, and determined.
- Make your case clearly and fully.
- Specifically state what you want from the company.
- Each time someone turns you down, thank him for his time, ask to be connected to his superior, and note that you'll report how well you were treated.
- Keep moving up the ladder until you get satisfaction.
- If you're offered a compromise settlement, negotiate, then accept.
- Threaten legal action only if you've exhausted all other avenues of appeal.

Returning a Meal in a Restaurant

83

STRATEGY

Very rarely should you have trouble returning a meal in a restaurant. Remember, these are service businesses that succeed by pleasing customers. If you're not happy with your experience, you won't be coming back. If you don't like a dish, call the waiter over and quietly give a specific reason for returning it (so the waiter can tell the chef and/or suggest something else for you), and you should have no problem. Obviously, you shouldn't eat half the dish before deciding you don't like it. Try to give a reason that's subjective, not objective. "Too spicy for me" is better than "overly spiced." That said, some restaurants don't empower the waiters to accept returns, so you may need to make the same presentation to the maître d'. However, if the maître d' doesn't immediately respond, you can make your dissatisfaction clear in a voice loud enough for diners at nearby tables (but not the whole room) to hear.

TACTICS

- **Attitude:** Don't hesitate to return a meal you're not happy with. You're the customer, and the restaurant's business is to please you.
- **Preparation:** Don't order something you know you're apt to dislike.
- **Timing:** Call the waiter over as soon as you know you're not happy with the meal.
- **Behavior:** Whisper to make it clear that you don't want to make a scene but know how to if need be. Give a specific reason for your dissatisfaction with the meal. Raise your voice only if both the waiter and the maître d' resist.

83. Returning a Meal in a Restaurant

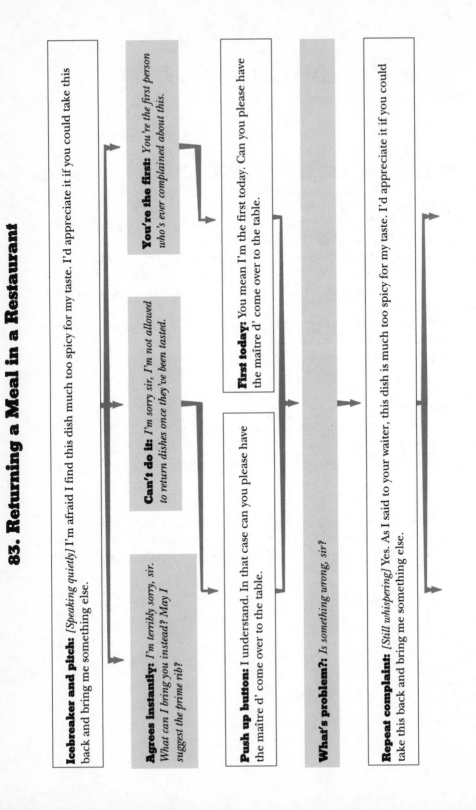

Icebreaker and pitch: *[Speaking quietly]* I'm afraid I find this dish much too spicy for my taste. I'd appreciate it if you could take this back and bring me something else.

Agrees instantly: *I'm terribly sorry, sir. What can I bring you instead? May I suggest the prime rib?*

Can't do it: *I'm sorry sir, I'm not allowed to return dishes once they've been tasted.*

You're the first: *You're the first person who's ever complained about this.*

Push up button: I understand. In that case can you please have the maître d' come over to the table.

First today: You mean I'm the first today. Can you please have the maître d' come over to the table.

What's problem?: *Is something wrong, sir?*

Repeat complaint: *[Still whispering]* Yes. As I said to your waiter, this dish is much too spicy for my taste. I'd appreciate it if you could take this back and bring me something else.

Agrees immediately: *I'm terribly sorry, sir. What can I bring you instead? May I suggest the prime rib?*

Won't do it: *I'm sorry, sir. Our policy is not to take dishes back once they've been tasted.*

Rejection: *[No longer whispering]* I'm sorry, too, because my policy is not to pay for dishes I cannot eat, not to ever return to restaurants that treat their customers rudely, and to warn everyone I know about restaurants that provide poor service.

KEY POINTS

- Be discreet, yet direct and specific with your waiter.
- If your waiter hesitates, ask to speak with the maître d'.
- Be equally discreet, direct, and specific with the maître d'.
- If you still meet resistance, make it clear you won't be paying or returning.

Suggesting an Overcharge Took Place

84

STRATEGY

Whether or not you think an overcharge was deliberate, you should always act as if it was an honest mistake. That way you keep from getting into a debate over honesty and allow the other party to save face if it was intentional. Your goal, after all, is simply to correct the bill, not to make a citizen's arrest. Even if you have documentation that there was an overcharge, this isn't a simple matter since an item of yours may be held hostage. You'll have to accept that if the other party has got your property and you don't want to go to court, you may need to compromise. Your best tactic is to repeat over and over again that you probably wouldn't have had the work done if you knew the cost would be this high. The other party, if he's a savvy business person, will relent and eat the cost. If he's antagonistic, the best you'll be able to do is come up with a workable compromise.

TACTICS

- **Attitude:** You have an edge if the other party isn't holding your property hostage. But if he is, accept that you have no more leverage than he does— if you want to get your item back without a day in small claims court.
- **Preparation:** Have evidence of the original estimate available, but also have in your mind an agreeable compromise figure.
- **Timing:** The timing will be dictated by the other party since he'll either be sending or presenting you with a bill.
- **Behavior:** Don't get angry. That will lead to an argument over motivation and possible wrongdoing. Instead, be forthright and determined, yet flexible enough to compromise.

84. Suggesting an Overcharge Took Place

Icebreaker and pitch: There's a mistake in my bill that needs to be corrected. The price I agreed to for the repairs to my lawnmower was $100, but this bill says $150.

Job was more complex: *That's because once we had the mower disassembled we saw it needed some additional repairs.*

Quote was wrong: *I don't know who told you it would only be $100—but they were wrong.*

Customer is always right: *I'm terribly sorry. I'll take care of it.* [Corrects bill.] *Sorry for the inconvenience.*

It's your staff: That may well be, but whoever it was works for you, not me. I wouldn't have left the mower here to be fixed if I knew that would be the price. I want to continue doing business with you, but I can't assume the cost for your staff's mistakes.

It's your problem: I never received a call telling me there were more problems and asking if I wanted to spend more to fix the mower. If I had received such a call I probably wouldn't have authorized the repairs. I want to continue doing business with you in the future, but I can't assume the cost for your staff's mistakes.

Offer thanks: Thanks so much for your help. Your customer-friendly attitude is one of the reasons I always bring all my work here and tell my friends to do the same.

Pay me for my work: *Look, I just want to be paid for what I did. Your machine needed these repairs. I can't release the machine unless I'm paid.*

Offer compromise: I'm sure you did what you thought you had to do. If the situation had been explained to me in advance perhaps I would have considered investing another $25 in the mower. But I wouldn't have wanted to spend another $50. After all, it's ten years old and a brand-new machine would cost me just a little bit more than this bill.

Won't compromise: *That's less than it cost me. I'll be losing money on the deal.*

Accepts compromise: *Fair enough. That will cover my costs. I'm sorry we had a problem.*

So am I: So am I. I'm not sure I would have left the mower here if I knew it would cost me that much. This is a case where I'm afraid we both have to pay because we didn't communicate with each other.

ADAPTATIONS

This script can be modified to:

- Renegotiate the price of a home repair or improvement

KEY POINTS

- Assume an honest error was made, but insist it's not your responsibility.
- If the other party tries to rationalize the higher fee, insist that's his problem.
- If the other party backs down immediately, thank him and indicate you'll be a repeat customer.
- If the other party blames his staff, insist that's his problem, not yours.
- If the other party asks to be paid his costs, offer a compromise.
- If the compromise isn't accepted at first, stick to your guns.

Requesting Better Service from a Professional

85.

STRATEGY

Far too many professionals forget that they are working for their clients. Whatever the poor service involves—whether they're being condescending to you, are rude, or aren't returning your calls promptly—you should put them on notice that it's not acceptable. Be prepared for them either to launch an attack of their own to regain control of the relationship, or to offer a half-hearted and meaningless apology. You have all the leverage here since you're the one paying the bills. Don't let them forget it; insist that either their behavior changes or you'll change professionals.

TACTICS

- **Attitude:** If you're paying the bills, you're the boss, regardless of how much more the pro may know about his field.
- **Preparation:** Have examples of the offending behavior in mind before the meeting.
- **Timing:** Do this as soon after poor service as possible. The best time is when you've just received, but haven't yet paid, a bill for services.
- **Behavior:** If possible, have this conversation face to face in your office or home so his status is clear. If that's impossible, have the dialogue over the telephone. *Do not* go to his office or place of business. That will just reaffirm his sense of mastery.

85. Requesting Better Service from a Professional

Icebreaker: Our relationship is important to me and something disquieting has happened that I need to speak to you about.

Open to conversation: *Our relationship is important to me too. What do you think is wrong with it?*

Attacks: *I've been meaning to speak with you, too. Your checks have been coming late and you've built up quite an outstanding balance. I need you to pay more promptly.*

Stonewalls: *I can't imagine what you mean. Everything we've worked on has turned out very well, I thought.*

Regain control: What you've just said is indicative of the problem: your attitude.

Voice complaint: I think sometimes you forget that you're working for me and are supposed to be responsive to my needs and wants. For example, it took you three days to return the telephone call to set up this meeting.

Accepts criticism: *I'm so glad you called this to my attention. You're one of my most important clients. I value our relationship. I promise you it won't happen again.*

Won't back down: *I'm afraid I'm very busy and my time is much in demand. You're expecting too much from me.*

Offers half apology: *I'm sorry you feel that way. That isn't my intent. But honestly, I'm doing the best I can. I'm very busy and sometimes it takes time to get back to people.*

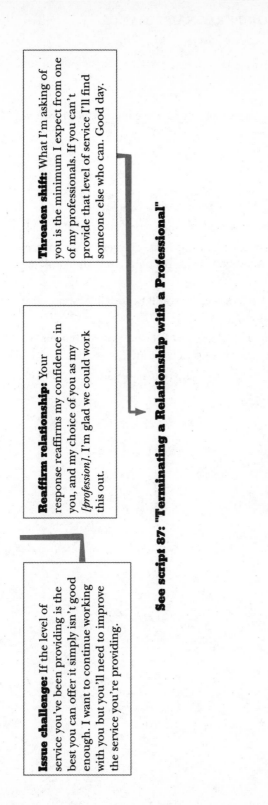

Issue challenge: If the level of service you've been providing is the best you can offer it simply isn't good enough. I want to continue working with you but you'll need to improve the service you're providing.

Reaffirm relationship: Your response reaffirms my confidence in you, and my choice of you as my *[profession]*. I'm glad we could work this out.

Threaten shift: What I'm asking of you is the minimum I expect from one of my professionals. If you can't provide that level of service I'll find someone else who can. Good day.

See script 87: "Terminating a Relationship with a Professional"

ADAPTATIONS

This script can be modified to:

- Speak with higher-ups at an organization or bureaucracy after you've worked your way up the ladder

KEY POINTS

- Be clear from the beginning that the relationship is in jeopardy.
- If the professional is open to conversation, voice your complaint.
- If the professional stonewalls or counterattacks, reassert your control by indicating that what just occurred is the problem, and then voicing your complaint.
- If the professional refuses to back down, say you'll be looking for another professional and end the dialogue.
- If the professional offers a half apology, put him on notice that his behavior must improve for the relationship to continue.
- If the professional accepts your criticism, reaffirm your relationship with him.

Setting a Professional's Fee

86

STRATEGY

No professional wants to lower his hourly fee since that's an admission his skills aren't as valuable as he has claimed. But it is possible to negotiate professional fees by taking into account options that don't require a reduction of the hourly rate. For instance, work can be delegated to lower-priced subordinates, or the time frame could be accelerated. It's also possible for a ceiling to be set on the fee, forcing the professional to be cost-conscious throughout the process. The best way to get a professional to negotiate in this manner is to note that you'd like to use him, but simply can't spend what he is asking, and would like him to recommend someone else. This lets the professional save face by suggesting staff or time reductions, or avoid having to say your job isn't worth his time. You can try to change his mind by implying that you'll be a source of future business or by suggesting time and staff savings yourself. Finally, after putting this much effort into the dialogue, insist on an answer during this meeting.

TACTICS

- **Attitude:** Never assail a professional's hourly fee. Instead, see if you can cut his hours or have lower-cost staffers do more of the work.
- **Preparation:** Have a ceiling in mind of what you're willing to spend on this project.
- **Timing:** Negotiate fees only after you're satisfied this is the person you want. This is a time-consuming, complicated dialogue that you don't want to go through every day.
- **Behavior:** The reason for price reductions should always be your willingness and ability to pay. That way you never question the price the professional has put on his services. Be direct, polite, and determined. But if you're turned down twice, don't ask again.

86. Setting a Professional's Fee

Icebreaker: You're one of the leading candidates for the job. If we can agree on a fee and a timetable that work for me I'd like to retain you. What is your hourly fee?

Quotes fee: *My hourly fee is $150. Work delegated to my associate is billed at $100 an hour. Work done by our nonprofessional staff is billed at $75 an hour.*

Ask for time frame: I'm not going to question your estimation of your worth. I guess the important question is how many hours do you think you'll be working on this project?

Quotes time frame: *Based on my past experiences, and barring unforeseen complications, I'd say this project will require ten hours of my time.*

Ask for recommendation: I don't know that I want to invest that kind of money in a project like this. Maybe I don't need someone as experienced as you. Can you recommend someone else who might be more appropriate for this project?

Offers name: *Why don't you give Judy Jones a call. I've worked with her and she's an excellent young professional.*

Saves face with staff: *Perhaps I can delegate more of the hands-on work to my staff and play more of a supervisory role on this project.*

Saves face with time: *Maybe we can figure out ways to accelerate the process so I don't need to spend quite that much time on the project.*

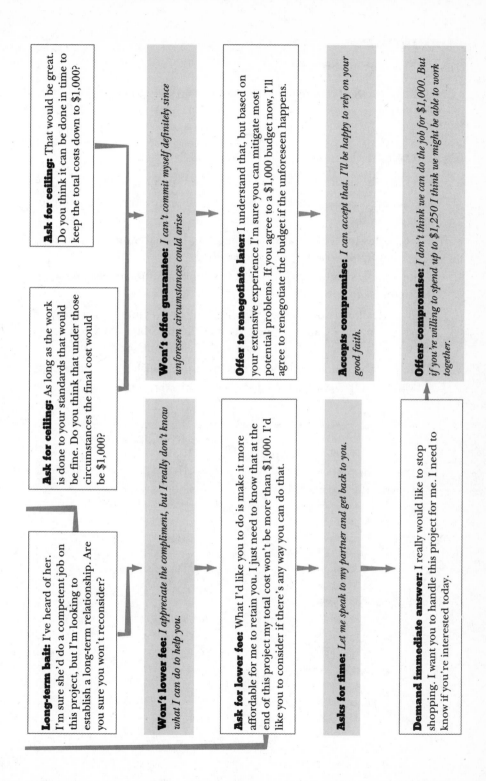

Long-term bait: I've heard of her. I'm sure she'd do a competent job on this project, but I'm looking to establish a long-term relationship. Are you sure you won't reconsider?

Ask for ceiling: As long as the work is done to your standards that would be fine. Do you think that under those circumstances the final cost would be $1,000?

Ask for ceiling: That would be great. Do you think it can be done in time to keep the total costs down to $1,000?

Won't lower fee: *I appreciate the compliment, but I really don't know what I can do to help you.*

Won't offer guarantee: *I can't commit myself definitely since unforeseen circumstances could arise.*

Ask for lower fee: What I'd like you to do is make it more affordable for me to retain you. I just need to know that at the end of this project my total cost won't be more than $1,000. I'd like you to consider if there's any way you can do that.

Offer to renegotiate later: I understand that, but based on your extensive experience I'm sure you can mitigate most potential problems. If you agree to a $1,000 budget now, I'll agree to renegotiate the budget if the unforeseen happens.

Asks for time: *Let me speak to my partner and get back to you.*

Accepts compromise: *I can accept that. I'll be happy to rely on your good faith.*

Demand immediate answer: I really would like to stop shopping. I want you to handle this project for me. I need to know if you're interested today.

Offers compromise: *I don't think we can do the job for $1,000. But if you're willing to spend up to $1,250 I think we might be able to work together.*

ADAPTATIONS

This script can be modified to:

- Set the fees of artists, decorators, designers, photographers, and other professionals

KEY POINTS

- Ascertain the hourly fee and the number of hours required.
- Ask for a recommendation of a lower-priced professional, blaming your budget, not the fee.
- If the professional saves face by suggesting delegating more to staff or streamlining the schedule, ask for a ceiling.
- If the professional won't provide a firm ceiling, offer to renegotiate if the unforeseen happens.
- If the professional doesn't suggest delegating or streamlining, but instead offers the name of another pro, dangle the possibility of a long-term relationship and suggest delegating and streamlining on your own.
- If the professional asks for time to think it over, push for an immediate decision, but be open to a compromise.

Terminating a Relationship with a Professional

87.

STRATEGY

Terminating a professional is more difficult than firing an employee. That's because your relationship with a professional is more intimate. He knows a great deal about your legal and financial life. It's possible you have developed a personal bond as well. If this termination isn't handled well, your former professional can make life difficult for you by holding onto your records and papers and procrastinating about any pending issues. The best strategy in this situation is to try to separate your personal and professional relationships. By saying you want to maintain your personal relationship, you keep from attacking the professional as a person and you also maintain some leverage, increasing the chance of a smooth transition. You also may want to drop the name of your spouse or partner during the dialogue, demonstrating that he isn't an avenue for an appeal.

TACTICS

- **Attitude:** Realize this will be awkward and uncomfortable for both of you, but the sooner it's done, the better off for all.
- **Preparation:** Have another professional already lined up so there's no turning back. Discuss the issue with your spouse or partner so he can't be approached with appeals.
- **Timing:** Hold this conversation as soon as you have lined up a replacement. Do this before office hours if possible. If not, do it as early in the day as you can.
- **Behavior:** This conversation is best done over the telephone. Just make sure you call the professional's place of business rather than his home. That will support your contention that this is strictly a business matter.

87. Terminating a Relationship with a Professional

Icebreaker and pitch: I have two important things to discuss with you. First, I need to end our professional relationship. Second, but equally important, I need to continue our personal relationship.

Antagonistic: *I'm not really surprised. But how do you expect us to remain friends when you're basically taking food out of my child's mouth?*

Aren't we friends?: I never thought our relationship was dependent on my paying you money. It simply would be better for me if I have someone else handling my account. *[Spouse or partner]* and I have found someone else to take the job on. You'll be getting a call from him in the next couple of days.

Seeks confrontation: *Are you firing me?*

Let's stay friends: Let me make myself clear. I want to continue our relationship but on a nonprofessional level. It would be better for me if I have someone else handling my account. *[Spouse or partner]* and I have found someone else to take the job on. You'll be getting a call from him in the next couple of days.

Seeks clarification: *What have I done wrong? You're one of my most important clients.*

Poor chemistry: It's not a question of right and wrong. It's a question of chemistry. Our professional relationship isn't working out for me. *[Spouse or partner]* and I have found someone else to take the job on. You'll be getting a call from him in the next couple of days.

Second chance: *Isn't there something I can do to get you to reconsider?*

Assigns blame: *Is this [spouse or partner]'s idea?*

No blame: I can't say it's any one person's idea. However, I can tell you we're both in accord.

Not rash: We've been thinking about this for the past month and weighing all our options. So I'm afraid the answer is no.

Gets angry: *After pandering to your whims, after working at night and over the weekends, after doing everything I could to help you, this is the thanks I get?*

Express thanks: Everything you say you've done for me is true, and I'm grateful. I hope we can continue our personal relationship because that's what's most important to me right now.

ADAPTATIONS

This script can be modified to:

- Terminate household help to whom your children are attached

KEY POINTS

- Be straightforward and clear, separating personal and business issues and taking the onus on yourself, not the professional.
- If the professional asks for clarification, offer generalities and note that you have someone else lined up already—you don't want to get into a debate.
- If the professional seems to be looking for a confrontation, repeat your pitch and note that you have someone else lined up already.
- If the professional seems antagonistic, stress the separation between personal and business issues and note that you have someone else lined up already.
- If the professional looks to assign blame or asks for a second chance, stress that there's no avenue for appeal and the decision is final.
- If the professional gets angry, express thanks for his past efforts, restate your wishes, and leave.

CHAPTER TWELVE

Lifescripts for
Creditors and Lenders

Asking a Creditor for More Time

STRATEGY

The key to getting more time from a creditor is to beat her to the punch. If you call her before there's a problem, you're demonstrating that you're aware of your obligations and are concerned. Most lending and credit organizations have standard procedures that allow for partial payments and skipped payments. However, expect that you will be pushed for total payment. Fend off such efforts, explain that your problem is temporary, demonstrate your willingness to eventually pay off the total debt, and indicate that you'll keep the creditor abreast of your changing circumstances—and you'll be able to reach a compromise.

TACTICS

- **Attitude:** Be contrite yet adamant about your inability to pay at this time.
- **Preparation:** Before you call, make sure you have your account number, balance, date of your last payment, and an idea of when you'll be able to resume normal payments.
- **Timing:** Call as soon as you know you'll have a problem paying the bill. The more warning you give, the more flexible the creditor will be.
- **Behavior:** Be as cordial as possible under the circumstances and insist on being treated the same way. When you feel you're being treated improperly, push the up button.

88. Asking a Creditor for More Time

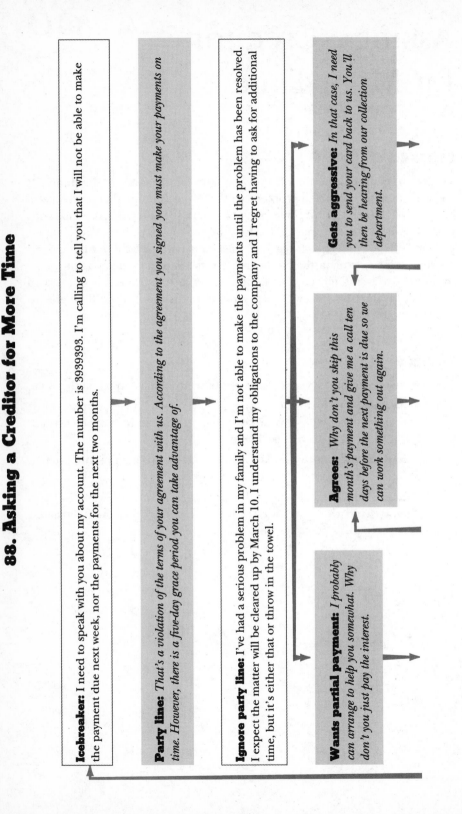

Icebreaker: I need to speak with you about my account. The number is 3939393. I'm calling to tell you that I will not be able to make the payment due next week, nor the payments for the next two months.

Party line: *That's a violation of the terms of your agreement with us. According to the agreement you signed you must make your payments on time. However, there is a five-day grace period you can take advantage of.*

Ignore party line: I've had a serious problem in my family and I'm not able to make the payments until the problem has been resolved. I expect the matter will be cleared up by March 10. I understand my obligations to the company and I regret having to ask for additional time, but it's either that or throw in the towel.

Wants partial payment: *I probably can arrange to help you somewhat. Why don't you just pay the interest.*

Agrees: *Why don't you skip this month's payment and give me a call ten days before the next payment is due so we can work something out again.*

Gets aggressive: *In that case, I need you to send your card back to us. You'll then be hearing from our collection department.*

Refuse: I'm sorry. I won't be able to make any payment this month.

Express thanks: Thank you. I won't be using the card until we clear this matter up. I will keep you abreast of my financial situation.

Push the up button: I'd like to speak with your supervisor please. I think it's unfair for you to react this way when I have a reasonable basis to ask for an extension.

Passes you on: *I'm going to connect you to Mr. Heep, my supervisor. His extension is 2525.*

ADAPTATIONS

This script can be modified to:

- Speak to your landlord about late rent payments

KEY POINTS

- State the facts of your case and say that you won't be making a payment.
- Ignore recitations of the party line and instead restate your case, stressing your willingness to meet your obligations when you can.
- If you're offered a month's grace period as a compromise, accept and agree to remain in touch.
- If you're asked to make a partial payment, refuse, restating that you'll be unable to make any payment this month.
- If you're offered no alternatives, push the up button until you reach someone with an open mind.

Arguing a Creditor Out of Collection

89.

STRATEGY

Being threatened with collection is no reason to cave in or panic. The last thing a creditor wants to do is to hand your account over to a collection agency. If that happens, she will only get part of whatever is collected—often less than 50 percent. And if putting you in for collection forces a bankruptcy, she could get nothing. The answer is to offer all your creditors the same plan, giving none preference over the others, yet agreeing to pay your obligations in full without interest. Odds are you'll get the time you need since no one creditor wants to be the one to push you over the edge. Therefore, this conversation is more a monologue than a dialogue.

TACTICS

- **Attitude:** Be contrite, frank, and clear in making your case.
- **Preparation:** Have a plan in place that will be offered to all your creditors.
- **Timing:** You'll probably have little control over the timing of this conversation.
- **Behavior:** Be honest and direct. There's little you can do other than make the facts of your situation clear, and point out the possible ramifications of a bankruptcy to all your creditors.

89. Arguing a Creditor Out of Collection

Issues threat: *Listen. We've worked with you for the past three months, but I'm afraid that unless you pay in full we're going to have to put your account in for collection.*

Make an offer they can't refuse: The company has been incredibly fair to me over the past three months and I appreciate what you've done. Frankly, I miscalculated the timing of when I'd get over my financial catastrophe. I'm afraid I'm going to need another six months. All my creditors that I've spoken with have agreed informally to give me the six months on the provision that I get 100 percent of my creditors to agree. Since I can't give preferential treatment to anyone, if you don't agree and put my account in for collection, I'll simply have to declare bankruptcy. That would probably result in the loss of my job and you'd have to write off my obligation. I don't want that to happen for my sake, for your company's sake, and for the other creditors' sakes. Please take this up with your superiors. If we're able to work this out I'll have my attorney send you the same confirming letter he has sent to my other creditors. I'll call you tomorrow.

ADAPTATIONS

This script can be modified to:

- Avoid repossession of property acquired under conditional or installment sales

KEY POINTS

- State the facts of your case and say you won't be making a payment.
- Ignore recitations of the party line and instead, restate your case, stressing your willingness to meet your obligations when you can.
- If you're offered a month's grace period as a compromise, accept and agree to remain in touch.
- If you're asked to make a partial payment, refuse, restating that you'll be unable to make any payment this month.
- If you're offered no alternatives, push the up button until you reach someone with an open mind.

Explaining a Prior Bankruptcy to a Lender

STRATEGY

Almost every lender has a policy of not lending to people who have previously declared bankruptcy. That's because they assume that a bankruptcy indicates an inability to manage your life and/or unwillingness to meet financial obligations. The key to making yourself an exception to this rule is to demonstrate that your bankruptcy was caused by circumstances entirely beyond your control and did not indicate inability to manage your life or unwillingness to meet your obligations. By getting to speak with someone who has some decision-making power, presenting a good case for yourself, and perhaps offering a cosigner, you should be able to overcome objections.

TACTICS

- **Attitude:** Accept that you're an automatic risk and therefore will face an uphill battle.
- **Preparation:** Have a simple explanation of your bankruptcy together with documentation of your current and future ability and willingness to re-pay loans. In addition, have a cosigner lined up before the meeting.
- **Timing:** Realize that you'll be automatically rejected, so before you even submit the application, ask for the name of a loan officer and set up a face-to-face meeting.
- **Behavior:** Meet with loan officers and lenders in person. Dress and act as you would for a job interview. Nothing about your manners or appearance should be at all unsettling to the most conservative of bankers.

90. Explaining a Prior Bankruptcy to a Lender

Icebreaker: Thank you for meeting with me. *[Name]* suggested I speak with you. I have a loan application that will be automatically rejected without preapproval since my credit file will show a bankruptcy. I need to discuss it with you.

Automatic no: *We do not make loans to bankrupts as a matter of policy.*

An exception: I'm aware of that, but I also know that under certain circumstances the top banks will make exceptions, and I think my case is such an instance. I declared bankruptcy due to medical bills resulting from a bout with cancer. I've since been cured. The bankruptcy resulted from something totally beyond my control and doesn't reflect any mismanagement of my personal finances.

Sympathetic no: *I'm sorry to hear of your illness and I'm glad you've recovered. You're right, we do make exceptions, but we don't want to take any risks with our depositors' money.*

Offer documentation: This wouldn't be a risk. I have a letter from my doctor outlining my case, a letter from my employer stating how much I'm paid and how secure my position is, and a letter from my landlord stating that I've never been late with the rent, even during my illness.

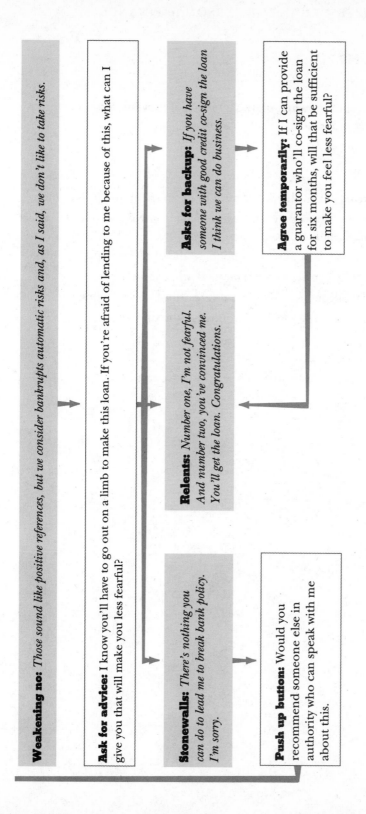

Weakening no: *Those sound like positive references, but we consider bankrupts automatic risks and, as I said, we don't like to take risks.*

Ask for advice: I know you'll have to go out on a limb to make this loan. If you're afraid of lending to me because of this, what can I give you that will make you less fearful?

Asks for backup: *If you have someone with good credit co-sign the loan I think we can do business.*

Agree temporarily: If I can provide a guarantor who'll co-sign the loan for six months, will that be sufficient to make you feel less fearful?

Relents: *Number one, I'm not fearful. And number two, you've convinced me. You'll get the loan. Congratulations.*

Stonewalls: *There's nothing you can do to lead me to break bank policy. I'm sorry.*

Push up button: Would you recommend someone else in authority who can speak with me about this.

ADAPTATIONS

This script can be modified to:

- Apply for insurance when there's a record of previous losses or negative information in medical files that can be explained

KEY POINTS

- Acknowledge your problem but push to be an exception to the rules.
- Show how the bankruptcy was beyond your control and doesn't reflect your financial abilities.
- Offer documentation of your willingness and ability to repay the loan.
- If the lender continues to reject you, ask what you can do.
- If the lender suggests a cosigner, push for this to be temporary.
- If the lender continues to reject you, push the up button.

Appealing a Loan Rejection

91.

STRATEGY

Loan decisions are judgments made on a set of facts. The best way to have such a decision reversed on appeal is to add to the set of facts. That way, you're not asking the lender to change her mind, you're just asking her to reconsider what amounts to a new application. The new facts should address the specific reason you were rejected. For instance, if you were turned down for insufficient income, your new application should show additional income that you overlooked. For this type of appeal to work, you'll need the personal intervention of someone in the bank who has the power to bend rules. That may require pushing the up button until you get high up the ladder.

TACTICS

- **Attitude:** Don't come as a supplicant. You're not asking the lender to change her mind, only to reconsider her decision based on facts you hadn't previously mentioned.

- **Preparation:** Have copies of your previous application, your rejection letter, and your new application with you. Make sure your new information directly addresses the reasons cited in the rejection letter.

- **Timing:** Have this meeting as soon after the rejection as possible.

- **Behavior:** Dress and act as you would for a job interview. Nothing about your manners or appearance should be at all unsettling to the most conservative of bankers.

91. Appealing a Loan Rejection

Icebreaker and pitch: Thank you for seeing me. I'd like to talk to you about a disappointing experience I had with your bank that I'm hoping you can help me with. I submitted this loan application *[offer copy]* and it was denied due to insufficient income *[offer copy of rejection letter]*. I think the denial was based on my presenting insufficient information. I've prepared a new application with documentation of sufficient income and I'd like the bank to reconsider its rejection.

Gets angry: *Are you suggesting we made a mistake? That rarely happens. My advice is to submit your application to another lending institution.*

Deflect anger: I'm surprised at your response. I came here in good faith. I had no idea that you, an important representative of the bank, would get angry at me. I'm not suggesting you made a mistake. I'd just like to be treated fairly; as a consumer who has a valid problem, I'm simply asking you to consider this additional information.

Unenthusiastic yes: *Okay. It looks pretty good. I'll take a better look at it when I have some time and I'll get back to you.*

Stress time pressure: Thank you. I knew you'd care when I made the facts clear. I have another request. There's some time pressure involved. If this loan is accepted right away I can save $2,000 on the price of the car. I'll need your help in expediting the process. Do you mind if I give you a call tomorrow?

Won't take risk: *I'd suggest you bring this new application down to Ms. Jones and let her put it back in the pipeline. You can tell her that I sent you.*

Stress importance: There's another issue here. Maintaining my credit and my good name are important to me; just as important as getting this loan approved. If I'm going to be denied I'd like to know it's based on the reasoned judgment of intelligent authorities such as yourself, rather than the system.

Accepts grudgingly: *I can't promise anything, but I'll do my best. Why don't you give me a call in a couple of days.*

ADAPTATIONS

This script can be modified to:

- Appeal any rejection of a request that's framed in a formal application

KEY POINTS

- Present new facts that address the specific reason you were rejected earlier.
- If the banker seems unwilling to get involved personally, stress how important this matter is to you and how you need an intelligent advocate.
- If the banker gets angry, say you're surprised, reiterate that you're not asking her to change her mind, only to consider a new set of facts, and demand to be treated fairly.
- If the lender accepts your application personally, add an element of time pressure to make sure it's not put on the back burner.

Asking for a Lower Interest Rate on Your Credit Card

92.

STRATEGY

The secret to getting a lower interest rate on your credit card is simply realizing that it's possible. Most banks have more than one rate. And many of those that have only a single rate will waive the annual fee for preferred customers. Make sure you speak with someone at the managerial level of the bank. If you use your card frequently, threaten to take your business elsewhere if the rate isn't lowered. If you don't use your card often, say the high rate is the reason.

TACTICS

- **Attitude:** This is a straightforward business discussion, so there's no need to feel nervous or fearful.
- **Preparation:** Know whether your account is active or not, where you could get a lower interest rate, and how much lower that rate would be.
- **Timing:** The time to have this conversation is before you're about to make a major purchase that you intend to pay off over a period of time—a vacation or furniture, for instance.
- **Behavior:** Dress and act as you would for a job interview. Nothing about your manners or appearance should be at all unsettling to the most conservative of bankers.

92. Asking for a Lower Interest Rate on Your Credit Card

Icebreaker: Thank you for meeting with me. I'd like to speak with you about my credit card account. As you'll see when you call my account up on your screen, I have very little activity on my card *[or]* I have a very active account.

Active account pitch: I would really regret leaving a bank I've done so much business with in the past, but unless you can lower your rate to a more competitive level I'm afraid I'll have to.

Little activity pitch: I would like to be a more active and profitable customer of this bank. The reason there's little activity is because I've found that your interest rates aren't competitive. I'm sure you know I can get a much lower rate from Greater Metro Bank.

Lowers rate: *We do value your business, and because of that I can offer you our preferred customer rate which is two points lower than what you're paying now.*

Lowers fee instead: *We do value your business, but I'm afraid we only offer that one rate. However, because you're a preferred customer I can eliminate the annual fee.*

Can't do it: *We do value your business, but I'm afraid we only offer that one rate. I'm sorry I couldn't be of assistance.*

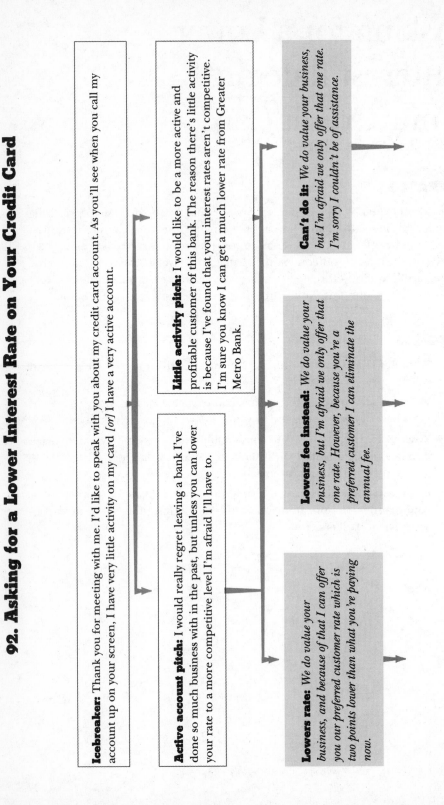

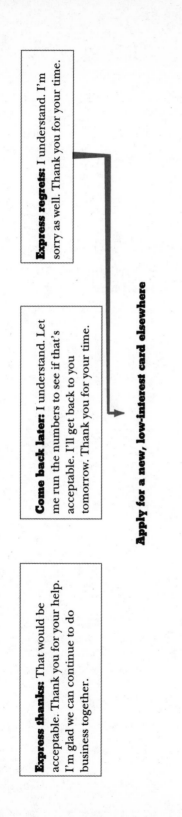

Apply for a new, low-interest card elsewhere

Express regrets: I understand. I'm sorry as well. Thank you for your time.

Come back later: I understand. Let me run the numbers to see if that's acceptable. I'll get back to you tomorrow. Thank you for your time.

Express thanks: That would be acceptable. Thank you for your help. I'm glad we can continue to do business together.

ADAPTATIONS

This script can be modified to:

- Eliminate the annual fee on a credit card account
- Reduce or eliminate the fees on a checking account
- Renegotiate insurance premiums

KEY POINTS

- Directly ask for a lower interest rate.
- If you have an active account, threaten to take your business elsewhere.
- If you have an inactive account, say the high rate is the reason.
- If the banker can't do it, apply for another card elsewhere.
- If the banker offers to eliminate the annual fee instead, ask for time to determine if that's acceptable.
- If the banker agrees, express thanks.

Handling a Telephone Call from a Bill Collector

93.

STRATEGY

Bill collectors are taught to be persistent to the point of rudeness. The key to dealing with one is to realize that her demands can usually be satisfied with a payment plan rather than immediate payment of the entire overdue balance. But in order to demonstrate that you're not going to pay the full amount right away, you'll need to be just as determined as she is. First, insist on getting time to formulate a payment plan. Second, push to negotiate the terms of the payment plan rather than total payment. Finally, call her bluff about your credit report and potential legal action. The former is going to be affected no matter what you do at this point. The latter doesn't make economic sense for the creditor if you're indeed willing to make steady payments on your debt.

TACTICS

- **Attitude:** Try not to be intimidated. As long as you're honestly willing to make some payment, you should have no fears of legal problems.
- **Preparation:** You won't be able to prepare for the initial call, but come up with a payment schedule by the time of your second conversation. Leave room in your offer for negotiations.
- **Timing:** You'll have no control over the timing of either telephone call.
- **Behavior:** Be as cordial as possible under the circumstances and insist on the same treatment. When you feel you're being treated improperly, push the up button.

93. Handling a Telephone Call from a Bill Collector

Opener: *This is Mrs. Jones from National Express. I'm calling about your overdue balance of $756.23. We need to get a payment for this right away. When can we expect your check?*

Ask for time: I realize my account is overdue. I'm experiencing some temporary financial problems. I'd like to go over my situation and call you back tomorrow morning with a plan for an alternative schedule.

Push the up button: I'd like to speak with your supervisor please.

Demands answer: *I'm sorry. I'm not allowed to do that. This is a serious matter and I need an immediate answer from you.*

Supervisor demands answer: *This is Mrs. Smith. We need an immediate answer from you. When will you be sending us your check for $756.23?*

Gives time: *Very well. My supervisor will call you back tomorrow morning to discuss this further. Please remember this is a serious matter. Good day.*

Demand more time: I've agreed you're due the money and I'd like to develop a workable plan to pay it back. But I simply can't do that without some thought. You may call me back tomorrow, when I'll have an answer for you. Good day.

Opener #2: *This is Mrs. Smith from National Express, calling about your overdue balance of $756.23. When can we expect to receive a check from you?*

Offer plan: As I mentioned yesterday, I've experienced a temporary financial setback. I would like to pay the balance off at a rate of $50 per month.

→

Not enough: *While I'm glad to hear you're willing to pay your debts, $50 per month won't be sufficient. I'm afraid I can't accept your suggestion. I'd like immediate payment in full.*

→

Best I can do: I wish I could make immediate payment in full but it's not possible. $50 per month is what I can afford to pay. I want to settle this bill but I won't promise something I can't deliver.

→

Rating will be hurt: *You realize that unless you make payment in full immediately your credit rating could be irreparably damaged.*

→

Aware of that: I'm well aware of that—that's why I offered an alternative plan. What is your problem with my plan? Do you have an alternative idea?

→

Call in lawyers: *This is a very serious matter. Unless you make full and immediate payment we will have to call in our lawyers.*

→

What's your suggestion: I'm sorry to hear that. I thought my offering an alternative plan would make legal action unnecessary. What is your problem with my plan? Do you have an alternative idea?

KEY POINTS

- Refuse to reach an agreement without first thinking over your position.
- If a bill collector demands an immediate answer, ask to speak to her supervisor or agree to a conversation the next day.
- Present your repayment plan, stressing that it's the best you can do.
- Steer efforts to get full payment into discussions of other repayment schedules.
- Deflect threats by offering your plan, or her counteroffer, as alternatives to other actions.

CHAPTER THIRTEEN

Lifescripts
for the Family

Discussing Funeral Planning with Your Parents

STRATEGY

It isn't easy discussing funeral plans with parents. Unless they're very ill or very pragmatic, they may see your efforts as morbid, overly pessimistic, unneccessary, and maybe even offensive. It's never easy coming to terms with your own mortality, and it's even harder when someone else is the one pointing it out to you. The best strategy is to use yourself as an example. Do your own planning and inform your parents of what you have done. Hope that they'll take the hint. If not, you'll have to be more direct. Remember, though, you can't do it for them. All you can do is suggest, prod, and provide information and advice. But it's up to them to take action. It's probably better if you have this conversation with one parent. Pick whoever is more pragmatic.

TACTICS

- **Attitude:** Don't feel as though this is solely for your benefit. By planning ahead, your parents are ensuring they'll have the kind of funeral they would like.

- **Preparation:** Plan your own funeral—it's not only good strategy, it's a sound choice financially and emotionally—and bring all the research and information you've gathered with you to this discussion.

- **Timing:** If possible, pick a time when you'll have the undivided attention of your chosen parent. Don't wait until you're sitting in a hospital room.

- **Behavior:** Be as matter of fact as possible—this isn't about death, it's about taking care of the living. If subtlety doesn't work, be more direct.

94. Discussing Funeral Planning with Your Parents

Icebreaker: Dad, I wanted to speak with you about something important. Bill and I have drawn up plans for our own funerals. We didn't want to put the burden on you or the kids. We just wanted to let you know about it. What do you think?

Denial: *How can you do that? I hate to even talk about stuff like that.*

Takes hint: *I guess maybe your mother and I should be thinking of doing the same thing.*

Unengaged: *Uh . . . sure. Whatever you want is okay with me and your mother.*

More direct pitch: Another reason I'm mentioning it to you is that we've saved a lot of money and aggravation by doing it now, and I think maybe you and mom should consider doing it as well.

Minor guilt trip: Believe me, I'm not crazy about it either. But we didn't want to lay this on the kids. They've got enough problems to deal with.

Major guilt trip: *If your kids really love you they'll take care of it. Look, it's part of life.*

Be blunt: Listen, Dad, we did it for our kids and we want you to do it for us. Please reconsider.

Procrastinates: *When I have some time I'll think about it and discuss it with your mother.*

Provide info: Here's all the information we came up with. Why don't you and mom look at it. If you have any questions or want to talk about it you can give me a call.

Push for action: That's what we thought at first. But then we realized we weren't doing it for ourselves, we were doing it for the kids, so we just sat down and did it.

ADAPTATIONS

This script can be modified to:

- Convince parents to downsize their assets in anticipation of qualifying for assistance for nursing home care

KEY POINTS

- Be subtle, using yourself as an example.
- If your parents take the hint, provide information and offer to help.
- If your parents are in denial, inject a small measure of guilt.
- If they respond with a larger degree of guilt, be blunt in your request.
- If your parents don't seem engaged, make a more direct pitch.
- If they procrastinate, push for immediate action.

Discussing Funeral Costs with Siblings

95.

STRATEGY

If the previous script failed, or you never got around to using it, and you're faced with having to arrange the funeral of a parent, you may have to deal with siblings who aren't as pragmatic as you. If you suspect that your siblings won't be pragmatic in this area, you're going to have to take on the job yourself and present it as almost a done deal. That might lead to some animosity, but as long as you haven't finalized the arrangements, you should be able to work things out. The degree to which you resort to "white lies" is a matter of your own conscience. Just remember, there's little chance for such fibs to be found out.

TACTICS

- **Attitude:** You're doing this for the estate, not the deceased. As long as the funeral is in keeping with their wishes and is dignified, there should be no question about appearances.

- **Preparation:** Do some preliminary research as to what a dignified funeral will cost. If your parents have spoken to you of their desires, refresh your memory and make some notes about the conversation.

- **Timing:** You'll have little control over the timing of this conversation. Try to have all the decision makers together and alone in one room.

- **Behavior:** Try to be a voice of reason in an emotional time. If you need to cut off extravagant expenditures, you can bring in the deceased as an ally. Otherwise, focus on the "here and now" and the pragmatic.

95. Discussing Funeral Costs with Siblings

Icebreaker and pitch: I'm pretty sure Dad would have wanted us all to work together on the funeral and get it behind us as soon as possible. I've made some telephone calls and have found that we can put together a dignified funeral and burial package for between $1,200 and $1,500. *[Note: if a plot must be purchased prices will be $2,000+ higher.]*

Appearances: *We can't be cheap about this. What would people think?*

No price tags: This isn't a question of being cheap. Money has nothing to do with it. We don't want to be taken advantage of by an unscrupulous funeral director. No one could accuse us of being cheap if it's a dignified funeral.

Would have wanted the best: *I know Dad would have wanted a big turn out. Don't you remember how he loved the bagpiper at Uncle Charlie's funeral?*

Deus ex machina: I didn't want to tell you this before, but he did talk to me about this. He said he didn't want to look like a fool like Uncle Charlie. He said he wanted a dignified and refined send off, not an ostentatious extravaganza.

Owe him the best: *We wouldn't be where we are today if not for Dad. We owe him the best funeral we can afford.*

Overpaying isn't payback: You're absolutely right—we owe Dad everything. But I think he would have been more concerned about Mom *[or]* our kids than the cost of his funeral. We can best repay him by looking out for their interests.

Closing: Here's a breakdown of the two packages I found out about. I can give the funeral home a call right now and get this business behind us.

KEY POINTS

- Be clear-headed and concerned with dignity and the estate.
- If your sibling is concerned with appearances, stress that dignity can't be quarreled with or criticized, while extravagance can.
- If your sibling sees the funeral as payback, stress that the best way to do that is to take care of the survivors and the estate.
- If your sibling seems eager to be extravagant, bring up the deceased's stated desire for dignity.

Discussing Parents' Elder Care Costs with Siblings

96

STRATEGY

When a parent requires some form of costly elder care, the financial burden often falls to the siblings, whether partially or fully, temporarily or for the rest of the person's life. Since every sibling's financial and life situation is probably different, what matters is not how much each sibling contributes, but that everyone contribute something. That's why the goal in this dialogue should be to get a contribution, preferably financial, regardless of size. The only issue should be the act of contributing, not the size of the contribution.

TACTICS

- **Attitude:** What counts is that everyone get involved, not that you are putting in more than your brother or sister. All other issues should take a backseat to the parent's needs.
- **Preparation:** Determine how much will be needed, and how much the parent will be able to contribute. Figure out your own affordability, but don't offer that number.
- **Timing:** Have the first conversation as soon as you realize the need. Try to place the call early in the day so your sibling has a full day and night to think about it.
- **Behavior:** Try to be a voice of reason in an emotional time. All other issues should take a back seat to your parent's needs.

96. Discussing Parents' Elder Care Costs with Siblings

Initial conversation

Icebreaker and pitch: The time we've worried about for so long has come. We have no choice. Mom can't take care of herself anymore. She has to go into a nursing home. *[or]* She needs someone to come in and take care of her. It's going to cost about $1,000 per month. She can only afford to pay about $400, so what will be left for the rest of us is $600. We need to figure out how much each of us can afford to contribute.

Accepts responsibility: *Let me think about it and get back to you.*

Questions need: *Come on. She has enough money. She doesn't need us.*

Pleads poverty: *I can't afford to help out. I'm sorry.*

Angry at you: *I'm not going to compete with you anymore. If I want to do something for Mom I'll do it on my own.*

Accepts . . . but: *Let me speak to my wife and get back to you.*

Demonstrate need: I thought so too, but then I took a look at her accounts. I don't know how, but the money has nearly run out.

Acknowledge pain: It's going to be tough for me too, but we have no choice. Let's just figure out how much we can truly afford.

Deflect anger: Don't punish Mom because you're angry with me. This is about her, not us. We can settle our differences.

Keep control: I'm sure you know we're under a lot of time pressure. I'll give you a call tomorrow morning.

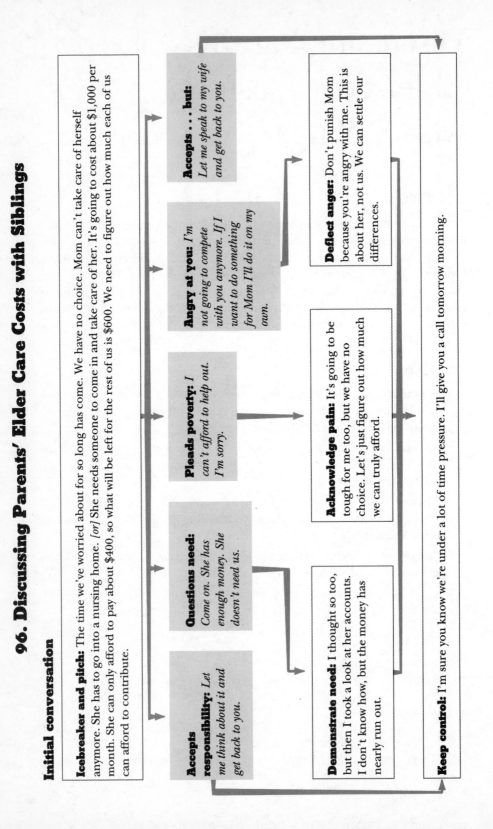

Follow-up conversation

Icebreaker: Have you figured out how much you'll be able to contribute to Mom's elder care costs?

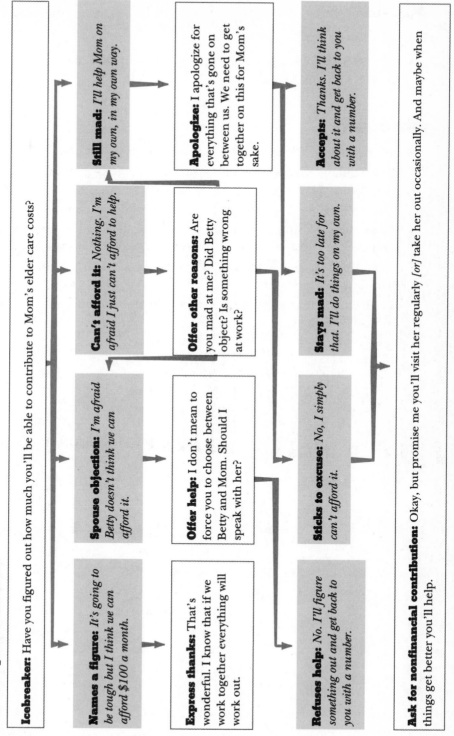

Names a figure: *It's going to be tough but I think we can afford $100 a month.*

Spouse objection: *I'm afraid Betty doesn't think we can afford it.*

Can't afford it: *Nothing; I'm afraid I just can't afford to help.*

Still mad: *I'll help Mom on my own, in my own way.*

Express thanks: *That's wonderful. I know that if we work together everything will work out.*

Offer help: I don't mean to force you to choose between Betty and Mom. Should I speak with her?

Offer other reasons: Are you mad at me? Did Betty object? Is something wrong at work?

Apologize: I apologize for everything that's gone on between us. We need to get together on this for Mom's sake.

Refuses help: *No. I'll figure something out and get back to you with a number.*

Sticks to excuse: *No, I simply can't afford it.*

Stays mad: *It's too late for that. I'll do things on my own.*

Accepts: *Thanks. I'll think about it and get back to you with a number.*

Ask for nonfinancial contribution: Okay, but promise me you'll visit her regularly *[or]* take her out occasionally. And maybe when things get better you'll help.

ADAPTATIONS

This script can be modified to:

- Request help from any family member or friend for another family member or friend who's in need

KEY POINTS

- Be clear and specific. Focus on the needs of your parent.
- If your sibling accepts some responsibility and names a figure, express your thanks.
- If your sibling questions the need for help, provide documentation.
- If your sibling pleads poverty, acknowledge the difficulty of contributing, ask if there are other reasons, and if necessary, ask for nonfinancial help.
- If your sibling is angry with you, ask for those issues to be set aside, or if necessary, apologize.
- If your sibling uses a spouse as a reason for not contributing, offer to speak with the spouse.

Splitting a Deceased Parent's Personal Property

97

STRATEGY

Splitting up a deceased parent's personal property is one of the most potentially disruptive situations covered in this book. That's because some children are looking to stake claims to the love (or sometimes, to the wealth) of a parent at the expense of the other children. Huge fights develop either over who gets the more financially valuable items or who gets the more emotionally valuable items. The best way to forestall this kind of dispute is to launch a preemptive strike. Find an item you know a sibling would like and present it to him or her. This sets the stage for noncompetitive sharing rather than sibling rivalry.

TACTICS

- **Attitude:** All the siblings need to feel that they're being treated equally—financially and emotionally—whether or not they feel they were treated equally by the parent when he or she was alive.
- **Preparation:** Find item(s) of the deceased that are both emotionally and financially valuable that you know your sibling(s) would like to have.
- **Timing:** Have this conversation as soon as you sense the issue of personal property is about to come up. It's important that you forestall any attempts by individual siblings to stake claims for themselves. If that happens, say you think you should wait until you've all had a chance to sit down, and then launch your noncompetitive preemptive strike.
- **Behavior:** Try to be a voice of reason in an emotional time. All other issues should take a back seat to preventing a battle among siblings.

97. Splitting a Deceased Parent's Personal Property

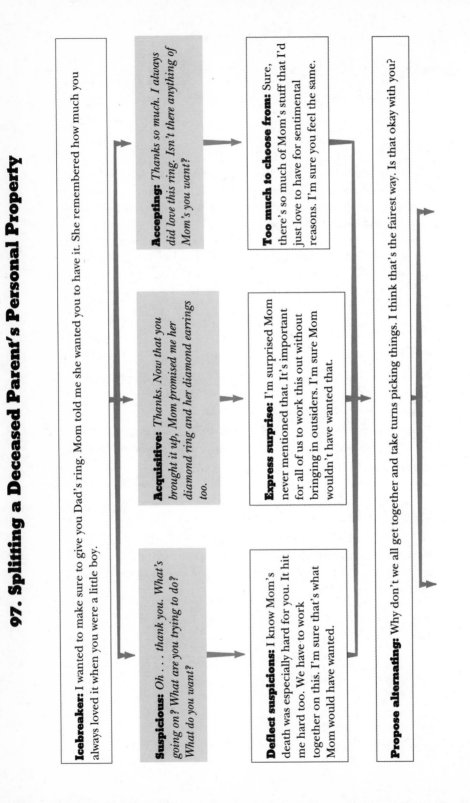

Icebreaker: I wanted to make sure to give you Dad's ring. Mom told me she wanted you to have it. She remembered how much you always loved it when you were a little boy.

Suspicious: *Oh . . . thank you. What's going on? What are you trying to do? What do you want?*

Acquisitive: *Thanks. Now that you brought it up, Mom promised me her diamond ring and her diamond earrings too.*

Accepting: *Thanks so much. I always did love this ring. Isn't there anything of Mom's you want?*

Deflect suspicions: I know Mom's death was especially hard for you. It hit me hard too. We have to work together on this. I'm sure that's what Mom would have wanted.

Express surprise: I'm surprised Mom never mentioned that. It's important for all of us to work this out without bringing in outsiders. I'm sure Mom wouldn't have wanted that.

Too much to choose from: Sure, there's so much of Mom's stuff that I'd just love to have for sentimental reasons. I'm sure you feel the same.

Propose alternating: Why don't we all get together and take turns picking things. I think that's the fairest way. Is that okay with you?

Disagrees: *Wait a minute. If I take this ring then you'll want to pick next. I don't think that's fair. Maybe I don't want the ring as much as something else.*

Agrees: *That sounds fine. You're right. I'm sure that's how Mom would have wanted it.*

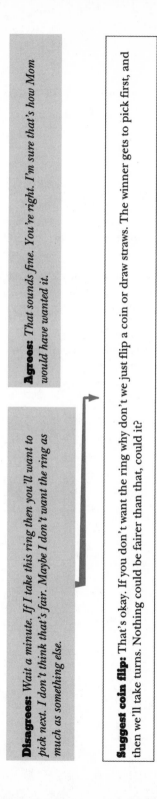

Suggest coin flip: That's okay. If you don't want the ring why don't we just flip a coin or draw straws. The winner gets to pick first, and then we'll take turns. Nothing could be fairer than that, could it?

ADAPTATIONS

This script can be modified to:

- Divide up any property when there's a perceived imbalance of power between the parties

KEY POINTS

- Launch a noncompetitive preemptive strike offering your sibling(s) something.
- If your sibling gets suspicious, acknowledge his special link with the parent (no matter how tenuous), but add that you're all in this together and propose taking turns.
- If your sibling acts greedy, express surprise, suggest unity would have been the deceased's wish, and propose taking turns.
- If your sibling accepts and suggests you select something, propose taking turns.
- If your sibling suspects he has been set up, offer to flip a coin or draw straws.

Offering Financial Help to Parents

98

STRATEGY

Offering financial help to your parents is touchy. Whether or not they need it, they're apt to feel uncomfortable accepting it. That's because it's a clear sign of role reversal. The parents are getting help from the child, instead of giving it. And such role reversal is seen as an indication of advanced age. There are also apt to be issues of pride and independence involved. The best way to overcome these emotional barriers is to present the gift as being of benefit to you, not just them. By accepting your help they're actually helping you. In addition, don't put any strings on the money—that cuts into your parents' independence and shows you don't trust their competence. Finally, if necessary, soften the ego blow by noting that yet another role reversal isn't out of the question.

TACTICS

- **Attitude:** Say that you're doing this because you can and you want to, not because they need it. The onus is on you, not them.
- **Preparation:** Determine how much you can comfortably give and turn it into a periodic payment rather than a lump sum.
- **Timing:** Have this conversation as soon as you sense they need the money and you've determined you can help.
- **Behavior:** Do not be at all condescending. Be grateful and dutiful. They're doing this for you, you're not doing this for them. They're helping you make amends.

98. Offering Financial Help to Parents

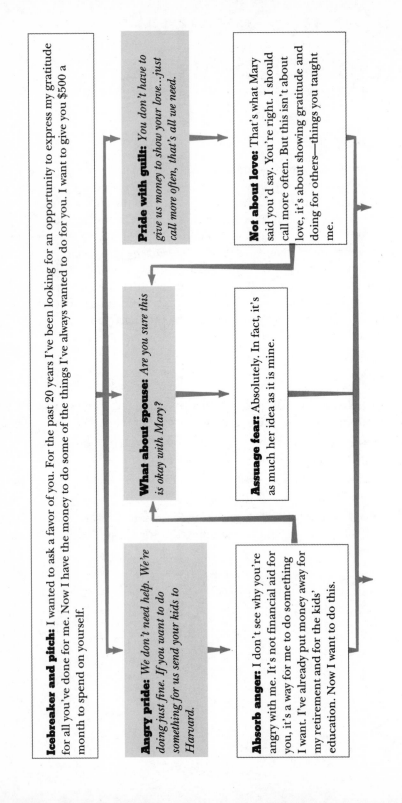

Icebreaker and pitch: I wanted to ask a favor of you. For the past 20 years I've been looking for an opportunity to express my gratitude for all you've done for me. Now I have the money to do some of the things I've always wanted to do for you. I want to give you $500 a month to spend on yourself.

Pride with guilt: *You don't have to give us money to show your love…just call more often, that's all we need.*

Not about love: That's what Mary said you'd say. You're right. I should call more often. But this isn't about love, it's about showing gratitude and doing for others—things you taught me.

What about spouse: *Are you sure this is okay with Mary?*

Assuage fear: Absolutely. In fact, it's as much her idea as it is mine.

Angry pride: *We don't need help. We're doing just fine. If you want to do something for us send your kids to Harvard.*

Absorb anger: I don't see why you're angry with me. It's not financial aid for you, it's a way for me to do something I want. I've already put money away for my retirement and for the kids' education. Now I want to do this.

Still hesitant: *This is very sweet of you, but what if you need the money in an emergency?*

I'll come to you: I've thought of that. If I have a problem I'll just come to you for help . . . as I always did in the past.

Softens ego blow: *Okay, since you put it that way. But why don't we make it a loan rather than a gift.*

No need: We don't need to because it already is like a loan. I know that if I ever needed help I could come to you . . . as I always did in the past.

Accepts ego boost: *You're right. We'll always be willing to help you in any way we can.*

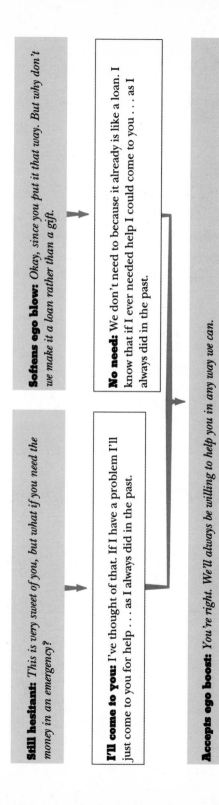

ADAPTATIONS

This script can be modified to:

- Remove pride from being an obstacle to your providing help to another

KEY POINTS

- Present this as something your parents can do for you.
- If they display angry pride, absorb the anger and reiterate your request.
- If they try to use guilt, deflect the attempt and reiterate your request.
- If they question your spouse's feelings, credit the spouse with the idea.
- If they remain hesitant, soften the ego blow by noting that you know they'd help you in the future if need be.

Asking a Parent for Money in an Emergency

99

STRATEGY

There are a handful of important considerations when asking your parents for money in an emergency. First, you must be sure they have the money. There's no way to get water from a stone, and if the money isn't there, it's actually destructive to everyone if you try to do the impossible. Second, make sure it really is an emergency, rather than a simple setback. Third, realize that the more financially responsible and independent you have been in the past, the more you're likely to get help. If you've made it a habit to go back to the nest for help, it's going to be tougher to get now that you really need it. It makes sense to approach one parent, rather than both. While your initial impulse might be to go to the one most likely to help, do the reverse. Otherwise you force a parent to choose between child and spouse. And, by going to the tougher parent first, you ensure that you'll have to go through the dialogue only once.

TACTICS

- **Attitude:** Be contrite, humble, apologetic, and specific in both your reason and your need.
- **Preparation:** Determine how much you need and when you need it by.
- **Timing:** Have this conversation as soon as you sense you'll need the money.
- **Behavior:** If you're going to get the money, you may have to truly humble yourself, so be prepared to prostrate yourself and accept whatever they dish out—that may be the price you have to pay for getting the money.

99. Asking a Parent for Money in an Emergency

Icebreaker and pitch: I probably wouldn't be in this situation if I'd spoken with you first, but I have a big problem that I need your help with. In order to maintain my health insurance coverage I need $1,000. I wonder if you could lend it to me.

Unsympathetic: *I don't have any money to give you. You'll have to go to a bank.*

Already tried: I've already tried the bank. They turned me down. I have nowhere else to turn. I'm not asking for a gift, I'm asking for a loan. I really need your help.

Still hesitant: *If the bank wouldn't trust you for the money why should I?*

Guilt trip: *I never see or hear from you unless you're in trouble.*

Make amends: I don't blame you for being angry with me—I'm angry with myself. I'm willing to talk about how often we see each other, but right now I have a very serious problem I can't solve without you. Will you help me?

Agrees to help: *Okay. I'll help you out. But you have to promise me this won't happen again. I'm not made out of money.*

Sympathetic: *What happened? How'd you get into trouble like this?*

Explain dire straits: I made the mistake of counting on the money coming from a job I was bidding on. The deal fell through and I have nowhere else to turn. Will you help me?

Offers partial help: *I can't give you $1,000 but I think I can give you $500. But you have to promise me it won't happen again.*

Ask for advice: Thanks so much for your help. I feel terrible about this. Would you have any ideas for where I could go for the rest of the money?

Offer thanks: Thank you so much. I feel terrible about this. I promise you I'll set aside an emergency fund so this won't happen again.

Guilt trip: Because you've known me longer and better. We have a relationship. I'm your son.

KEY POINTS

- Humbly and contritely present a specific request, if possible flattering them in the process.
- If your parent asks for an explanation, give as much information as you can, taking full and total responsibility for the situation.
- If your parent tries to use guilt, absorb it, accept any blame, but reiterate your need for help.
- If your parent is unsympathetic, persist, even if it means using guilt of your own.
- If your parent offers partial help, express thanks, and ask for advice on where you could get the rest of the money.
- Provide whatever future assurance you're asked for.

Asking a Parent for Money in a Nonemergency

100

STRATEGY

For an adult, the secret to being able to borrow money from your parents in a nonemergency is to establish this as a continuation of the earlier parent/child relationship. (It's tougher if you're married, but it can be done. Just leave your spouse at home.) Make sure you're not asking for something for someone else—even if it's your children. It should also be for a specific item that would have a positive impact on your life in a number of ways that are quantifiable. It's easier to ask for money for something if it has a utilitarian purpose. Of course, your parents have to have the money or the credit rating, and you must truly need the funds.

TACTICS

- **Attitude:** Be contrite, humble, apologetic, and specific in both your reasons and your needs.
- **Preparation:** Determine how much you need. Have a list of reasons why this money will help improve the quality of your life. Be prepared to explain why you can't go elsewhere.
- **Timing:** Don't have this conversation within 6 months of buying yourself some luxury item. Have the conversation in your parents' home on the weekend to help reaffirm the parent/child bond. Speak with the parent you suspect will be tougher—that way, you'll only have to go through this once and won't create conflict between your parents.
- **Behavior:** Don't get angry, no matter what is said. If you want to succeed, it's better to grovel and be ashamed than it is to be proud.

100. Asking a Parent for Money in a Nonemergency

Icebreaker and pitch: Dad, I need your help again for something I can't afford to do myself. I'd like to get a car so I don't have to take the bus to work any more. That would cut at least an hour off my daily commute. I think it would really improve the quality of my life, but I need your help in order to do it.

Anger: *The only time you come over [or] talk to us is when you need money.*

Absorb anger: I know it may look that way, but I love you very much. You're the only people I could turn to for help.

Still angry: *Do I look like a bank? Go ask a bank for the money like the rest of the world.*

Poverty: *I wish we could help, darling, but we just don't have the money.*

Co-sign: I'd never ask if I thought it would hurt you. But I thought you could co-sign a loan for me.

Fearful: *But what if we need the money back [or] you can't pay back the loan?*

Criticism: *What do you need a car for? I took the bus to work for 20 years.*

Provide more reasons: I knew you'd say that. That's why I've studied the issue and come up with some numbers. Besides cutting time off my commute and improving the quality of my life, it will save me money in the long run [or] help me in my career [or] keep me healthier [or] make my trip a lot safer [etc.].

In-laws: *Have you asked your in-laws for help, too, or just your own folks?*

No defense: You know they wouldn't [or] couldn't help. I can't go to them . . . you know that.

Spouse: *What does your husband think about your coming here? How come he's not here too?*

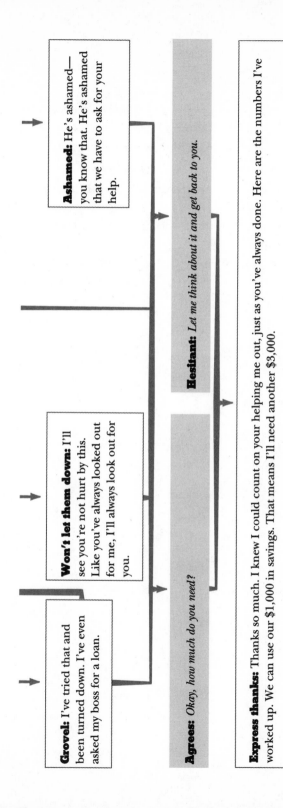

Grovel: I've tried that and been turned down. I've even asked my boss for a loan.

Won't let them down: I'll see you're not hurt by this. Like you've always looked out for me, I'll always look out for you.

Ashamed: He's ashamed—you know that. He's ashamed that we have to ask for your help.

Agrees: *Okay, how much do you need?*

Hesitant: *Let me think about it and get back to you.*

Express thanks: Thanks so much. I knew I could count on your helping me out, just as you've always done. Here are the numbers I've worked up. We can use our $1,000 in savings. That means I'll need another $3,000.

KEY POINTS

- Humbly and contritely present a specific request, if possible flattering your parents in the process.
- If your parent asks for an explanation, give as much information as you can, offering specific reasons why the money will benefit you objectively.
- If your parent gets angry, absorb the anger and restate your appeal.
- If your parent pleads poverty, ask him to cosign a loan instead.
- If your parent is critical of your idea, present additional documented benefits and show intense research.
- If your in-laws or spouse are brought up, absorb the hints and reaffirm the parent/child relationship.
- Whether your parent agrees or hesitates, express your thanks and add further details to the request.

Discussing Wedding Expenses with Parents

101.

STRATEGY

Wedding plans, more often than not, are based on emotions rather than logic. Despite my own belief that it's foolish to let emotions play such a large role in a major transaction, I felt obligated to offer a script for such a common problem. This dialogue is exceptional in being one of the few in this book that centers on an emotional rather than logical argument. That needn't weaken your case, if you take some precautions. Make sure you have this conversation during a relaxed time. Both you and your future spouse should be present so as to minimize anger, reduce the rivalry between the sets of parents, and stimulate their pride. However, you should do all the talking to your folks while your future spouse simply sits next to you in silent support, and vice versa. This plays on the parent/child bond. Don't go into this looking for either a traditional breakdown of expenses or a 50–50 split between the sets of parents. Instead, assume costs will be split among you, your parents, and your future in-laws, based on what you can each afford.

TACTICS

- **Attitude:** Be excited, emotional, and grateful, yet determined.
- **Preparation:** Determine what the approximate cost will be and how much you and your future spouse will be able to contribute.
- **Timing:** It's best to hold this conversation on the weekend, in your parents' home, when you will all have a chance to sit down together and talk for at least an hour or two.
- **Behavior:** Don't get angry, no matter what is said. Acknowledge that your decision is based on emotions rather than logic, but don't acknowledge that's wrong in this instance. View each objection as an obstacle that can be overcome through joint efforts.

101. Discussing Wedding Expenses with Parents

Icebreaker and pitch: We just wanted you to know how happy we both are and how grateful we are. After all, the two of you have been our role models for what a good relationship should be. We wanted to bring you up-to-date on the wedding plans, discuss some ideas with you, and tell you to what extent we'll need your help.

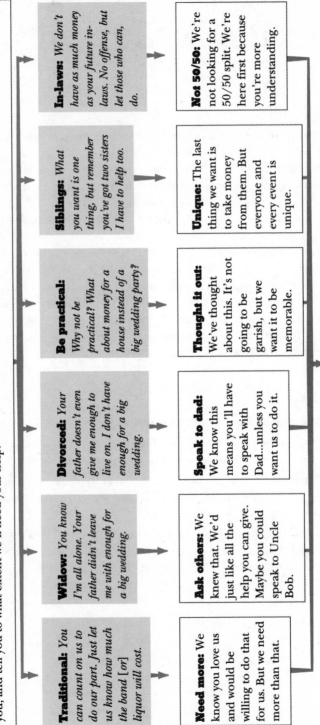

Traditional: *You can count on us to do our part. Just let us know how much the band [or] liquor will cost.*

Widow: *You know I'm all alone. Your father didn't leave me with enough for a big wedding.*

Divorced: *Your father doesn't even give me enough to live on. I don't have enough for a big wedding.*

Be practical: *Why not be practical? What about money for a house instead of a big wedding party?*

Siblings: *What you want is one thing, but remember you've got two sisters I have to help too.*

In-laws: *We don't have as much money as your future in-laws. No offense, but let those who can, do.*

Need more: We know you love us and would be willing to do that for us. But we need more than that.

Ask others: We knew that. We'd just like all the help you can give. Maybe you could speak to Uncle Bob.

Speak to dad: We know this means you'll have to speak with Dad...unless you want us to do it.

Thought it out: We've thought about this. It's not going to be garish, but we want it to be memorable.

Unique: The last thing we want is to take money from them. But everyone and every event is unique.

Not 50/50: We're not looking for a 50/50 split. We're here first because you're more understanding.

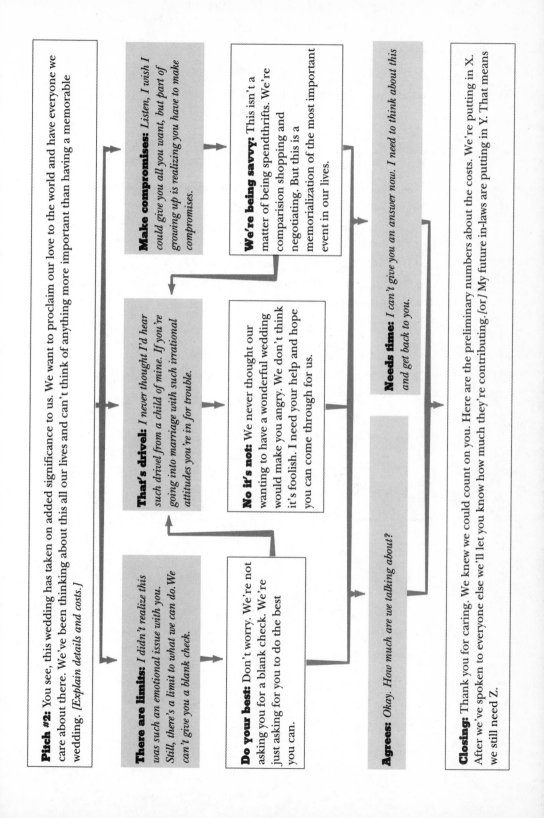

Pitch #2: You see, this wedding has taken on added significance to us. We want to proclaim our love to the world and have everyone we care about there. We've been thinking about this all our lives and can't think of anything more important than having a memorable wedding. *[Explain details and costs.]*

There are limits: *I didn't realize this was such an emotional issue with you. Still, there's a limit to what we can do. We can't give you a blank check.*

Make compromises: *Listen, I wish I could give you all you want, but part of growing up is realizing you have to make compromises.*

That's drivel: *I never thought I'd hear such drivel from a child of mine. If you're going into marriage with such irrational attitudes you're in for trouble.*

We're being savvy: This isn't a matter of being spendthrifts. We're comparision shopping and negotiating. But this is a memorialization of the most important event in our lives.

Do your best: Don't worry. We're not asking you for a blank check. We're just asking for you to do the best you can.

No if's not: We never thought our wanting to have a wonderful wedding would make you angry. We don't think it's foolish. I need your help and hope you can come through for us.

Needs time: *I can't give you an answer now. I need to think about this and get back to you.*

Agrees: *Okay. How much are we talking about?*

Closing: Thank you for caring. We knew we could count on you. Here are the preliminary numbers about the costs. We're putting in X. After we've spoken to everyone else we'll let you know how much they're contributing./or] My future in-laws are putting in Y. That means we still need Z.

KEY POINTS

- Express your love and gratitude, say you're bringing your parents into the planning process, and explicitly say you'll need financial help.
- Responses centering on the traditional breakdown of costs should be directly challenged.
- Responses focusing on the widowed or divorced status of the parent should be met with offers to intervene.
- Responses that dwell on obligations to other siblings should be answered by stressing that every situation and person is unique.
- Pleas for pragmatism should be deflected by stressing that you're not being impulsive.
- Shots at future in-laws should be answered with flattery.
- Whether you get a firm commitment or not, act as if you did, offer specifics, and express your thanks.

Suggesting a Prenuptial Agreement with Your Future Spouse

102

STRATEGY

The secrets to minimizing potential problems with suggesting a prenuptial agreement are to say that the idea came from a third party and to frame the matter as one of mutual protection. The timing of this discussion is important. You want to bring the matter up after you have agreed to get married but well before the actual wedding. That way it doesn't look as if you're making the marriage conditional on the prenuptial agreement, or having last-minute second thoughts. Try to have this conversation as part of an overall discussion of financial matters. Don't have this conversation in a public place. You want your future spouse to feel able to talk freely.

TACTICS

- **Attitude:** Be matter-of-fact about the issue. Look on it as a formality, like getting a marriage license or updating your life insurance coverage.
- **Preparation:** Be ready to offer a specific reason for needing a prenuptial agreement. Protecting children from a previous marriage is the most readily accepted reason for having a prenuptial. Keeping a family business within a family is also a widely accepted reason for having a prenuptial. Disparities in age or wealth are less accepted reasons.
- **Timing:** It's best to hold this conversation after a formal engagement but well before the date of the wedding.
- **Behavior:** Have this discussion in a private place to allow for free expression of feelings. Raise the issue, give a reason, and try to pass the matter on to attorneys as quickly as you can.

102. Suggesting a Prenuptial Agreement with Your Future Spouse

Icebreaker: I got an interesting call from my attorney today. She asked if we had discussed a prenuptial agreement yet. I told her we hadn't even thought about it, but she said there were a bunch of reasons we should consider one.

Family business pitch: She reminded me that the business has been in my family for more than 50 years and for that reason shouldn't be considered part of our marital assets . . . at least until we had a child.

Child from previous marriage: She reminded me that my [or] our primary concern has to be my [or] our children. I [We] need to insure that while the assets we acquire together should be ours, whatever assets I [we] bring to the marriage should belong to my [our] children.

Disparity in age or wealth: She suggested that because of the disparity in our ages [or] assets, we should keep our individual assets separate until we're sure the marriage will work [or] we have a child.

Trust objection: *Our relationship should be founded on trust. That's how marriages work. Don't you trust me?*

Pessimism objection: *A prenuptial agreement plants the seeds for divorce. It's wrong to start a marriage off looking toward divorce.*

Trust counter: Of course I do, but I don't think this is a question of trust. It insures that if, heaven forbid, anything happens, we will both have assets to fall back on.

Pessimism counter: I don't know. By working out any possible conflicts now we don't have to worry about them later on. These issues will never come between us in the future.

Let the lawyers handle it: That's why the one thing I insisted to my attorney is that you and I don't get involved in this process and that we let the lawyers take care of it. I don't want this to come between us.

KEY POINTS

- Blame a third party for coming up with the idea.
- Offer a specific reason for drafting an agreement, and frame it as mutual protection.
- If your future spouse objects on grounds of trust, reaffirm your love and stress that this is a financial, not an emotional, issue.
- If your future spouse objects on grounds of pessimism, stress that this resolves potential problems in advance.
- Try to turn the matter over to professionals as quickly as possible.

Negotiating a Big-Ticket 103.
Purchase with Your Spouse

STRATEGY

There are times in every relationship when there are differences of opinion about how to spend money. These conflicts are most common when the purchase is a luxury that's valued more by one partner than the other. There are a couple of secrets to getting your spouse to agree to such a purchase. First, from the very beginning acknowledge that this is an indulgence for you. Second, if you've no other choice, offer to give another indulgence up in exchange for this one. Just make sure this is also a solo pursuit.

TACTICS

- **Attitude:** Be upfront about this being a selfish whim—but stress that it's still something you want.
- **Preparation:** Have a concession in mind before you begin the conversation. It needn't cost exactly the same amount, but the closer the better.
- **Timing:** Have this conversation at home, in private, at a relaxed time—maybe the weekend. Of course, if you've indulged a whim of your partner's just recently, that would help.
- **Behavior:** This isn't something to get emotional about. Keep it light, even humorous if possible. Your body language and manner should say that this really isn't that big a deal—but you'd really appreciate it.

103. Negotiating a Big-Ticket Purchase with Your Spouse

Icebreaker and pitch: I'd like to do something that's important to me but isn't to you. In fact, you may even think it's a bit foolish, even though it matters so much to me. I know you think our current television is fine, but when I was over at Wendy's watching the soaps on her new set I couldn't believe how much better it was and how much we were missing out on. I'd like to buy a bigger set. I know you may not agree, but I'd like you to indulge me.

Angry: *Are you nuts? Our television's perfectly fine. Buying a new one would be an obscene waste of money.*

Deflect anger: Not to me. I knew you'd be upset, but I didn't expect you to overreact. Are you angry with me about something else?

Fearful: *I'm just worried about spending so much money. What if we have an emergency and need that extra cash?*

Admit concerns: I've thought about that too. You're right about the need for an emergency fund. But I think I've come up with a solution.

Offer a concession: How would it be if I quit the bowling league. That way it would be a wash and we wouldn't lose anything.

Guilt: *I hope you've really thought this out. I was counting on using that money for something for both of us.*

Admit selfishness: I have thought it out. You're right. I am being selfish. But I promise I'll make it up to you.

Hesitates: *I don't know. It's a lot of money.*

Agrees: *Okay, since it means so much to you.*

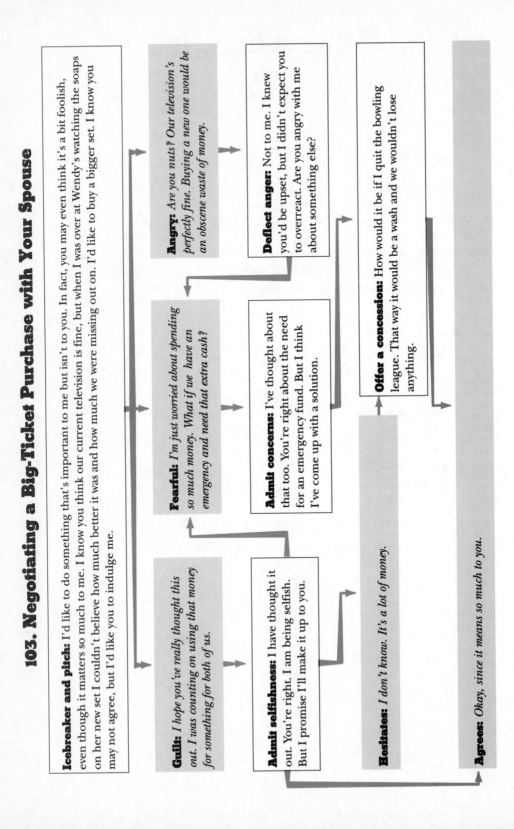

ADAPTATIONS

This script can be modified to:

- Obtain consent to lend money to a parent or sibling
- Obtain consent to spend any money for a purely personal luxury item or service
- Obtain consent to be absent from home for a period in order to do something

KEY POINTS

- Admit from the start that this desire is neither shared nor practical.
- If your partner uses guilt, readily admit selfishness, but promise to reciprocate.
- If your partner gets angry, deflect the anger by asking if he is upset with you about something else.
- If your partner expresses fears about money, or continues to object, offer to give up another personal indulgence in exchange for this new one.

Debating Vacations with Your Spouse

104.

STRATEGY

Sometimes it's impossible to come up with a compromise vacation site. For instance, if one partner loves relaxing in the sun and sand while the other longs to visit a stimulating city, there's no way both can be satisfied. The answer, of course, is to take separate vacations or for one partner to make a sacrifice. The best way to gently lead your partner to these two alternatives is to start by making a selfless offer of your own. Whether or not the bait is taken, it lays the groundwork for a reciprocal gesture later on.

TACTICS

- **Attitude:** You're asking for a sacrifice so be prepared to make one of your own in exchange.
- **Preparation:** Be willing to take separate vacations if need be, or to delay your desired trip for a year if that's what it takes.
- **Timing:** Have this conversation at a time when you're free to talk openly and you have some uninterrupted private time.
- **Behavior:** This isn't something to get emotional about. However, it is something that would make you happy and that you're willing to go to some lengths to accomplish.

104. Debating Vacations with Your Spouse

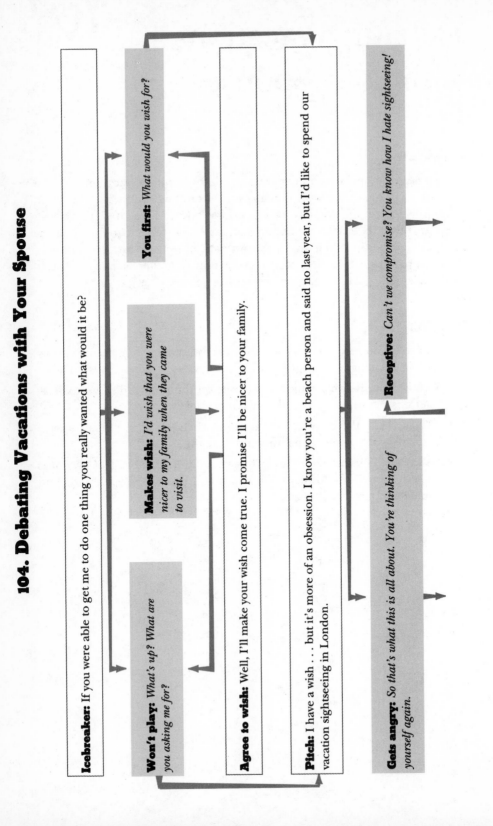

Icebreaker: If you were able to get me to do one thing you really wanted what would it be?

Won't play: *What's up? What are you asking me for?*

You first: *What would you wish for?*

Makes wish: *I'd wish that you were nicer to my family when they came to visit.*

Agree to wish: Well, I'll make your wish come true. I promise I'll be nicer to your family.

Pitch: I have a wish . . . but it's more of an obsession. I know you're a beach person and said no last year, but I'd like to spend our vacation sightseeing in London.

Gets angry: *So that's what this is all about. You're thinking of yourself again.*

Receptive: *Can't we compromise? You know how I hate sightseeing!*

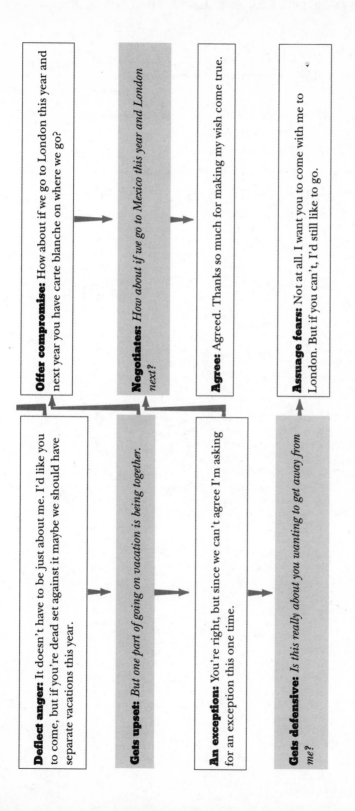

Deflect anger: It doesn't have to be just about me. I'd like you to come, but if you're dead set against it maybe we should have separate vacations this year.

Offer compromise: How about if we go to London this year and next year you have carte blanche on where we go?

Gets upset: *But one part of going on vacation is being together.*

Negotiates: *How about if we go to Mexico this year and London next?*

An exception: You're right, but since we can't agree I'm asking for an exception this one time.

Agree: Agreed. Thanks so much for making my wish come true.

Gets defensive: *Is this really about you wanting to get away from me?*

Assuage fears: Not at all. I want you to come with me to London. But if you can't, I'd still like to go.

KEY POINTS

- Offer to answer a wish of your partner's in exchange for getting a wish of yours.
- If your partner gets angry, deflect the anger and suggest separate vacations.
- If your partner gets defensive, assuage fears.
- If your partner seems receptive, offer a compromise.
- If your partner offers a counterproposal, accept as long as it achieves your goal.

Discussing Potential Relocation with Your Spouse

105

STRATEGY

In today's job market it's not unusual to have to shift locations in order to advance in your career. Couple that with the fact that in many families today both spouses have careers, and relocation becomes a major issue in a marriage. This is a complex matter that can't be solved in one session using a simple script. The key is to establish as early as possible that the move is very important to you, determine where the primary obstacles will be, and lay the groundwork for an acceptable compromise. Those are the goals of this script. By the way, the earlier in the process you bring this issue up with your partner, the more successful you'll be.

TACTICS

- **Attitude:** You're asking your partner to become part of the process of coming up with a solution. You're in this together. This isn't a win/lose adversarial matter.

- **Preparation:** Realize that this is just the beginning of the discussion, but come up with some preliminary information and develop a few sketchy solutions to obstacles.

- **Timing:** Have this conversation as early in the process as possible.

- **Behavior:** Treat all objections, no matter how seemingly trivial or emotional, as serious and worthy of discussion. Frame this, not as a discussion of whether or not you should take the job, but of how you can overcome the obstacles involved in your taking the job. Focus on solving problems, not deciding whether or not to accept the offer.

105. Discussing Potential Relocation with Your Spouse

Icebreaker and pitch: There's something important we need to talk about. I was offered a job today by Public Servants Inc. in Washington D.C. If it was just a career decision there would be no question of my taking it, but this is a real lifestyle choice we need to discuss.

Job objection: *I know it's selfish of me, but I don't want to move. I love my job—I don't think I could ever get another one like it. If we move I'll have to start all over again.*

Family objection: *I know you've always wanted this job and it's the best move you could make. Wherever you have to go, I'll go. But what are we going to do about the kids and Mom and Dad?*

Housing/roots objection: *I know you've always wanted this. It's just that I hate to give up this house—we just got it into shape.* [or] *It's just that I hate to leave this town. We've made such good friends and have really put down roots here.*

Suggest compromises: The last thing in the world I want to do is to tell you to leave your job; to have one of us sacrifice their career for the other. If there's nothing equivalent down there, maybe we could look at finding a place somewhere in the middle. Or maybe I should look into getting a studio apartment down there and coming home on the weekends.

Obstacles, not problems: You're not kidding about those being big issues, but I think they're obstacles we can overcome. The recruiter faxed me some preliminary information about the schools in the area and we can investigate them together. As for your folks, we'll just have to figure out a way we can see them often.

Housing/roots counter: I know. I love this house *[or]* town too. But the recruiter faxed me some information about lovely new developments *[or]* old houses around D.C. we could look into. *[or]* But I'm sure we'll make new friends, and we'll still be able to keep in touch with our friends here.

Work together: Our marriage is more important to me than any job. I know we can come up with ways to overcome all the obstacles this could create.

ADAPTATIONS

This script can be modified to:

- Discuss one spouse's desire to have a child or adopt a child when the other has expressed reservations

KEY POINTS

- Indicate as early as possible that you just received the offer and you want to accept it, but need to discuss it with your partner.
- If your partner raises job-related objections, suggest a number of possible compromises, stressing that neither of you should have to compromise career goals for the other.
- If your partner raises family-related objections, agree those are important issues, but present them as obstacles you can jointly overcome.
- If you partner raises housing and roots-related objections, offer some preliminary information on the opportunity to find similar housing in the new area, and affirm your belief that you can maintain old connections and make new ones too.
- Remember your goal is to set the stage for compromise and problem solving, not to win a debate.

Raising the Issues of AIDS Testing and Safe Sex Practices

106.

STRATEGY

It's very uncomfortable discussing AIDS testing and/or safe sex practices with a potential sex partner. By bringing the topic up, you're not only raising the issue of potential sexual relations, but you're also probing for very personal information. The best way to ease into this subject is, rather than asking directly, ask if it's okay to ask. That offers the other person the opportunity to suggest you're jumping the gun. If he says it's okay to ask, then you can cautiously raise the issues of concern.

TACTICS

- **Attitude:** Put discomfort and fear aside. It's better to get rejected or be embarrassed than it is to be infected with the AIDS virus or to have that fear unresolved.
- **Preparation:** *Get tested yourself!*
- **Timing:** Have this conversation when you sense that there's a mutual physical attraction.
- **Behavior:** Indicate you're not embarrassed or uncomfortable about having this discussion. If the other person is, either back down or take the lead, depending on whether your potential partner is saying it's unnecessary or indicating it's uncomfortable.

106. Raising the Issues of AIDS Testing and Safe Sex Practices

Icebreaker and pitch: I really enjoy being with you and I'm looking forward to spending more time together in the future. I'm not making any suggestions, but how do you feel about discussing AIDS?

Slow down: *I don't think that's really necessary at this stage in our relationship.*

Fearful or angry: *What do you mean? What are you asking me?*

Timid agreement: *Uh . . . well why not . . . I guess . . . sure, we can talk about it.*

Back down: I'm not suggesting we need to talk about it now. I just needed to let you know that if the time comes I won't feel uncomfortable discussing it with you.

Fearful, defers: *Uh . . . um . . I'm not really sure. What do you think?*

Offer options: Well, what are your feelings? Do you believe that using condoms is sufficient or do you believe everyone should be tested?

Offers opinion: *Since I give blood every couple of months I'm tested regularly. Thank God they've all been negative. But I do think it makes sense for everyone to be tested as well as to use condoms. What do you think?*

Offer opinion: I think in this day and age everyone should be tested. I myself was tested last year, and the results were negative. It made me feel a lot better.

ADAPTATIONS

This script can be modified to:

- Request consensual sex
- Define the nature of a relationship when you're unsure

KEY POINTS

- Indicate that you take the relationship seriously.
- Focus on talking about the issue, not the issue itself.
- If you're told to slow down, back off.
- If you're invited to ask questions, whether timidly or angrily, ask.
- If you meet further timidity, offer your own opinions.

Breaking an Engagement

107

STRATEGY

It's never going to be easy to break an engagement, no matter how well you script the encounter. The secret here is to accept clear and total responsibility for ending the relationship. Stress that the problem is with you, not your former fiancée. Don't make any concessions—they're just false hopes. Instead, make it clear this is your final decision. Absorb any anger; it's understandable under the circumstances and probably even healthy.

TACTICS

- **Attitude:** Sometimes you've got to be cruel, or at least blunt, to be kind. There's no easing into this, and half measures simply prolong the pain.
- **Preparation:** Be sure this is what you want to do.
- **Timing:** Have this conversation as soon as you know you don't want to get married.
- **Behavior:** Do this somewhere your former fiancée will feel free to get emotional. Hear him out, but continually reiterate that it's over. Once the other person begins to get angry, feel free to leave the scene.

107. Breaking an Engagement

Icebreaker and pitch: This is very difficult for me to say, but it's very important. I can't marry you. You are a wonderful, caring person and you deserve someone who loves you with all their heart. I thought that person was me when I proposed to you *[or]* accepted your proposal. But now I know that I don't feel that way. I love you, but I'm not in love with you. I'm sorry if this hurts you, but in the long run we'll both be better off apart.

What did I do?: *What did I do wrong? I love you. Tell me and I'll fix it. I can change. I swear.*

Not you, me: It's not you. It's me. There's nothing wrong with you . . . I'm just not in love with you. You shouldn't have to change. You'll find someone who loves you for who you are. But that's just not me.

Gets angry: *How could you do this to me? I can't believe how selfish you are. What am I going to tell everyone? The wedding is only two months away! There's someone else, isn't there!*

Absorb anger: You have every right to be angry. I'm not being selfish, however. I'm doing this for both of us. There's no one else. A little embarrassment now is better than making what I now know would be a terrible mistake and getting married.

Delay instead: *I know it's been tense between us lately, but maybe that's because of the wedding plans. What if we postpone the wedding and try to work things out?*

Inevitable: That would only be delaying the inevitable. I know that I don't want to marry you. Time isn't going to change that. I think it's better we end things now and get on with the rest of our lives.

ADAPTATIONS

This script can be modified to:

- Announce the desire to separate or get divorced
- End any intimate relationship

KEY POINTS

- Assume the blame, accept the responsibility, and stress that it's better for both of you.
- If he asks for another chance, stress that he deserves to be loved unconditionally.
- If he asks for the wedding to be postponed rather than canceled, say that that is only delaying the inevitable and stress that it's best to sever the relationship now.
- If he gets angry, absorb the anger but reiterate that this is what's best for both of you.

Ending a Personal Relationship

108

STRATEGY

One of the hardest things in the world to do is to end a relationship or acquaintance that's gone sour. The feelings we have for people we've known for some time stand in the way of successfully severing the bond. That's because in order to truly end the friendship, you're going to have to be a bit cold and blunt—especially if the other party can't take hints. Try not to get into debating the reasons for the split and instead, stress that you just don't have the time or energy or desire to maintain the relationship. As with breaking an engagement, this is an instance where you've got to be willing to absorb some retaliatory shots to get the job done.

TACTICS

- **Attitude:** Sometimes you've got to be cruel, or at least blunt, to be kind. There's no easing into this, and half measures would simply prolong the pain.
- **Preparation:** Be sure this is what you want to do.
- **Timing:** Have this conversation as soon as you know you don't want to remain friendly.
- **Behavior:** Do this somewhere the other person will feel free to get emotional. Hear him out, but continually reiterate that it's over. Once the other person begins to get angry, feel free to leave the scene.

108. Ending a Personal Relationship

Icebreaker and pitch: This is very difficult for me to say, but it's very important. I don't want to have any contact with you anymore. I don't have the time or desire to maintain what I perceive to be a very draining and high maintenance relationship. Frankly, this relationship isn't worth what it's costing me in time and energy. My decision is final. Please don't call me, write, stop by, or try to get anyone else to intercede. You still have my best wishes, but I don't want to have any relationship with you.

What did I do?: *What did I do wrong? I cherish our relationship. Tell me and I'll fix it. I can change. I swear.*

Not you, me: It's not you. It's me. I simply don't have the time or energy for this kind of relationship. You shouldn't have to change.

Gets angry: *How could you do this to me? After all I've done for you. I was there when you needed me, and now you're dumping me. You've got some nerve.*

Absorb anger: I understand your anger. Relationships should not be based on perceived obligations. I'm sorry. I no longer want to have any contact with you.

Issues threats: *I'll get even with you for this. Believe me, you'll regret the day you turned on me and stabbed me in the back. You haven't heard the last of me.*

Deflect threat: Please don't spoil our past relationship by issuing threats that will force me to speak with an attorney. I simply don't want to be in contact with you. Let's end it at that okay?

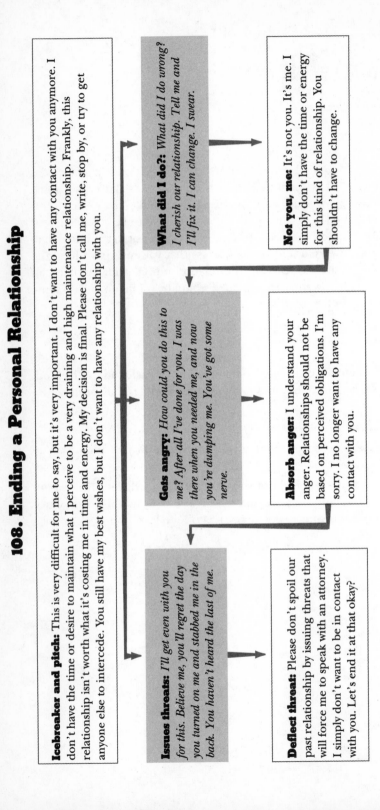

KEY POINTS

- Simply say the friendship isn't worth the effort it requires and you've chosen to end it.

- If the other person asks for another chance, stress that he deserves a friendship that is unconditional.

- If other person gets angry, absorb the anger but reiterate that the relationship is over.

- If the other person issues threats, deflect them by saying that this is spoiling the past relationship, and indicate you won't simply turn the other cheek.

Asking Your Spouse to Lose Weight

109

STRATEGY

The key to getting your spouse to go on a diet or launch an exercise campaign is to make it a joint effort designed to prolong and improve your relationship. By taking the burden on yourself and beginning with self-criticism, you may be able to minimize any anger and break through any denial. But be ready to be more direct if need be. These direct prods will be better received if they're based on health rather than appearance reasons.

TACTICS

- **Attitude:** You're doing this for your partner's own good as well as your own, so don't be afraid to be direct if necessary.
- **Preparation:** Have some specific instances you can point to as indicating the need for both of you to get into better shape or lose weight.
- **Timing:** Have this conversation when you have time to be alone together and will be uninterrupted—but not over a meal. Try during a long car ride.
- **Behavior:** Act as you normally have in the past whenever you've discussed something important to you. For instance, if your relationship is a joking one, feel free to use humor. Just make sure to stress the importance of a definite joint effort.

109. Asking Your Spouse to Lose Weight

Icebreaker and pitch: Honey, I wanted to tell you that I've decided to join a gym and go on a diet. I was looking at a picture of us from last year and I couldn't believe how much weight I've gained. I want to stay attractive to you and I also want to be healthy so we can live a long life together. Hey, if you'd like you can come with me to the gym . . . it will give us a chance to spend more time together.

Don't need it: *Honey, you look great to me. Sure we're both a year older. And maybe we've put on a few pounds, but that's just part of getting older. At least we're aging together.*

Offer specific: What about the other week when we both were having such a hard time walking up the hill from the mall? And I just don't think we're looking as good as we did in the past when we were in better shape.

Gets angry: *Are you saying I'm fat? Maybe my shape has changed, but I'm still in as good shape as I was back in college. If you think that of me you've probably fallen out of love with me. Is that what this is all about?*

Absorb anger: I'm not saying you're any more out of shape than I am. And the only reason I'm saying it is because I love you so much I want you to be around for a long time to come. But to do that we'll both have to get back in shape.

Doesn't take hint: *Sure, honey. Whatever you want to do is fine. I don't think I'll be joining you though, but don't let that stop you.*

Be more direct: Honey, I think we both should go. To be honest I think we both could stand to get back into shape. And besides, that way you'll be sure to stay healthy so you'll be around as long as I am.

ADAPTATIONS

This script can be modified to:

- Ask your spouse to break an annoying or unhealthy habit

KEY POINTS

- Take the action you want your spouse to take, saying you're doing it (partly) for him and suggesting it's something you can do together.
- If your spouse says neither of you need to diet, offer a specific that shows you both do.
- If your spouse doesn't take the hint, be more direct.
- If your spouse gets angry, absorb the anger and stress that you want a long life together.